SECULAR STEEPLES

SECULAR STEEPLES

*Popular Culture
and the
Religious Imagination*

CONRAD OSTWALT

TRINITY PRESS INTERNATIONAL
A Continuum imprint
HARRISBURG · LONDON · NEW YORK

Copyright © 2003 Conrad Ostwalt

Trinity Press International, P.O. Box 1321, Harrisburg, PA 17105

Trinity Press International is a member of the Continuum International Publishing Group.

Cover image: Photograph by David Sandman. Our thanks to Skip Hicks for the generous use of the marquee at the Allen Theatre, Annville, Pennsylvania, www.allentheatre.com.

Cover design: Corey Kent

Library of Congress Cataloging-in-Publication Data

Ostwalt, Conrad Eugene, 1959–
    Secular steeples : popular culture and the religious imagination /
Conrad Ostwalt.
        p. cm.
Includes bibliographical references and index.
    ISBN 1-56338-361-6 (pbk.)
    1. Popular culture—Religious aspects. 2. Religion and culture. 3. Secularism.
I. Title.

BL65.C8 O88 2003
291.1'7—dc21   2002153594

Printed in the United States of America

07 08 09   10 9 8 7 6 5 4 3

for

Heather Lien

"my lotus flower is blossoming"

CONTENTS

ACKNOWLEDGMENTS

American secular culture is saturated with religion and religious messages. I am not sure if I arrived at this conclusion through my academic reflection or because my youth was dominated by religious and moral teachings and primed me to view the world in this way. Nevertheless, I believe the unique history of America has encouraged a culture that is at once thoroughly secular in its organization while essentially religious in its orientation. I began years ago to explore this dual character of culture through my teaching and writing. This book continues that investigation.

I began formal research for this book during the autumn of 1996 during a one-semester leave from teaching at Appalachian State University. For this time, I thank my colleagues in the Philosophy and Religion Department and Dr. Donald Sink, who was then the dean of the College of Arts and Sciences. Since then, research and writing for this book took place mainly at night, on weekends, and during summer beach holidays. And for this time, I thank Mary and Heather.

Nevertheless, my writing of this book encompasses much more than the past six years—many of my teachers will recognize their influence in my words, and I thank them for the intellectual journey begun so long ago. In particular, Dr. Grant Wacker and Dr. Peter Kaufman have been my mentors and friends since I was a teenager. They helped pry open my eyes to the world around me. Dr. Wacker continued as my teacher of American Religions through graduate school. Dr. Wesley

Kort became an important mentor during graduate school and provided me tools for cultural analysis. Dr. Joel Martin and Dr. Carolyn J. Medine are cherished friends and continue to inform my work on American religion, film, and literature.

So, as expected, my colleagues and teachers have contributed to this book, but so have many students. Christy Lohr continues to help me explore the richness of American literature and theology. James Casey, Jennefer Hill, and Lonnie Grimes have all searched libraries and popular culture looking for books, articles, songs, and videos of relevance. Finally, Carl Larsen was an invaluable graduate assistant during the 2001–2002 academic year, checking notes and bibliographical references. Dr. Pat Beaver, director of the Appalachian Studies Program at Appalachian State University, made Carl available to me during that year.

I am grateful to my previous publishers for their cooperation in my using or reprinting previously published works here, including *After Eden: The Secularization of American Space in the Fiction of Willa Cather and Theodore Dreiser* (Bucknell University Press, 1989); *Screening the Sacred: Religion, Myth, and Ideology in Popular American Film,* ed. Joel Martin and Conrad Ostwalt (Westview Press, 1995); and *Love Valley: An American Utopia* (Popular Press, 1998), reprinted by permission of The University of Wisconsin Press. In addition to drawing in general upon these sources, some material is reproduced by permission and is acknowledged in the appropriate notes. Some of the material in this book was published previously in journals and appears here in edited or altered form. Again, appropriate acknowledgment appears in the notes, but I offer my thanks here to the following journals for permission to reprint material: *North Carolina Humanities* for permission to reprint a short vignette about Love Valley; *The Southern Literary Journal* and the University of North Carolina at Chapel Hill Department of English for permission to reprint an edited version of my article, "Witches and Jesus: Lee Smith's Appalachian Religion" (1998); *The Journal of Religion and Film* for permission to reprint portions of articles published previously with that journal; and *Currents* and Continuum Press for permission to reprint an edited version of "Celluloid Religion: Reading Religion Scholars Watching Films: A Supplementary Response to Alice Bach's 'Cracking the Production Code: Watching Biblical Scholars Read Films.'"

Of course, I owe thanks to my current publisher, Trinity Press International, for support in bringing this book to publication. In particular, Henry Carrigan, editorial director, and Amy Wagner, managing editor, have provided learned assistance and wise counsel through their input and guidance.

Finally, I offer my most sincere thanks to my family, to whom I am in greatest debt and from whom I receive the greatest blessing. To Mary, thank you for believing in me. And to Heather, thank you for reminding me of the value of seeing the world from the floor. For that insight, I dedicate this book to Heather.

Appalachian State University
Boone, North Carolina
December 2002

INTRODUCTION[1]

Imagine an old monk, bent and nearly blind from years of hunching over ancient manuscripts by candlelight. His fingers are deformed and stained from his careful grip on pen or quill. He stays at his task for a lifetime because his call to preserve a sacred object provides divinely inspired determination and energy. Compare this image to that conjured by a contemporary monastery with its electronic scriptorium. Computer screens emit a mysterious blue glow that replaces the dim, yellowed light of candles. Monks hunch over keyboards instead of over manuscripts, and rather than faithfully reproducing sacred words, they design Web pages for worldly corporations and provide information about their order through their own Web site.[2] The sacred task has changed, the tools include the most sophisticated and worldly technology, and the once isolated monastic life has been linked to the outside world via the World Wide Web.

Now, imagine any number of medieval cathedrals, their splendid architectural details rising to the heavens to extol the glories and greatness of an almighty God. Imagine the mystery and awe surrounding the sacred spaces of those cathedrals, the Dome of the Rock, the Wailing Wall, or a Buddhist shrine. Compare this to the image of a family of four retreating to the vestibule of a large suburban church to eat lunch in a fast-food restaurant located just outside the sanctuary. Or imagine the re-creation of sacred space in what was once PTL's Christian theme

park, Heritage, U.S.A., where sacred space was defined by a reconstructed American town based on a conservative Christian ideology. In
the first contemporary image, a fast-food culture invades our sacred
spaces; in the second, the sacred space was Main Street, U.S.A., not the
church or the mosque or the synagogue. Sacred space has changed, in
function and in organization, just as the tasks of our monks have changed.

Finally, imagine a family singing the seder service, gathered around
the dining room table, or the Primitive Baptist preacher's singing-style
sermon[3] or the Hallelujah chorus of George Frederick Handel's *Messiah*.
These very traditional and orthodox invocations use auditory manipulation and musical forms to tell the divine story. Compare these images
to a seductive young woman asking musical questions about God to
MTV viewers or to a scantily clad singer resurrecting a Christian saint
through song and dance.[4] Music as a medium for information about the
divine has remained constant—the content of the message and the origin of its production have changed. And in the MTV image, the per-
former acts independently of a religious institution or tradition to raise
the question of God's nature.

In contemporary American society, there is no doubt that religion has
changed, that an intimate relationship exists between religion and popular cultural forms. This change and the accompanying involvement of
religion with culture make it difficult to know where religion stops and
the secular world begins. Was PTL's Heritage, U.S.A., a sacralization of
secular America or a secularization of the Christian message? These
questions, these images, and the relationship between contemporary culture, religion, and ethics have prompted a debate of at least five decades
in duration, perhaps one that has extended for five centuries or more.
The debate is about secularization—what is it, is it occurring, and what
are the implications for religious faith?

This debate has produced several common assumptions about secularization and its effects on religion. Since the 1960s the predominant
thesis has come from sociologists of religion and has been known as the
secularization thesis. The early assumptions of this thesis suggested that
secularization is a process that will eventually free humanity from religious manipulation and control, that enlightenment, science, or other
social institutions will replace religion or make religion irrelevant or at
least less relevant.[5] This predominantly sociological view of religion is
one that many contemporary religious organizations have taken to heart
in their attempts to be more relevant to their constituents. Nevertheless,
some contemporary sociologists challenged the view but now seem
content that religion is not destined to disappear. Peter Berger, who

contributed much to the secularization debate in the 1960s, himself questions the major premises of the secularization thesis. Berger writes that the "core premise" of the theory, "modernization necessarily leads to a decline of religion," is wrong and needs revision.[6] Berger goes on to say the notion of "counter-secularization" is of prime importance and religions that really succeed in the contemporary situation are those that do not accommodate to the secular world.[7] Mark Chaves argues that secularization should not be understood as "declining religion" but rather as "the declining scope of religious authority."[8] Still other writers attack the secularization thesis more aggressively. Andrew Greeley takes the secularization paradigm to task,[9] while sociologists like Rodney Stark, William Sims Bainbridge, Daniel Bell, and others look for other models or for more helpful ways to view secular culture's relationship to religion.[10]

The upshot of the current thinking on secularization is that religion is not simply going to capitulate to the advance of secularism—but religion is still viewed as precarious or as a less-than-legitimate way of understanding reality. Once again, a predominant scholarly, particularly sociological perspective suggests that in a secular society, which is how we understand contemporary Western society, rational people should not take religion seriously.[11] The assumption again is based on the notion that the importance of religion will decrease as society becomes more secularized. Both of these assumptions posit an antagonistic relationship between secular culture and religion. This might be true if by religion one means traditional religious faiths and institutions.[12] But most religious studies scholars define religion in much broader terms, and some sociologists have recognized the necessity to broaden our understanding of the sacred. N. J. Demerath suggests that rather than focusing on religion, sociology should be looking at the sacred and at various possible sources for the sacred. Sometimes this will be religion and sometimes it might be something else, possibly some aspect of secular culture.[13] All of this suggests that there need not be an all-or-nothing dichotomization of religion and the secular and that in some ways our oppositional presuppositions concerning religion and the secular are misguided and misleading. One of the assumptions to be tested and challenged in this volume is the presupposition that religion and secular society exist in a necessarily antagonistic relationship to one another. Certainly this can be the case, especially with traditional religious institutions, but the evidence simply does not support the notion that religious and secular worldviews cannot exist side by side. In fact, in most cases if not all, as with Christianity since at least Constantine, religion and secular culture exist in a tandem codependency.

While my current work recognizes its genesis in my reaction to the secularization thesis, and while I am influenced by recent attempts to revise, rescue, or debunk the old thesis, this book should not be considered a sociology of religion. I am not trying to enter the debate on paradigms here, nor am I trying to advance new theoretical positions on the future of religion. Rather, I am more interested in how religion functions in relation to secular society and, conversely, how secular society reacts to or recognizes religious organizations. One of the major arguments of this book hinges on the idea that the secular and the religious worlds can and do coexist. In fact, they have always coexisted. If they do not feed off one another, certainly they affect one another. The whole secular/sacred polarization needs to be reconsidered in light of the relationship between religion and culture. For whatever else it is, religion must take up secularity as a necessity. Even if the subject matter of religion is another world, religion's task is to exist as relevant in this world; thus, by definition, religion is a part of the secular world just as religious institutions are by nature secular institutions (they reside in and operate in this world, not in a transcendent one).

For years, sociologists have viewed religion as Peter Berger's "sacred canopy,"[14] a worldview human beings have constructed to give reality meaning.[15] This view assumes that since religion deals with ultimate meaning, it covers all aspects of life and leads to religious authoritarianism, and that religion, being other-worldly directed, is a derived reality construction and is suspect if not deceptive.[16] In more recent studies such secularization thought is undergoing revision. Perhaps it is time to think of society in terms of a "secular canopy" rather than a sacred one. Religion, as a cultural form that operates in this world, falls under a secular umbrella with all other cultural forms. All cultural products, including religion, are affected by and must conform to the exigencies of secular life, although religion's content or subject matter includes speculation about the transcendent, the sacred. Because of this secular umbrella, we should not be surprised when we witness intimate connections between religion and other cultural forms. In fact, religion should be understood as a secular cultural form. That its object is transcendence or the ethical ideal or an otherworldliness no more invalidates this than the goal of an aesthetic ideal denies that art is a secular cultural form, not to mention that other secular forms can deal with the sacred.[17]

Of course, many will say that considering religion a secular cultural form is a condition of contemporary secular society and proves the secularization thesis. That argument rests on the assumption there was once a sacred society, generally thought of in the Western tradition to be medieval sacred society. If medieval Christendom seems to run counter to understanding religion as a secular cultural form, this is not evidence that religion is other than a secular cultural product, because the medieval church, as the self-proclaimed gatekeeper to the afterlife, was the most secular institution of its time. Real sacrality would be better found in the folk religions and superstitions of the peasants, that is, in the popular religious practices of the time.[18]

This work attempts to move away from the idea that religion as a sacred ideal must be at odds with secular society and that religion will diminish as secularization continues. I hope to shift the discussion away from paradigms and, following Mark Chaves[19] and others, focus on the functional authority of religion in society. For example, secularization might not destroy religion, but it might shift the authority away from religious institutions to other elements of society. The religious impulse will not disappear with secularization if, as many believe, humans have a fundamental religious consciousness.[20] However, where we find religion and how religion operates in society might change as authority structures within society shift. For example, if it is true that the institutional church is losing authority in contemporary society as Chaves suggests,[21] we should not be surprised to find religion expressed with new vitality outside the institutional church, in new religious movements,[22] or in "secular" cultural forms like literature, film, or art. So even if religious institutions lose authority, the power of religion does not diminish in scope—the location of that power might, however, shift in focus.

If the first major theme of this book is that secularization does not destroy religion, that religion will persist across cultural forms, the second theme, and a corollary to the first, is that secularization occasions a shift in the locus of authority to express religious ideals. Authority might shift from traditional religions to new religions or from institutional religion to some other cultural form: governmental institutions (secular state), the entertainment industry, the media, the publishing industry. This work assumes the shift in authority to be an ongoing result of secularization in the West, so much so that religion in the postmodern West has become reactionary. Religion in a secular world has in some cases lost the power to reify a culture and has found itself in the position of reacting to a culture that occasionally assumes the tasks previously reserved for religion.

A third major theme addresses another commonly held assumption about religiosity in contemporary society. Many commentators believe that European society is more thoroughly secularized than American society. This assumption is based on statistics that measure church membership

and attendance as well as less official anecdotes concerning public religion in American culture. This work argues that secularization is a reality both in America and in Europe—not necessarily to varying degrees,
but in different ways. This in part is a result of the history of organized
religion in America, in particular as it relates to disestablishment of the
churches. Because of disestablishment in America, religious institutions
since the American Revolution have been unable to ascend to the level
of elite power institutions as they did in Europe. Since the process of
secularization as understood in this study depends on shifting loci of
power, secularization would necessarily proceed differently in America
than in Europe. Because in America religious institutions have been
excluded from the elite power structure of government, religion in
America has always tended toward popular culture and thus is dispersed
more thoroughly through secular components of society. This might
help to explain in part why American intellectuals seem more anxious to
investigate popular culture and religion than their European counterparts.

In *Selling God: American Religion in the Marketplace of Culture*, R.
Laurence Moore argues that because of disestablishment, religion in
America became popularized in order to compete in a free market.[23]
The open-market theory is found elsewhere in sociology (e.g., R.
Stephen Warner) and religious studies (e.g., Nathan Hatch) to explain
the evolution of religious traditions in America.[24] Religion operating in
a free-market environment finds itself competing with entertainment for
attention and often adopts the stance of entertainment in order to thrive.
As a result, religion in America is more worldly and secular than religion
in Europe, where historically religion has not had to compete.
Secularization has proceeded differently, and in America we witness religion that is more attune to the secular environment and a popular culture that is more infused with religious images. In a sense, then, America
is more thoroughly secularized than Europe in that religion appears in
secular, popular culture and the church has become more like the secular world. This is perhaps one reason church attendance is higher in the
United States—because America, including American religion, is more
secularized than Europe, not less so.

The comparison of the European and American situations brings up
the fourth and final major theme to run throughout this work. This
introduction began with a series of images that asked the reader to imagine the confused boundaries between religion and the secular in contemporary society. As Paul Nathanson suggests, increasingly we witness
not confused boundaries but "flexible" ones between "religion and secularity."[25] From Nathanson's "flexible boundaries," we see secularization

taking place in two directions in contemporary society. First, there is a tendency for religious institutions to employ secular and popular cultural forms like television and the movies to make religious teachings relevant for a modern audience.[26] In this instance, we see contemporary religion making concessions to secular cultural forms and becoming more like society in general in the struggle to stave off obsolescence. As Bernard Meland points out, theological works such as John A. T. Robinson's *Honest to God,* Paul Van Buren's *The Secular Meaning of the Gospel,* and Harvey Cox's *The Secular City* demonstrated this dynamic some thirty years ago.[27] The end of the nineteenth century and early part of the twentieth witnessed this dynamic in the Social Gospel's attempt to build super churches, and contemporary society sees this development in the creation of "megachurches." This first direction of secularization across boundaries makes religion reactionary to secular culture and comes as a result of religion's perceived loss of authority or relevance in society.

The second way secularization is proceeding is by the dispersion of the religious sensibility through a variety of cultural forms. When religious institutions no longer dominate culture, they lose their grip on what might otherwise be their prerogative—the religious sensibility and striving of humanity toward the sacred. With this loss of prerogative, religious concerns find expression in other cultural forms so that cultural products perceived to be secular can carry authentic and meaningful religious content and deal with sacred concerns. In fact, I would argue, much in the vein of theomusicologist Jon Michael Spencer,[28] that secular and popular culture might contain more authentic belief than official religious theologies, because it is in the popular culture that one can encounter belief and values apart from and freed from paternalistic religious doctrine and dogma.

Both ways secularization takes place in contemporary society originate with the loss or perceived loss of authority or relevance by religious institutions. This supports the contention that secularization has more to do with shifting structures of power in society than it does with the disappearance of religion. The second way secularization occurs will receive the most attention in this study by focusing on how religious sensibilities are spread out through the cultural spectrum. To use N. J. Demerath's phrasing, this might be referred to as the "sacralization" of society.[29]

The remainder of this introductory chapter will focus on developing these four themes and contextualizing a more thorough study of the second way secularization occurs in contemporary society—through the dissemination of the religious impulse in a variety of cultural forms external to traditional religious institutions and expressions. The underlying

assumption is that human beings are religious and will express themselves religiously in a variety of cultural forms that have relevance and
meaning to them. If institutional religious traditions are among those
forms, we will find vital religious institutions; if they are not relevant and
meaningful (and even if they are), the religious impulse will find expression elsewhere. In any event, we should not be surprised to find interaction between religion and other cultural forms. Just as Western
civilization nurtured state Christianity, just as Christianity co-opted
pagan practices, we should expect to see a fusion of the religious and the
secular. So monks using computers, Christian singers employing rock
rhythms, and coffee in the vestibule should not surprise us—nor should
the suggestion that religious images, messages, and content can be found
at the movie house, in the pages of popular novels, and in the lyrics of
pop music. This work on secularization is about the relationship between
culture and religion.

THE SECULARIZATION PARADIGM AND ITS REVISION

The predominant paradigm for understanding secularization as a process
comes to religious studies via sociology and has defined the discussion
to one degree or another since the 1960s. This paradigm has several features, chief among them the assumption (shared by religious studies) that
religion views sacred reality as a wholly different order from the secular
world and that the two worldviews are necessarily mutually exclusive
and antithetical. In the following pages, I attempt to reconstruct the
main features of this model as it developed from the sociological study
of religion, suggest additional recent revisionist ideas to the paradigm,
examine the sources or causes of the secularization process, and posit a
different way of thinking about secularization that does not require a
polarization of secular and sacred but allows a commingling of the two.

For the most part, the term *secularization* is used in two ways: 1) to
describe the process of making religion more worldly, which is how religious leaders often use the term, and 2) to describe the process of a contemporary growing irrelevance of religion.[30] In either usage, the term is
ideologically charged. In the first instance, secularization is often
attacked from religious circles as a compromise to those parts of culture
and society that are antithetical to religion. In the second usage, the term
is often employed by anti-religion idealists who view religion as an out-
dated and repressive cultural system. In either case, secularization as a
process is understood as the enemy to religion;[31] even more insidiously,
this antagonism has behind it an ideology of its own that is often referred

to as secularism, an ideology that is anti-religious at its base.[32] Just as religions sponsor worldviews, secular ideologies suggest certain ways of viewing the world, and these secular worldviews often compete directly with religious ways of understanding reality.[33] Religion apologists counter the secular worldviews by claiming that such views abandon humanity to alienation[34] and are responsible for a modern crisis of faith, a situation that leaves postmodern society in limbo concerning order— a situation where postmoderns might no longer be able to understand reality or gain meaning from their world.[35]

In this book, I will be less concerned about secularism as an ideology and more interested in secularization as a process that offers the key to understanding the relationship between the secular and the sacred and even the relationship between religion and culture. As a process, secularization does more than simply signal surface changes in habit or custom: it is a cultural process akin to "religionization" that helps define how human beings make sense of their world.[36] Thus, whatever else it might be, secularization involves and helps direct how we relate to the cultural forms in society, including religion. The predominant sociological secularization model is summarized by Paul Nathanson and others as a process that 1) is essentially modern in scope, 2) will lead to the demise of religion or its power, and 3) is an irreversible and chronological societal and historical process of Western civilization.[37]

This model stems from the Enlightenment notion that, in the words of Andrew Greeley, "the progress of science, technology, education, and . . . modernization"[38] will eventually make religion unnecessary. In the earlier years of secularization theory, Peter Berger took this so far as to posit a "secularization of consciousness," leading to a worldview in which "an increasing number of individuals . . . look upon the world and their own lives without the benefit of religious interpretations."[39] If this model is correct, if indeed the Enlightenment and the scientific revolution will answer all the questions for humanity that religion at one time tried to answer, if there is a secularization of consciousness going on, then we can expect a shift in the structure of belief: religious beliefs will be adequate for fewer and fewer people as a meaningful explanation of reality.[40] As Stephen Carter points out, we can expect to see a society where the culture rejects the idea of the supernatural, ridicules religious devotees, trivializes religion, and replaces supernatural explanations with supreme reason.[41] Although certain of these characteristics show up in contemporary U.S. and European society, there is still no consensus that the secularization model does indeed explain postmodern society. In fact, as we shall see, there is much evidence to counter that assumption.

If the secularization model described above is correct, we should be able to see religion losing social significance at the institutional level. Religious institutions not only would lose their power to enforce belief and behavior with individual constituents of religious communities but also would lose power over other institutions such as government.[42] In short, religion, as institution and as individual belief, would become marginal to the point of irrelevance in a technological civilization.[43] Furthermore, if the secularization model is accurate, according to Bryan Wilson, secularization will lead to a "transfer of property, power, activities, and both manifest and latent functions, from institutions with a supernaturalist frame of reference to (often new) institutions operating according to empirical, rational, pragmatic criteria."[44] According to Steve Bruce and Roy Wallis, this process might include differentiation (where other institutions will take on the roles religion once handled) as well as individualization and fragmentation of religion into increasingly less powerful and smaller units.[45] In *The Sacred Canopy,* Peter Berger argues this would eventually leave a society with cultural artifacts displaying a lack of religious content.[46] Bernard Meland even suggests the process could be a conscious one that leads to an effort to build a secular state where pluralism and toleration replace religious hegemony and bigotry and where separation of church and state allows for greater "justice to an entire citizenry of a culture."[47]

This secularization model, which predicts the inevitable and irreversible decline of religion as a condition of social processes initiated in modern Western culture, is now being revisited, questioned, and revised, at least in part because the data do not support that religion is becoming increasingly irrelevant. Poll after poll, study after study suggests that religious observance in America is as strong as ever. At the beginning of the 1990s, 90 percent of Americans claimed to be religious;[48] evidence indicates that church adherence increased in the nineteenth century and remained steady during the twentieth, and contributions to religious organizations continue to increase steadily, even when adjusting for inflation.[49] These figures are based largely on a traditional definition of religion. If a focus on popular religious practice were measurable, one might find an even greater level of religiosity in American life.[50] Thus, advocates of the secularization theory are forced to make concessions about the American situation and put forth revisions to some of its premises. And even in Europe, where the numbers suggest a much less impressive religiosity and where public religion is less visible, the secularization paradigm is not necessarily supported. For the European situation to support the model, there must have been at one time a Europe that was not secular, that was defined by a sacred worldview. The popular image of a sacred medieval European society is the product of history written from the perspective of medieval elite society, which was controlled by the church. Therefore, we have no reliable evidence that religious life in Europe has declined since the Middle Ages.[51] We can, however, rest assured that there was never a Western civilization that was "not secular,"[52] and that the secular did not simply arise in Europe in the fifteenth to seventeenth centuries.

If we cannot demonstrate that religion is declining, what do we do with our secularization paradigm? Must we abandon it as a way of understanding the relationship between religion and culture in the contemporary world? Certainly not. However, it does seem that certain of its major tenets need revision. The major problem with the dominant theories about secularization lies in their intransigence. For many, such as Jeffrey K. Hadden, secularization has become as much a doctrine as a theory and represents a cultural elitist attitude that expects religion to vanish.[53] Andrew Greeley echoes this sentiment when he says, "'Secularization' . . . is the religious faith of the secularized."[54] Greeley goes so far as to say adamantly that secularization is not occurring, that religion is just as important individually and institutionally as it ever has been in the past, and that declining religious affiliation is not proof that religiosity is in a state of decline.[55] Greeley and Hadden are joined by others such as Laurence Iannaccone, Rodney Stark, William Sims Bainbridge, Mark Chaves, and Peter Berger, who all challenge the secularization paradigm to one degree or another and call for its revision.[56]

It seems that we must question the notion, at least for the time being, that religion is becoming less viable or less important in contemporary society. We will talk about the mode of expression of religion later. It also seems that the notion that secularization is a modern phenomenon must also be discarded. Surely, Christianity in Constantine's empire experienced as much secularization—becoming more worldly—as do contemporary religious expressions. We might also conjecture that religion is a characteristic of humanity and is fundamental to a way of being and that human beings have always been religiously oriented and always will be.[57] Thus, we can consider religious striving a constant, but that does not mean religion is unchanging. And it might be that what we often think of as the decline of religiosity is nothing more than a natural evolution of religious being.

The idea of religious evolution is not new. As W. Warren Wagar points out, theologians and religious studies scholars as diverse as Martin Marty, Harvey Cox, Rudolf Bultmann, and even Dietrich Bonhoeffer

have suggested that a decline in belief in the supernatural and of the
institutional expression of religion does not mean that religious faith
might not arise anew "in some reconceived but still authentic form."[58]
These theologians challenge us to think differently about secularization
and about religion so that we might view religion in broader terms, as
individual faith rather than as institutional expression, as a more basic
way of thinking about the sacred in general.[59]

In this context, where we can think about religious evolution without theorizing the extinction of religion, we can look at secularization
as an agent for change, as do Stark and Bainbridge in their enlightening
study, *The Future of Religion: Secularization, Revival and Cult Formation*.
Stark and Bainbridge argue that secularization happens constantly in
religious communities, sometimes leading to the collapse or weakening
of some religious traditions, even the dominant ones. Nevertheless, religion does not disappear or become irrelevant, nor does religion forfeit
all its functions to secular institutions; new religions surface, sects
become churches, cults form, the religious landscape shifts and evolves,
and secularization becomes a "harbinger of religious change," not of its
demise.[60] They identify a pattern wherein secularization is always happening, religious communities are supplanted by other new religions
when they become too worldly, and secularization leads either to revival
or to religious innovation, in other words, religious change.[61] We might
add to their pattern that other cultural forms can and do participate in
the communication of religious meaning when traditional religions
wane and even when they do not. We need to broaden our categories so
that religious institutions are not the only cultural forms seen as partic-
ipating in the religious enterprise.[62] So in the context of religious evolution as a result of the secularization process, we can think about
literature, film, music, art, and other cultural products, along with traditional religious structures and new religious groups, as vehicles that carry
and transport our religious longings, rituals, and beliefs.

So we can think in new ways about secularization. It need not destroy
religion, nor is it necessarily antagonistic to religion. It might be a cata-
lyst for change, but secularity can also be a partner with traditional religions and religious institutions in the process of making known the
sacred. Secularization and religious devotion are not necessarily inversely
related; that is, one does not have to suffer for the other to prosper.[63] We
can think about religion and secularity, indeed religion and culture, as
maintaining Nathanson's "flexible boundaries," where secularity and religion are on the same continuum rather than antitheses of one another.[64]
Finally, we can recognize that much of the debate over secularization has

been misdirected. Secularization theory might hold for institutional expressions of religion, but even then not universally. This should come as no surprise, because religion has always found expression through secular institutions like the Christian church. The religious impulse remains constant—that religious nature of humanity that, through its quest for the sacred, results in the creation of religions and religious institutions. Humanity's religious impulse also finds expression through many secular cultural forms, including but not limited to the church and other religious institutions.

As we look at the evolutionary nature of religious development, one element of change stands out as the type of secularization taking place in Western religions in particular. This element has to do with religious authority relative to other cultural institutions[65] and is where the secularization paradigm is most instructive. It seems that even though religious devotion is as strong as ever, or at least not measurably weaker, and that religious bodies are not disappearing, there is a sense in which religious institutions do not exercise the degree of control and authority over society they once did in Western culture. This can be seen, for example, in the secularization of American education from a situation where Christianity once enjoyed a privileged position in higher education to its current state as a peripheral or excluded philosophical component of secular education.[66] This shift should not be conceived as a loss of religious efficacy, however, but as a loss of worldly authority, because usually when a religious institution exercises control it is because that institution acts as a secular institution, controlling law, government, and even education.

Mark Chaves has argued persuasively that secularization results in a decline in religious authority when religious authority is defined "as a social structure that attempts to enforce its order and reach its ends by controlling the access of individuals to some desired goods, where the legitimation of that control includes some supernatural component."[67] Therefore, for Chaves, "secularization is most productively understood not as declining religion, but as the declining scope of religious authority."[68] This view has validity when we consider that antagonism between secular institutions and religious ones usually centers on the locus of power. Thus, we can look at the contemporary American situation, for example, and see a tug-of-war of sorts between religious institutions and political institutions because the separation of religion and state made that power struggle inevitable. If at one time religious institutions had the power not only to direct secular matters but also to nourish spiritual needs, then we can say that secularization has occurred to the extent that religious institutions seem to have lost some of their ability to direct secular matters, although certainly not all of it. However, we must not equate this loss with the disappearance of religion from public life, because we still see the evidence of the religious quest in our art, music, literature, civil religion, and other cultural forms.

This brings us to our rethinking of the dominant secularization paradigm. We certainly do not want to discard it, because there is evidence that secularization is taking place in that religious institutions are becoming more like the rest of secular society, less "other," and we do note a decline in the ability of religious institutions to affect secular matters authoritatively even if we do not witness a decline in religiosity itself. What we are left with is a model of secularization that views religion, secularity, and other cultural forms on the same interactive continuum. We see shifts in functions of these forms and a shift in the location of authority in culture in such a way that secularization entails and perhaps initiates transition in culture and evolution of religion without its necessary extinction. This evolution has resulted in changes in the ways humans are religious and often in the ways humans express themselves religiously, so we get a constant infusion of new religious expressions, new religions, revivals of religions, and new vehicles for the expression of the religious imagination. Oftentimes these new vehicles for expression come from outside the traditional religious institutions and draw upon other cultural forms that may or may not be formally related to religious institutions. As a result, we often find popular cultural forms taking on some of the tasks of traditional religions in this constantly evolving, shifting secular landscape. In later chapters, this book explores some of those popular cultural forms to see if and how religious longings and questions arise outside traditional religious institutions in what we normally consider "secular" forms of culture. It might be that in our postmodern context, with shifting authority structures, popular cultural expression of religiosity is more important, more available, and more powerful than traditional expressions of religious truth.

THE ORIGINS OF SECULARIZATION

However we perceive secularization in Western civilization, there is little doubt it is occurring and affecting religion and other cultural forms. We can understand those effects better if we try to locate the source of the secularization process. As I mentioned above, in the Western tradition, religious institutions have always been secular or have evolved into secular institutions. The history of Christianity, its antagonism to and then acceptance by the Roman Empire, the Orthodox tradition's state church, the Catholic Church's involvement in secular matters throughout the Middle Ages, Protestantism's various experiments with state-church relations, and modern developments that have changed the face of Christianity all testify to the evolution of religion in light of secularization. So in some sense, it will profit little to search for the origins of secularization in the Western tradition—the impulse to secularize has been there from the beginning, and secularization's beginnings correspond with the beginnings of Western religions.

Peter Berger suggests the seeds of secularization are to be found in the nature of Western religion, in the oppositional relationship Western religion draws between itself and the rest of society, and particularly in the idea of transcendence, which polarizes the transcendent and profane realms. Berger argues that the biblical concept of a transcendent God leads to "disenchantment of the world" and the separation of the world from the sacred realm.[69] Later, as this transcendent philosophy developed into the Christian tradition, the tendency to create an oppositional relationship between religion and society was heightened by the institutionalization of the church. Berger argues when the church separated itself from the rest of reality by locating all "religious activities and symbols in one institutional sphere," it defined the rest of the world as separate, profane, and secular.[70] Nevertheless, as David Martin points out, European religious patterns evolved from the Roman model of a partnership between Caesar and God, an idea that led to the commingling of the sacred sphere the church defined and the secular sphere the church set apart.[71] So when looking for the roots of secularization in Western traditions, we need look no further than Western religion itself. Indeed, Western religion sponsors the divided worldview that allows reality to be divided into secular and sacred realms in the first place.

Nevertheless, in addition to this general origin of secularization, we might argue that Western religions are in a specific phase of secularization, particularly if we look at secularization as involved in the ongoing evolution of religion. This view generally points to the Enlightenment as the genesis of the current phase of secularization that is changing the way religiosity is communicated and understood in society and changing the role and function of traditional religious institutions. Based on the work of John Sommerville, Vernon Pratt, Olivier Tschannen, and others, this phase of secularization can be generally characterized by societal and institutional differentiation, pluralism of belief and disbelief, confusion of boundaries between secular and sacred, and the transfer of activities between cultural forms.[72] The following pages will outline the major events, institutions, activities, and ideologies flowing out of the massive transitions in European society during the fifteenth through the seventeenth centuries that seem to exert continued influence on the contemporary evolution of Western religion.

If we look beyond the nature of Western religious experience as the origin of the secularization impulse, we can look at the specific historical phase of secularization that confronts contemporary Western religions. In particular, as the power of the Catholic Church began to wane in the fourteenth century, we might argue that the modern phase of secularization began as the Middle Ages came to a close. The Catholic Church, which during much of the Middle Ages defined and controlled social order, power, and thought, entered into a period of decline marked by the Avignon papacy and the Great Schism. The weakened church never regained its far-reaching ability to control society; nevertheless, it attempted through futile measures to maintain a tight control over society and religion. When the Protestant Reformation movements succeeded, the Catholic Church realized its privileged position as a power broker in Western Europe had been seriously compromised.

This period, from approximately 1300 to 1550, can be understood as a transition period for the Catholic Church and for Western Christendom in general. Many argue this became a crucial time in the secularization process because institutional differentiation became a necessity.[73] With the loss of ecclesiastical prerogative came the dismantling of the feudal system (which favored the church with its vast landholdings), the rise of nationalism, the flourishing of a middle class, the growth of self-governing towns, and a revolutionary spirit that was in many cases directed at the church and its power structure. As broad, sweeping changes flooded Europe, the power structures of the Middle Ages fell apart. The institution that best defined that structure, the church, did not emerge unscathed. The ties between church and state began to unravel, and religion in the West was forced into a new role.[74] According to W. Warren Wagar, at the end of the Middle Ages, out of the rubble left by these movements, "the foundations of modern Europe were laid," and this foundation supported the weight of a new secular edifice.[75]

The edifice that emerged from the general social, economic, and religious upheaval of 1300 to 1550 included the Catholic Church, an institution that was less powerful than before but that also gave new legitimacy to secular institutions and to secular thought. Secularism defined the mood of the day as the rush of revolution provided excitement for burgeoning new governments. The church was often intransigent in its reaction and moved into a posture of reaction. No longer occupying a position that allowed it to define and control life in Western Europe as it once did, the church's reactionary stance helped establish the process of secularization we recognize at present. As loyalties were transferred from ecclesiastical power brokers to nationalistic ones, the church suffered in power and prestige and feared the fate of irrelevancy. The Catholic Church has since sought ways to define itself in relation to the "world" rather than defining the world. In the Catholic Reformation, the First Vatican Council, the modernist movement, and the Second Vatican Council, the Catholic Church struggled to understand itself over against the secular world. Long gone was the powerful, all-encompassing institution of the Middle Ages that had the power to define the secular world over against the church.

We might say the sources of Western secularization included the sweeping socioeconomic changes in Europe between 1300 and 1550 and the reactionary stance the Catholic Church assumed in response to these changes. However, it is perhaps unfair to characterize the Catholic Church as an unyielding institution that heightened the secularization of Europe by refusing to acknowledge the great transitions affecting European life. Something much greater and more broadly conceived was happening to Western Europe that changed the worldviews of Europeans. The European Enlightenment provided a philosophical basis for a new, secular worldview that not only succeeded in secularizing the Continent but also provided the free thought tradition that led to English secularism[76] and ultimately to the Enlightenment traditions and religions that characterized the American Revolutionary period. The modern prejudice against religion, if such exists as a characteristic of a secular society, might have begun, according to Stephen Carter, with "the Enlightenment, when the Western tradition sought to sever the link between religion and authority."[77] The Enlightenment's emphasis on and reliance on reason made Christianity seem unreasonable, based as it is on revealed truth. Thus, we could argue that one of the results of secularization, mistrust of religion in general, stems from the Enlightenment emphasis on reason.[78]

Beyond the mere emphasis on the rational as opposed to revelatory experience, the Enlightenment was accompanied by an epistemological revolution sponsored by the seventeenth-century scientific revolution. The scientific revolution, particularly the rise of natural science championed by Newtonian physics, changed the way the West perceived the world. Natural science ushered in a new paradigm, a new worldview, that disrupted, if not in some cases destroyed, what Bernard Meland calls the "mythos of the West."[79] Natural science introduced and legitimized a worldview that had no need to resort to supernatural phenomena or explanations to explain reality.[80] This whole movement put the church in an awkward stance: either Christianity would accept naturalistic explanations for the workings of the universe and thus invalidate the basis of revealed religion and some of its long-accepted precepts, or the church would retreat into a defensive stance, reject naturalist explanations, and thereby render itself irrelevant in the modern world. In many ways, this has been the dilemma of the Christian church since the scientific revolution, and either choice on the part of the church results in secularization: either the church becomes more secular by accepting scientific ways of thinking, or the church heightens the sacred-secular antagonism by entrenching itself against science. The church has employed both strategies at certain times during its history.

Newton's "mechanization of nature" made the divine, as the divine previously had been perceived, somewhat obsolete. Many scholars claim this led to a decline in religious belief as science began to assume some of the roles previously reserved for God; what Vernon Pratt calls the "naturalization of the supernatural"[81] made religion a less reasonable pursuit for Enlightenment-minded Europeans. As God became less a reality, human beings suddenly found themselves alone in the universe, and what Meland calls the "idealization" of humanity resulted.[82] However, this created another existential dilemma for human beings. On the one hand, with the supernatural out of the way, human beings were supreme; yet on the other hand, the scientific revolution changed the way human beings could think of themselves. The scientific revolution pushed humanity to the periphery—no longer could humanity think of itself as the focus of God's created order. Rather, the Copernican revolution removed the Earth from the center of creation to the periphery, and the Darwinian revolution heightened this anxiety when it came to the biological sciences. Humanity found itself in the precarious position of no longer being the favored of God's creation but instead the result of random and natural events[83]—without God's providential care, humans were alone in the universe. This is why religion did not crumble and has not disappeared in the wake of advancing science; even though science created a crisis for revealed religion, it failed to answer fundamental existential problems of humanity and even heightened human anxiety about contingency.[84]

The scientific revolution made religion seem unreasonable, and since European intellectuals were in an Enlightenment frame of mind, science certainly created problems for Western religions as natural explanations impinged on the territory of the supernatural. The boundaries were malleable, and they were shifting. This is one way religion became more secularized. Stark and Bainbridge claim that as it became increasingly more difficult to defend supernatural explanations, theologians began to make fewer and fewer claims for the supernatural in order to avoid conflict with science.[85] We see concessions grudgingly made by the church in such situations as the Darwinian challenge. We also see religion reacting against this trend with such movements as Christian fundamentalism. In any event, the scientific revolution forced secularization by placing the church in a dilemma: either become more secular or become less relevant. As we shall see, this dilemma still faces many contemporary Christians.

Yet another likely source of secularization in Western society can be found in the French Revolution, as well as in the American Revolution and other revolutionary movements of the late eighteenth century.[86] The French Revolution helped nationalism to materialize in Europe by replacing the old monarchy model (undergirded by divine right) with a new democratic model fueled by the middle class. The democratic ideals of the resulting Republic not only undercut the divine rights of kings and thus helped sever church and state but also led to greater toleration of religion and eventually to a greater pluralism of belief in Western society, one of the characteristics of secularism.[87] One can see a parallel phenomenon in the American Revolution and the separation of church and state in the United States. The French example perhaps resulted in the greatest degree of secularizing tendencies because there was a purposeful move to secularize life in the French Republic. Since the Catholic Church opposed the Revolution, the church quickly became a symbol of the Old Regime, and the newly formed Republic tended to view the church as an impediment to progress. So there were active efforts in the Republic to replace religious ethics with secular ones and to oppose the church as a social institution.[88] With the French Revolution, we see the increasing marginalization of religious thought in everyday life as secular concerns dominated during the revolution itself, and we see the increase of religious pluralism as democratic principles took hold. Both of these elements are characteristic of the modern phase of secularization in Western society.

Earlier we saw how Catholicism probably contributed to secularization in the late Middle Ages and during the Enlightenment period. However, Protestantism is probably an even greater culprit in the secular enterprise than the Catholic Church, so much so that William Lloyd Newell dubbed "modernity . . . the secular child of Protestantism."[89] A quick look at the central tenets of Luther's reform demonstrates how

Protestantism participated in and served as a source of secularization in Western Christianity. As Paul Nathanson points out, when Luther claimed that God is known through Scripture alone, he effectively "desacralized" the church[90] by making the revelatory experience less necessary. As Timothy B. Husband and Jane Hayward remind us, when Luther attacked good works as a means of salvation, he "separated . . . earthly endeavors from . . . eternal life"[91] and heightened the tension between the secular and sacred realms. And when Luther declared the existence of a priesthood of believers, the democratization, and thus the secularization, of religion was complete—with the priesthood of believers there need be no sacred hierarchy. The democratizing effects of Luther's reform and of Protestantism in general paralleled some of the social upheaval in European society at the time and contributed to the secularization of European life.

These are a few of the possible sources of the modern phase of the secularization of Western society. Many more possibilities exist. For example, David Martin argues that secularization is a Christian phenomenon and then discusses various types of secularizing tendencies based on revolutionary events and patterns,[92] leading us to a multitude of revolutionary movements that could serve as sources of secularization. Others point to the nineteenth-century Industrial Revolution as one of the harbingers of modern secularization.[93] We have neither the time nor the space to pursue these directions, but the above examples should suffice to illustrate where some of the characteristics of the modern phase of secularization in Western religion originated. From the nature of Western religion itself, to the revolutionary political and economic changes in Europe, to the epistemological transition accompanying the scientific revolution, to the basic tenets of Protestantism, these and other changes have produced a process of secularization that results in institutional differentiation, pluralism of belief, permeable boundaries between the sacred and the secular, and the transfer of religiosity to other cultural forms, to politics, science, literature, and more. Following this general orientation to the secularization process, I will now examine the relationship between religion, culture, and secularization in the European and American settings and discuss the two dominant directions secularization is taking in contemporary society.

One of the major extensions of the secularization thesis is that Britain and Europe are more thoroughly secularized than the United States. Why is this? The main assumption of the paradigm is that as secularization occurs, religion will become irrelevant and will eventually diminish. Thus, a measure of the degree of secularization is the level of religious observance in a society. Many observers of European and American religion make the claim that America is a much more religious society than Britain or the Continent. And indeed, if the political influence, membership, and public expressions of religiosity measure the degree of secularization, then America does seem to be less secularized than Europe. Many commentators note the degree to which intellectual life in Britain, Scotland, and France was secularized by the eighteenth century.[94] Others warn against generalizing about secularization in Europe and suggest that the degree of secularization in Europe differs drastically from country to country. For example, cites Andrew Greeley, Ireland and Poland have a very high degree of religious participation.[95] Still others warn about making judgments concerning religiosity based on measures such as membership rolls and the appearance of religion in the public realm. For example, Stephen Carter suggests that Americans have mixed feelings about religion. Whereas there is an abundance of public religion in America, Americans do not take religion seriously and treat it as "a hobby."[96] If Carter is right, then we cannot be sure that statistics demonstrate anything about the religiosity of the United States compared to Europe.

Nevertheless, the numbers seem to support at least a superficial acceptance of and practice of religion as part of American culture that outpaces religious life in most parts of Europe. Although American intellectual life demonstrated some of the same secularizing tendencies in the eighteenth century as European intellectual life, the twentieth century seems to suggest that religion in America is more vital than ever and perhaps an even more important component in American society than secular aspects like politics.[97] Since Alexis de Tocqueville noted the level of religious observance in the United States and its role in maintaining a thriving democracy,[98] American religious studies scholars have been theorizing about the abundance of religion in American life. Over half of Americans claim to attend church regularly, some 85 percent believe the Bible is divinely inspired, public ritual is filled with religious rhetoric, and even popular music contains religious images.[99] The ever-present American civil religion suggests that U.S. society is godly and moral,[100] making it difficult to be irreligious in the United States. Sociologists like Peter Berger recognize the level of apparent religiosity in America. Berger writes, "The majority of Americans are as furiously religious as ever—and very probably more religious than they were when de Tocqueville marveled at this quality of American life."[101] How can we account for this apparent disparity, and what does it mean for the current study?

A major argument accounting for the seeming vital religiosity in America focuses on the disestablishment of religion in America as the key to its religious vitality. According to R. Laurence Moore, state religion, as it was practiced in Europe for much of the modern era, relieves religion from the necessities of the marketplace.[102] The flip side of the coin is that when religion loses its privileged position in society through disestablishment, as was the case in America, then religion is forced to compete not only against other religions but also against other cultural forms.[103] So in American society, religion has found itself in the position of wooing its clients for allegiance, often against rival suitors as diverse as Friday night dates and Sunday afternoon football games. Many scholars, like Moore, believe this competition increases religious participation in America.[104] If this is true, then disestablishment helps us understand the high level of religiosity in America; however, it does not help us understand, as Greeley points out, the high levels of religious participation in countries where religion is established.[105]

At least partly because of disestablishment in America, religion has never occupied the position of an elite power establishment in post-revolutionary America as it did in Europe. Since religion had to compete against secular institutions and secular forms of entertainment, the church in America has tended to favor popular culture and has been more closely tied to secular concerns than in Europe. In Europe, the church occupied a privileged position as part of the cultural elite and maintained a position aloof from popular cultural forms. As an institution, the church came under attack or at least under suspicion during the French Revolution and since then has become an institution falling out of favor in the popular culture. This indicates there have been two different trends in secularization in America and in Europe. In America, secularization is expressed through the church aligning itself with popular, secular cultural forms and becoming more like them. In Europe, secularization is expressed through the rejection of an elite institution by the populace; thus, attendance and religious fidelity are apparently lower than in America. Secularization is taking place in opposite directions: the church is moving toward popular culture in America; popular culture is moving away from the church in Europe. With this scenario, one could even argue that America is the more thoroughly secularized society as its church becomes increasingly akin to popular and secular cultural forms. According to R. Laurence Moore, this helps account for the vitality of American religion.[106]

Thus, to mount a study of secularization in the context of religion and culture, one area of investigation must be how religion surfaces in and is reflected by popular cultural forms as well as by elite institutions. This book seeks to do just that, and the following pages contain reflections on how religion and culture relate in society and how secularization in postmodern American society takes place in two directions: 1) traditional religion becomes more like secular cultural forms, and 2) religious concepts find expression in popular cultural forms beyond the traditional institutions.

RELIGION AND CULTURE

This work assumes that religion is a crucial part of a larger cultural system and exists in relation to other cultural forms within a society. Borrowing from Clifford Geertz's famous "web" analogy, religion is one strand among many cultural strands that are interrelated in society.[107] As Robert Booth Fowler points out, religion is a cultural form that is integrated into life, society, and culture, and from thinkers as diverse as Max Weber, Emile Durkheim, de Tocqueville, and H. Richard Niebuhr, we see that religion shapes, undergirds, reflects, challenges, and critiques the social order and other cultural forms.[108] Of course, other cultural forms also shape, undergird, reflect, challenge, and critique religion, so Geertz's web is a dialectical one.

Religion's relationship to culture raises questions about the function or uniqueness of religion as a cultural form; that is, is religion any different than other cultural forms? As a cultural form, religion resembles other cultural products; however, religion's subject matter[109] directs its attention to otherworldliness, and it functions, according to James Moseley, to "express . . . culture's relation to a primordial, fundamental order or ground of reality, often imagined as a divine being." Religion functions as "an anchor of meaning" that often regulates behavior and morality.[110] When religion does this institutionally, religion is expressed through traditions that relate to the world through secular organizations like the church. Of course, other cultural forms can function similarly and thus function religiously without being categorized as religion. Religion, therefore, should be considered a cultural form that is directed toward the sacred and that exists in dialectical relationship with other cultural forms that sometimes explore religious content. This is not a reductionist definition that allows everything in culture to be classified as religion. Rather, it recognizes that cultural forms can act religiously just as religion can be expressed through a secular institution like the church.

Religion is necessarily entangled with secular culture, and attempts to dichotomize secular and sacred realms in society blur this crucial relationship. Religion, according to Greeley, is intimately connected to culture because it emerges as a "story" within a culture, a type of cultural story that operates communally,[111] that does not discount the possibility of private religious expression but merely suggests that religion has a communal component. Religion evolves as a culture evolves and changes in respect to cultural changes—sometimes religion changes the culture, but religion must always relate to the rest of the culture if it is to remain vital.[112] If religious expression runs too counter to other cultural trends, it runs the risk of being rejected by the rest of the cultural system as fundamentalism was culturally rejected in America in the 1920s because of its intransigent stance against modernism.[113]

Because religion and culture are indelibly connected, we must be careful to study religion and culture, as Jon Butler reminds us, in relation to "particular historical settings among real people in real places across real centuries."[114] Too often religious leaders and religious studies investigators place religion in cultural contexts other than its own, perhaps because religion is perceived to be the repository of eternal truth and thus immune from the vagaries of historical process and change. Religion has always been connected to, part of, and affected by the culture of which it is a part. If religious traditions attempt to remain aloof from contemporary culture, they will cease to be dynamic and relevant. When religious institutions absolutize beliefs and values, often in opposition to other aspects of the culture, they run the risk of stagnating the culture or of stagnating the tradition and becoming culturally irrelevant.[115] Thus, religion finds itself in the awkward position of competing in the cultural marketplace and aligning itself with a society's popular cultural forms.[116]

R. Laurence Moore's *Selling God: American Religion in the Marketplace of Culture* demonstrates very effectively how religion must compete with other cultural forms if it is to remain viable in a culture. According to Moore, religion becomes entangled with popular culture in various ways, often by first opposing it, but it almost always seems to find a way to embrace cultural trends in the competitive quest to remain relevant. When religion is popularized, it becomes closely aligned with entertainment and is sometimes virtually indistinguishable from secular amusements. Our consumption of culture includes our consumption of religion, and religion must be made palatable to remain current.[117] One of the most effective ways religion can compete for popular consumption is through mass media. The mass media offer both a challenge and a great potential for religion, threatening to lure away the interests of potential religious adherents and at the same time offering a means of reaching more people more effectively.[118] It is easy to see from the era of televangelism how the latter occurs, and author Quentin Schultze warns how the former can become problematic. According to Schultze, contemporary families do not communicate enough and depend too heavily on media information. Schultze believes that the media have invaded life and have impinged on the ability of families to communicate meaningfully, and he advocates using popular media as a stimulus for communication rather than as a detriment to it.[119]

This trend in the popularization of religion as a cultural product signals a new era of secularization that differs from that described as the modern era of secularization. If the modern era of secularization promised the disappearance of religion, the new era, the postmodern era of secularization, promises the increasing relevance of religion expressed through popular cultural forms. In this way, perhaps Langdon Gilkey's premonition that the latter part of the twentieth century might witness "the beginning of the decline of the Enlightenment"[120] might come to fruition in the changing forecast for the future of religiosity. Reflecting on postmodernism as a method and as a description of contemporary society can help us better understand this new era of secularization marked by the popularization of religion.

POSTMODERN CULTURE AND THE POPULARIZATION OF RELIGION

The Enlightenment and the modern era focused knowledge toward the empirical. Thanks to the scientific revolution, life and nature became explainable, understandable, mundane. As with secularization in the modern age, we witnessed a loss of mystery, a loss of awe, a loss of the sacred myth that infused life with transcendent possibilities. The result is a Western society that has been demystified, and this has changed religion. For example, traditional religion has seen the rise of fundamentalism in the twentieth century, and fundamentalism, at least in the Christian tradition, focuses on the empirical. When fundamentalist Christianity demands an inerrant Bible, for example, it wants a standard of truth that allows no ambiguity, no mystery, no myth. In other words, it demands a faith based on empirical proof, on fact, and on historical evidence.

The postmodern world no longer needs a scientific revolution to drive its premises; rather, its premises are the result of that revolution. Postmodernism is driven by the technological revolution, pluralism, and new threats to Western life. Whereas the scientific revolution demystified life by offering objective standards of truth, postmodern culture threatens to depersonalize life by championing diversity over conformity, heterogeneity over community. The call to diversity threatens to polarize society into insular camps and identities based on race, gender, affiliations, and ideologies. Technology, from air-conditioning to e-mail, makes this separation possible, threatens to insulate us from personal contact, and frees us from the necessity of community building. This depersonalization threatens to cut us off from familiar ways of considering the mysteries and myths formerly housed in religious traditions and in institutionalized religious rituals.

Yet even when this secularization and the loss of mystery occur, the religious sensibility does not disappear, and the need for mystery is dispersed through areas of life besides traditional religions. As religious beings, we desperately search for myths in other places, in art, literature, film, and a variety of cultural forms. If secularization has demythologized our religion, then it has also remythologized our culture, and we find ourselves needing mystery, needing to think in some other way than empirically, needing to visualize in some other way than literally—we need and nurture this remythologization. This volume represents an exploration of our ability to nurture such abilities to think and visualize in some other ways than literally. Contrary to realist and fundamentalist assumptions, we want to continue to believe things are not always as we see them and hear them. If institutional religions no longer allow that belief, the religious sensibility will search for it elsewhere, and our postmodern world might find itself with a secular religiosity that has co-opted some of the functions formerly reserved for religious institutions.

The result is a postmodern society "defined by paradox"—a society that is "uncomfortable with religion" and the sacred, but one that is confronted with religious categories and images through various modes of popular culture. As the secularization of society continues, so does the dissipation of functions formerly reserved for religious institutions. We find popular culture functioning in some of the same ways as institutionalized religious ritual, so that popular culture is the entity that provides the context for understanding values, belief systems, and myths.[121]

Postmodernism describes a perceived condition of our contemporary society, particularly as it relates to popular culture. John Storey's *An Introductory Guide to Cultural Theory and Popular Culture* traces the development of postmodernism through various theoretical thinkers such as Jean-Francois Lyotard, Jean Baudrillard, and Frederic Jameson. According to Storey, a new pluralism is supposed to be one of the characteristics of our contemporary society following the collapse of modernism. Modernism was marked by the distinction between high culture and popular culture, including a suspicion of popular culture, which became associated with anarchy, and high culture, which reflected the ruling and bourgeois classes. Modernism became associated with "Truth" and standardized hermeneutics, while popular culture was associated with democracy and anarchy.[122] Postmodernism as a theory and method tends toward popular culture as the material for investigation. Postmodernism thus makes the study of popular culture more accessible and legitimate.

According to Storey, a landmark study that emphasizes this change is Jean-Francois Lyotard's *The Postmodern Condition*. Lyotard distinguishes between metanarrative and narrative in his assessment of the collapse of modernism and the rise of postmodernism. Lyotard asserts that metanarratives are universalist stories that focus on and provide an overarching meaning and order to produce a type of homogeneity of culture. Metanarrative characterized the modernist era, with its standardization of culture, taste, and belief. However, in postmodernist culture, metanarratives are collapsing and being replaced by narratives, the voices of the periphery, the voices of difference and plurality. Postmodernism thus produces a culture of heterogeneity and diversity, where truth is no longer recognizable with a capital "T." Postmodernism signals the end of objective truth and replaces it with a culture without truth standards.[123]

Storey views the work of Jean Baudrillard as a continuation of the work of Lyotard and has investigated the possible consequences of the collapse of objective Truth. Baudrillard argues that postmodern culture operates in the realm of the "hyperreal" through "simulation," the blurring and merging of the imaginary and reality. With the collapse of objective Truth, claims Baudrillard, postmodern society has difficulty distinguishing simulation from reality, so that postmodern society experiences a crisis of belief as objective sources of authority and certainty lose efficacy. When this happens, the hyperreal can become more real than the real and postmoderns might have a difficult time separating depictions of reality from the real thing. If the film *JFK* comes to represent a new myth for the assassination of President John F. Kennedy, then the hyperreal has merged into the real; if we confuse movie violence with the real thing, then simulation has taken on primary meaning; if Disneyland becomes Americans' primary experience of their country and its history, then Baudrillard's point demonstrates the postmodern tendency to blur the lines and to confuse the distinctions between reality and simulation.[124] It is easy to imagine how traditional religious authority structures, science, or other systems making truth claims can collapse and be replaced by "simulated" realities. When this happens, not only does the concept of Truth or reality suffer, but story also loses its power as we transfer our illusions of objective truth onto cultural forms that should operate mythically. Nevertheless, when we turn to these simulations, we turn toward popular cultural forms for truth.

Finally, according to Storey, Frederic Jameson adds to the discussion by defining postmodern culture as a culture of "pastiche"—a culture that finds truth and value only in a nostalgic representation of the past. Postmodern culture suffers from "historical amnesia" and cannot distinguish real history from a nostalgic representation of stereotypes about an imagined past. This postmodern tendency creates false representations about truth that we have difficulty processing.[125] Examples of this "historical amnesia" abound in contemporary films like *Dances with Wolves,* where nostalgic representations of history are paraded as real history and accepted as such by the culture.[126] What Jameson and others demonstrate is that popular cultural forms have the power to construct realities and myths—art becomes life; representation becomes reality.

If these assumptions about postmodern culture are accurate, then such a culture will value popular cultural forms as its main source of cultural meaning, myth, and legitimization. In the examinations that follow, one item for consideration will be the differing attitudes toward the study of popular culture in America and Europe. It seems that European intellectuals are less open to the value of studying popular culture as a source of meaning. Does their attitude mean that Europe as a society is less characterized by postmodern elements than U.S. society? Perhaps it suggests that European scholars accept what many of the postmodern theorists hypothesize: namely, that postmodernism represents a decay of culture and a demise of society. This demise is expressed not only in how a culture views history but also in the way a culture views ultimate reality. In such a culture, it is as easy to receive truth from the movie house as from the synagogue or church. When this happens, we witness what David Jasper has referred to as the "absorption of the sacred into the profane," which might be, as Jasper has suggested, "a kenotic move."[127] Certainly, if postmodern society infuses the profane or the secular with sacred significance, the kenosis is complete and the response of the religious institutions in such a society is to embrace the sacred by embracing the profane. This leads us to the two ways secularization occurs in postmodern society.

THE TWO DIRECTIONS OF SECULARIZATION

If the modern era promised the disappearance of religion through secularization, the postmodern era promises the increased visibility of religion, although not necessarily in traditional packages. Contemporary American culture witnesses secularization occurring in two directions: 1) the churches and religious organizations are becoming increasingly more attune to the secular environment, particularly to popular culture, and are in some cases trying to emulate it in the effort to remain relevant; 2) popular cultural forms, including literature, film, and music, are becoming increasingly more visible vehicles of religious images, symbols, and categories. These two directions of secularization demonstrate the blurred or malleable boundaries between religion and culture—the sacred and the secular—that define the relationship of religion and culture in the postmodern era.[128]

First, if we focus on the American Christian community in particular, it is clear that some segments of the population are drawn by church traditions that are closely aligned to secular and worldly culture. R. Laurence Moore suggests this occurs because religion in America has had to sell itself to compete and defines secularization according to religion's "commodification," not its disappearance.[129] Others understand this alignment with the secular in light of Christianity's perceived obligation to act in the world.[130] Regardless of the motivations behind the trend, it seems this pattern puts religion in a reactive stance, where religions that work best are the most effective in dealing with the crises or trends of a society.[131] Religion tends to do this through revival and innovation, according to Rodney Stark and William Sims Bainbridge in *The Future of Religion: Secularization, Revival and Cult Formation*.[132] As R. Laurence Moore makes clear, in American Christianity this spirit of innovation is clearly seen throughout its history, from George Whitefield's ability to make sermons entertaining, to Charles G. Finney's guidelines for mounting a successful revival, to the hedonistic air of some nineteenth-century camp meetings, to twentieth-century televangelists, to Heritage, U.S.A.-type theme parks.[133] In every case, these religious innovations were designed to allow Christianity to compete for popularity and remain relevant, and they led to the church's taking on aspects of worldliness. Perhaps the most conscious efforts of ecclesiastical innovation to remain relevant came from the Social Gospel movement in the late nineteenth and early twentieth centuries. The Social Gospel movement wanted to reform all aspects of life (work, education, entertainment, etc.) in order to protect Christianity's relevance in the modern world.[134]

In the attempt to remain relevant in contemporary society, more and more churches are employing popular cultural forms from the media and technology to raise religious questions in a way that parishioners will embrace.[135] This seems to be particularly effective in attracting young

people to church. Jacqulyn Weekley puts it this way: "Archaic terminology doesn't resonate with the younger generations because they've been
brought up with technology. If the church doesn't use the language
they're familiar with, then we're perceived as having no relevance in
their lives."[136] And in an article in *Christianity Today*, Timothy C. Morgan
demonstrated the extent of this perceived need for using technology in
the church. The title of the article itself suggests the church's way of
thinking when it comes to keeping up with the times: "Cyber Shock:
New Ways of Thinking Must Be Developed for the Church to Keep
Pace in the Coming Information Age."[137]

The emphasis on media and technology is probably nowhere clearer
than in the "megachurch" movement that increased in popularity during
the 1990s in the United States and even in Europe. Megachurches are
huge suburban churches with membership roles in the thousands that
seek to be relevant by sponsoring elements of secular life, including
technology and media-produced presentations and entertainment,
within the walls of a church. In any particular week, a member of a
megachurch might go bowling, attend an aerobics class, play basketball,
seek family counseling, and attend a multimedia presentation—all
within the church's confines.[138] American church historian Bill Leonard
calls the megachurch movement the "Wal-Martization of American religion"[139] by noting the megachurch philosophy is to provide for every
need of the potential consumer. Finally, the megachurch worship service
tends to be high energy and includes entertainment forms such as contemporary music, plays, and skits, while youth programs might include
church-made music videos, arcade games, and laser light shows—the
emphasis seems to be on entertainment to keep a high level of interest.[140]
The megachurch movement is an international trend. The movement's
model church, Willow Creek Community Church in suburban
Chicago, boasts some twenty-seven thousand worshipers on Easter
morning.[141] But even in smaller communities in traditional Bible Belt
settings, the megachurch influence is alive and well, with community
churches modeled on Willow Creek using secular entertainment like
popular movies or business tools like PowerPoint to preach the gospel.[142]

These examples suggest that many contemporary religious traditions
have adopted a reactionary stance toward technology, popular culture,
and the secular world, employing elements of popular culture in an "If
you can't beat 'em, join 'em" mentality in order to remain competitive
and relevant in contemporary society. Perhaps no better illustration is
needed than the one that introduces this book: the monks of the
Monastery of Christ in the Desert in Chama River Canyon, New

Mexico, who stay connected to the world via the World Wide Web. On the one hand, like ancient monasteries, this one is no different in providing the monks retreat from the secular world and materialism. On the other hand, the monks are not afraid to use secular technology as a tool to remain relevant and to prosper.[143] As we see more and more examples of religion becoming more like secular culture, we witness the first direction secularization is taking in postmodern culture. This phase of secularization seeks to regain what was lost in the modern phase of secularization—relevance and power.

The second direction of secularization involves the spreading of religious messages, symbols, and concerns in other cultural forms besides the traditionally religious. When traditional religious institutions lose their power, and even when they do not, religiosity will express itself in other parts of the culture, oftentimes in popular cultural forms. So in the contemporary secularization movement, not only do we see religious institutions becoming more like the secular world, we also see secular forms of entertainment and culture carrying religious messages. If this is true, then secularization in the postmodern age could result in a wider dissemination of religious messages than ever through a broader base of cultural vehicles. Rather than witnessing religion diminish, we might witness a culture of religious saturation where religious symbolism and questions are dispersed throughout the cultural landscape.[144] Many religious elements are expressed through secular forms characteristic of culture and time period. This does not mean that everything can be religion but that many different aspects of culture can provide a forum for religious discussion.[145] Thus, in our cultural studies, which include the study of literature, art, film, music, and so on, we expect to find a religious dimension beyond the traditional that extends to the popular level[146] because myth and ritual can be expressed through story and aesthetic expression as well as through doctrine.

Oftentimes religious leaders adopt certain popular forms of culture to express religious truth when they recognize that those forms can command the attention of the public. Thus, even though some such forms might be initially suspect (for example, Hollywood and popular novels), they can also provide an excellent vehicle for carrying religious messages.[147] In these cases, the "sacralization" of secular forms is purposeful and direct. In other cases, the sacralization of secular cultural forms might be simply a product of the dialectical relationship between religion and other cultural forms because they have the ability to express a cultural worldview as well as the personal attitudes and beliefs of the artists and creators of cultural products.[148] This is why, as R. Laurence

Moore suggests, Mark Twain could declare that religion came more from the "despised novel" than from the "drowsy pulpit."[149] But this is also why many secular products of culture can carry sacred significance—from civil religion to modern fiction with apocalyptic messages.[150] One thing is certain, with the constant pressure to censure popular cultural forms, the public perceives these forms to have the power to shape and define morality, attitudes, and ethics. In this sense at least, they carry religious significance and aspirations.

LOOKING AHEAD: SECULAR/SACRED PORTALS

This book began with an image of twenty-first century monks slaving away at keyboards that connect them to the outside world through cyberspace and the World Wide Web. Technology has provided them with a way to connect with the world without involving themselves in the world. This real-life image reminds me of a series of commercials for a photocopy machine years ago: a monk produced perfect copies of an ancient manuscript in record time by using a photocopy machine and his fellow monks thought it was a miracle. This real-life example and the humorous commercial message tell us something about our culture. They demonstrate on a fundamental level how the secular has intruded upon the sacred realm or how the sacred has been subsumed into the profane. The examples also suggest that how we receive the truth has changed—if secularization has not changed the fundamental religious need of humanity to ask ultimate questions, perhaps it has altered the way we seek answers to those questions. Rather than relying solely on revelation, the inbreaking of the sacred, we rely on reification, the secular manufacturing of truth. The pages that follow examine how secularization has occurred in two directions in contemporary American culture, helping the reader understand his or her own religious sensibilities, cultural involvement, and perhaps even future trends and possibilities for religion and culture.

Without trying to be exhaustive, I have chosen to limit the investigation to three areas (windows or portals to truth) that have been constant in Western culture and, more precisely, in American culture. Thus, the examination will focus on American popular culture and the American religious imagination but is based on Western ways of searching for meaning. Throughout the history of Western religion, there have appeared human windows to the transcendent—attempts to see beyond and experience truth, wholeness, holiness, God. Three of these portals—space/place, text, and image—arise time and again in the attempt to conceptualize the transcendent. The portals also provide avenues for secular stories as well. Places, texts, and images tell stories both sacred and secular, and regardless of whether the place, text, or image is sacred or secular, we often find these portals attempting to establish some truth. The temple and the secular monument, Scripture or state constitution, art, both sacred and secular—all of these participate in telling stories, myths, and foundational truths about humanity's relationship to the divine and to society. These portals, sacred and secular, establish an inter-connectedness, a dialogue, a constant interchange about reality. Perhaps the definition of truth will differ, but these sacred and secular windows function similarly—to provide a sense of meaning and order to life.

In ancient, medieval, and premodern Western societies, space, its organization and humanization, allowed a sense of place to grant mean-ing. In cultures where literacy was largely absent or limited, places (such as the magnificent cathedrals of Europe) allowed a portal to truth, to the transcendent, for those without the written word. As such, space consti-tutes a type of pre-text to meaning in the West, replaced during the modern era by text as narrative meaning, which replaced spatial mean-ing as a primary portal of truth. As literacy rose in the modern era, text became the primary medium for humanity's deepest yearnings. We see this most clearly expressed religiously in Luther's reliance on "Scripture alone" for authority, and expressed generally with the technology offered by the printing press. Now our postmodern era witnesses the decline of textual supremacy as images, television, movies, virtual reality, and image-rich Web pages compete with and, some believe, supplant text as the primary conveyance of meaning in our culture—supported, of course, by the advent and popularization of new technologies. In one sense, we have reached back beyond text to the pre-textual situation, coming full circle so that our post-textual reliance on images mirrors our pre-textual dependence on spatial orientation.[151]

This does not suggest mutual exclusiveness during historical periods. Quite the contrary. The human quest for meaning takes place through all three portals, sometimes in concert. For example, images such as Christian art were an integral part of spatial orientations in a pre-textual situation, just as text is a critical part of a post-textual, postmodern film. Nor does it suggest that other components of culture are absent in the quest for meaning. Rather, I am suggesting that a sense of place, text, and image has contributed and does contribute to the process of building and perpetuating myths, which seem to lie at the heart of humanity's search for meaning. Sense of place, text, and image participate in a cul-ture's storytelling and represent three and only three of the various ways humans seek and express truths. At some times and in some places, one or another may tend to dominate, but all three are present in the cultural sacred and secular myths that help define what cultures hold to be true.

In the following pages, I look at each portal and examine the secular-sacred dialogue taking place in contemporary America. The dialogue illustrates the claim in this chapter that secularization should be seen as taking place in two directions: secularization equals secularizing the sacred as well as sacralizing the secular. This secularization of space, text, and image, regardless of its origination or direction, constitutes the relationship between religion and culture that steers our search for meaning.

NOTES

1. The evolution of the theory of secularization presented in this chapter and book runs throughout my work in two previous books. My thanks to the publishers of those books for their cooperation in my use of previously published material. See Conrad E. Ostwalt Jr., *After Eden: The Secularization of American Space in the Fiction of Willa Cather and Theodore Dreiser* (Lewisburg, Pa.: Bucknell University Press, 1990) and Conrad E. Ostwalt Jr., "Conclusion: Religion, Film, and Cultural Analysis," in Joel W. Martin and Conrad E. Ostwalt, Jr., eds., *Screening the Sacred: Religion, Myth, and Ideology in Popular American Film* (Boulder: Westview Press, 1995).

2. Claudia Glenn Dowling, "A Light in the Desert," *Life*, June 1996, 72.

3. Howard Dorgan, *Giving Glory to God in Appalachia: Worship Practices of Six Baptist Subdenominations* (Knoxville: University of Tennessee Press, 1987), ch. 2.

4. Joan Osborne's "One of Us" and Madonna's "Like a Prayer" music videos.

5. This understanding of the relationship between religion and secularization exists throughout the scholarly literature. For a good articulation of the predominant attitude, see Bernard Eugene Meland, *The Secularization of Modern Cultures* (New York: Oxford University Press, 1966).

6. Peter Berger, "Secularism in Retreat," *The National Interest* (winter 1996/97): 4.

7. Ibid., 5, 6.

8. Mark Chaves, "Secularization as Declining Religious Authority," *Social Forces* 72, no. 3 (March 1994): 749, 750. Other writers such as David Yamane support this line of thinking and uphold the old secularization thesis while incorporating newer revisions and insights. See David Yamane, "Secularization on Trial: In Defense of a Neosecularization Paradigm," *Journal for the Scientific Study of Religion* 36, no. 1 (1997): 109–22. The roots of this revision can be seen as early as the mid-1970s in works such as Bryan Wilson's "Aspects of Secularization in the West," *Japanese Journal of Religious Studies* 3, no. 4 (December 1976): 259–76, where Wilson points to religion's powerlessness in Western contemporary society (276).

9. Andrew Greeley, "The Persistence of Religion," *CrossCurrents* 45, no. 1 (spring 1995): 24–41.

10. See Rodney Stark and William Sims Bainbridge, *The Future of Religion: Secularization, Revival and Cult Formation* (Berkeley: University of California Press,

1985); Daniel Bell, "The Return of the Sacred? The Argument on the Future of Religion," *British Journal of Sociology* 28 (December 1977): 419–49; and Robert Booth Fowler, *Unconventional Partners: Religion and Liberal Culture in the United States* (Grand Rapids, Mich.: Eerdmans, 1989).

11. Stephen L. Carter, *The Culture of Disbelief: How American Law and Politics Trivialize Religious Devotion* (New York: Basic Books, 1993), 15–16.

12. See Carter, *The Culture of Disbelief.* This is how he understands religion. See also Wade Clark Roof and William McKinney, *American Mainline Religion: Its Changing Shape and Future* (New Brunswick, N.J.: Rutgers University Press, 1987).

13. See N. J. Demerath III, "Varieties of Sacred Experience" (presidential address at the Society for the Scientific Study of Religion, Boston, November 1999), *Journal for the Scientific Study of Religion* 39, no. 1 (March 2000): 1–9.

14. Peter L. Berger, *The Sacred Canopy: Elements of a Sociological Theory of Religion* (Garden City, N.Y.: Doubleday, 1967).

15. Ibid., 27–28.

16. See also Bryan Wilson, "Secularization: The Inherited Model," in *The Sacred in a Secular Age: Toward Revision in the Scientific Study of Religion,* ed. Phillip E. Hammond (Berkeley: University of California Press, 1985), 9–20; and David Martin, *The Religious and the Secular* (New York: Schocken Books, 1969).

17. See Demerath, "Varieties of Sacred Experience."

18. See Greeley, "Persistence of Religion." See also Demerath, "Varieties of Sacred Experience"; and James Mathisen, "From Civil Religion to Folk Religion: The Case for American Sport," in *Human Kinectics,* ed. S. J. Hoffman (Champaigne, Ill.: University of Illinois Press, 1992).

19. Chaves, "Secularization as Declining Religious Authority."

20. See E. M. Adams, *Religion and Cultural Freedom* (Philadelphia: Temple University Press, 1993), 1–4; Owen Chadwick, *The Secularization of the European Mind in the Nineteenth Century* (Cambridge: Cambridge University Press, 1975), 432. Even if religion is connected to neurosis as Freud thought, it is still a fundamental human characteristic. See Sigmund Freud, *The Future of an Illusion,* trans. and ed. James Strachey (New York: W. W. Norton), 1961.

21. Chaves, "Secularization as Declining Religious Authority."

22. See Stark and Bainbridge, *The Future of Religion,* for the idea that revival and new religion formation could result from the secularization process.

23. R. Laurence Moore, *Selling God: American Religion in the Marketplace of Culture* (New York: Oxford University Press, 1994).

24. See R. Stephen Warner, "Work in Progress toward a New Paradigm for the Sociological Study of Religion in the United States," *American Journal of Sociology* 98, no. 5 (March 1993): 1044–93; and Nathan O. Hatch, *The Democratization of American Christianity* (New Haven, Conn: Yale University Press), 1989.

25. Paul Nathanson, *Over the Rainbow: The Wizard of Oz as a Secular Myth of America* (Albany: State University of New York Press, 1991), 17–18.

26. Ibid., 17.

27. See Meland, *Secularization of Modern Cultures,* 45–46.

28. Jon Michael Spencer, *Blues and Evil* (Knoxville: University of Tennessee Press, 1993).

29. See Demerath, "Varieties of Sacred Experience," 3.

30. See W. Warren Wagar, "Introduction," in *The Secular Mind: Transformations of Faith in Modern Europe*, ed. W. Warren Wagar (New York: Holmes & Meier, 1982), 2.

31. Berger, *The Sacred Canopy*, 106.

32. See Wilson, "Secularization: The Inherited Model," 11; Greeley, "Persistence of Religion," 41; and James Drane, *The Possibility of God: A Reconsideration of Religion in a Technological Society* (Totowa, N.J.: Littlefield, Adams & Co., 1976), 98–99.

33. See Ninian Smart, *Beyond Ideology: Religion and the Future of Western Civilization* (San Francisco: Harper & Row, 1981), 208ff.

34. See Drane, *The Possibility of God*, 99–100.

35. See William Lloyd Newell, *The Secular Magi: Marx, Freud, and Nietzsche on Religion* (New York: Pilgrim Press, 1986).

36. See Chadwick, *Secularization of the European Mind*, 14–15, 156; and Wagar, "Introduction," 2.

37. See Nathanson, *Over the Rainbow*, 14.

38. Greeley, "Persistence of Religion," 38.

39. Berger, *The Sacred Canopy*, 108.

40. Steve Bruce, ed., *Religion and Modernization: Sociologists and Historians Debate the Secularization Thesis* (Oxford: Clarendon Press, 1992), 6.

41. Carter, *The Culture of Disbelief*, 6, 23–24, 277.

42. See Chaves, "Secularization as Declining Religious Authority," 752; and David Martin, *A General Theory of Secularization* (New York: Harper & Row, 1978), 12. See also Wilson, "Secularization: The Inherited Model."

43. See Nathanson, *Over the Rainbow*, 14; and Meland, *Secularization of Modern Cultures*, 116.

44. Wilson, "Secularization: The Inherited Model," 11–12. See also Olivier Tschannen, "The Secularization Paradigm: A Systematization," *Journal for the Scientific Study of Religion* 30, no. 4 (1991): 395–415. See Nathanson, *Over the Rainbow*, 14, for his use of this quotation.

45. Roy Wallis and Steve Bruce, "Secularization: The Orthodox Model," in *Religion and Modernization: Sociologists and Historians Debate the Secularization Thesis*, ed. Steve Bruce (Oxford: Clarendon Press, 1992), 11, 22.

46. Berger, *The Sacred Canopy*, 107–8.

47. Meland, *Secularization of Modern Cultures*, 36–42. The quotation is found on p. 42.

48. R. Laurence Moore, *Selling God*, 4. Moore cites a report on a survey conducted by the Graduate School of the City University of New York, *New York Times*, 10 April 1991.

49. Roger Finke, "An Unsecular America," in *Religion and Modernization: Sociologists and Historians Debate the Secularization Thesis* (ed. Steve Bruce; Oxford: Clarendon Press, 1992), 163.

50. See Mark Hulsether, "Interpreting the 'Popular' in Popular Religion," *American Studies* 36, no. 2 (fall 1995): 129–31. See also Jon Butler, *Awash in a Sea of Faith* (Cambridge: Harvard University Press, 1990).

51. Martin, *The Religious and the Secular*, 10ff.

52. Chadwick, *Secularization of the European Mind*, 4. See also Hammond, *The Sacred in a Secular Age*.

53. Jeffrey K. Hadden, "Desacralizing Secularization Theory," in *Secularization and Fundamentalism Reconsidered: Religion and the Political Order*, vol. 3 (ed. Jeffrey K. Hadden and Anson Shupe; New York: Paragon House, 1989), 3–4.

54. Greeley, "Persistence of Religion," 39.

55. Ibid., 25–26, 29–31, 39.

56. See Laurence Iannaccone and Rodney Stark, "A Supply Side Reinterpretation of the 'Secularization' of Europe," *Journal for the Scientific Study of Religion* 33, no. 3 (1994): 230–52; Stark and Bainbridge, *The Future of Religion;* Chaves, "Secularization as Declining Religious Authority," 749–74; and Berger, "Secularism in Retreat," 3–12.

57. Meland, *Secularization of Modern Cultures*, 117.

58. Wagar, "Introduction," 4. See also Harvey Cox, *The Secular City: Secularization and Urbanization in Theological Perspective* (New York: Macmillan, 1966); and Martin E. Marty, *The Modern Schism: Three Paths to the Secular* (New York: Harper & Row, 1969), 11.

59. See Frank J. Lechner, "The Case Against Secularization: A Rebuttal," *Social Forces* 69 (1991): 1103–19; Chaves, "Secularization as Declining Religious Authority," 749, Chadwick, *The Secularization of the European Mind;* and Hammond, *The Sacred in a Secular Age*.

60. Stark and Bainbridge, *The Future of Religion*, 429–30.

61. Ibid., 1–2.

62. See Demerath, "Varieties of Sacred Experience."

63. Peter Iver Kaufman, "Religion on the Run," *Journal of Interdisciplinary History* 25, no. 1 (summer 1994): 85–86. See also C. John Sommerville, *The Secularization of Early Modern England: From Religious Culture to Religious Faith* (New York: Oxford University Press, 1992).

64. Nathanson, *Over the Rainbow*, 318.

65. See Chaves, "Secularization as Declining Religious Authority."

66. George M. Marsden and Bradley J. Longfield, eds., *The Secularization of the Academy* (New York: Oxford University Press, 1992), 5, 13–41.

67. Chaves, "Secularization as Declining Religious Authority," 755–56.

68. Ibid., 749.

69. Berger, *The Sacred Canopy*, 110–18. The quotation is found on p. 118.

70. Ibid., 123.

71. Martin, *A General Theory of Secularization*, 100–1.

72. Sommerville, *Secularization of Early Modern England*, 3–5. See also Vernon Pratt, *Religion and Secularization* (London: Macmillan, 1970), 1–5 and Tschannen, "The Secularization Paradigm."

73. See Timothy Husband and Jane Hayward, *The Secular Spirit: Life and Art at the End of the Middle Ages* (New York: E. P. Dutton, 1975), 11.

74. See Wagar, "Introduction," 6.

75. Ibid., 5. See also p. 12.

76. David Nash, *Secularism, Art and Freedom* (Leicester: Leicester University Press, 1992), 8–27.

77. Carter, *The Culture of Disbelief*, 7.

78. Ibid.

79. Meland, *Secularization of Modern Cultures*, 15, 58ff. See also Arnold Toynbee, *An Historian's Approach to Religion* (New York: Oxford University Press, 1956).

80. Wagar, "Introduction," 9. See also Pratt, *Religion and Secularization*, 11–20.

81. Pratt, *Religion and Secularization*, 13.

82. See Bernard Eugene Meland, *The Realities of Faith: The Revolution in Cultural Forms* (New York: Oxford University Press, 1962), preface.

83. Drane, *The Possibility of God*, 87–89.

84. Stark and Bainbridge, *The Future of Religion*, 430–4.

85. Ibid., 432–33.

86. Wagar, "Introduction," 8.

87. See Meland, *The Secularization of Modern Cultures*, 35; Smart, *Beyond Ideology*, 209–11.

88. Phyllis H. Stock, "Proudhon and *Morale Independante*: A Variation of French Secular Morality," in Wagar, *The Secular Mind*, 102ff.

89. Newell, *The Secular Magi*, xiv.

90. Nathanson, *Over the Rainbow*, 311.

91. Husband and Hayward, *The Secular Spirit*, 12.

92. See Martin, *A General Theory of Secularization*, 1–8 in particular.

93. Wagar, "Introduction," 5–6.

94. See David Spadafora, "Secularization in British Thought, 1730–1789: Some Landmarks," in Wagar, *The Secular Mind*, 36.

95. Greeley, "Persistence of Religion," 34–35, 27.

96. Carter, *The Culture of Disbelief*, 44–45, 51.

97. See Fowler, *Unconventional Partners*, 2. See also Kenneth D. Wald, *Religion and Politics in the United States* (New York: St. Martin's, 1986), 9.

98. Alexis de Tocqueville, *Democracy in America*, ed. Harvey C. Mansfield and Delba Winthrop (Chicago: University of Chicago Press, 2000).

99. See Hulsether, "Interpreting the 'Popular' in Popular Religion," 127. See also Paul Boyer, *When Time Shall Be No More: Prophecy Belief in Modern American Culture* (Cambridge: Belknap Press of Harvard University Press, 1992), 2–3, 13–15; and George Gallup Jr. and Jim Castelli, *The People's Religion: American Faith in the 90s* (New York: Macmillan, 1989).

100. Carter, *The Culture of Disbelief*, 51ff., 67.

101. Peter L. Berger, "Religion in Post–Protestant America," *Commentary*, May 1986, 4; and Berger, "Secularism in Retreat." See also Fowler, *Unconventional Partners*, 3; and Butler, *Awash in a Sea of Faith*.

102. Moore, *Selling God*, 67ff.

103. Ibid., 11. See also Hulsether, "Interpreting the 'Popular' in Popular Religion," 128.

104. See Moore, *Selling God*; Roger Finke and Rodney Stark, *The Churching of America, 1776–1990: Winners and Losers in Our Religious Economy* (New Brunswick, N.J.: Rutgers University Press, 1992); Laurence Iannaccone, "The Consequences of Religious Market Structure: Adam Smith and the Economics of Religion," *Rationality and Society* 3 (April 1991): 156–77; Warner, "Work in Progress toward a New Paradigm," 1044–93.

105. Greeley, "Persistence of Religion," 27.

106. Moore, *Selling God*, 10.

107. Clifford Geertz, "Thick Description: Toward an Interpretative Theory of Culture," in Clifford Geertz, *Interpretation of Cultures* (New York: Basic Books, 1973), 3.

108. Fowler, *Unconventional Partners*, 3.

109. Moore, *Selling God*, 8.

110. James G. Moseley, *A Cultural History of Religion in America* (Westport, Conn.: Greenwood Press, 1981), 161–62. See also Geertz, *The Interpretation of Cultures*, 87–125.

111. Greeley, "Persistence of Religion," 36.

112. Moore, *Selling God*, 9, 275.

113. See George M. Marsden, *Fundamentalism and American Culture: The Shaping of Twentieth-Century Evangelicalism 1870–1925* (Oxford: Oxford University Press, 1980), vi, 3ff.

114. Butler, *Awash in a Sea of Faith*, 4.

115. Adams, *Religion and Cultural Freedom*, 25, 56.

116. See Moore, *Selling God;* and Allen C. Guelzo, "Selling God in America: How Christians Have Befriended Mammon," *Christianity Today*, 24 April 1995, 27–30.

117. Moore, *Selling God*, 5–6, 13ff., 91, 120, 221–22. See also Michael T. Gilmore, *American Romanticism and the Marketplace* (Chicago: University of Chicago Press, 1985), and Hatch, *The Democratization of American Christianity*.

118. See Moore, *Selling God*, ch. 8; and Hulsether, "Interpreting the 'Popular' in Popular Religion," 128–29.

119. See Paul Galloway, "Media Are Poor Substitute for the Family," *Chicago Tribune;* repr. in *The Charlotte Observer*, 3 June 1996, 9A. See also Quentin Schultze, *Winning Your Kids Back from the Media* (Westmount, Ill.: InterVarsity Press, 1994).

120. Langdon Gilkey, *Society and the Sacred: Toward a Theology of Culture in Decline* (New York: Crossroad, 1981), 3–4.

121. Ostwalt, "Conclusion," 157–58.

122. See John Storey, *An Introductory Guide to Cultural Theory and Popular Culture* (Athens: University of Georgia Press, 1993), 154–59.

123. See Storey, *Cultural Theory and Popular Culture*, 159–61, and Jean–Francois Lyotard, *The Postmodern Condition: A Report on Knowledge* (Manchester: Manchester University Press, 1984).

124. Storey, *Cultural Theory and Popular Culture*, 162–65, and Jean Baudrillard, *Simulations* (New York: Semiotext(e): 1983). For the *JFK* reference, see Ostwalt, "Conclusion," 156.

125. See Storey, *Cultural Theory and Popular Culture*, 166–72; and Frederic Jameson, "Postmodernism, or the Cultural Logic of Late Capitalism," *New Left Review* 146 (1984); "The Politics of Theory: Ideological Positions in the Postmodernism Debate," in *The Ideologies of Theory Essays*, vol. 2 (London: Routledge, 1988); "Postmodernism and Consumer Society," in *The Anti-Aesthetic: Essays on Postmodern Culture*, ed. Hal Foster (Port Townsend, Wash.: Bay Press, 1983), 111–25.

126. See Ostwalt, "Conclusion," 156–57; see also Conrad Ostwalt, "*Dances with Wolves*: An American *Heart of Darkness*," *Literature/Film Quarterly* 24, no. 2 (1996): 209–16.

127. David Jasper (paper presented at the Southeastern Conference for the Study of Religion, Columbia, S.C., March 1996).

128. See Ostwalt, "Conclusion."

129. Moore, *Selling God*, 5.

130. Gabriel Vahanian, *The Death of God: The Culture of Our Post–Christian Era* (New York: George Braziller, 1961), 60–66.

131. See Newell, *The Secular Magi*, xiv.

132. See Stark and Bainbridge, *The Future of Religion*, 435–86.

133. Moore, *Selling God*, 3, 41–42, 44, 49, 50–52, 251–52, and ch. 9.

134. Ibid., 209–18.

135. Nathanson, *Over the Rainbow*, 17.

136. Jacqulyn Weekley, quoted in Julie Slaven, "Lights! Camera! Religion!" *The Charlotte Observer*, 1 June 1996, G1, G4.

137. Timothy C. Morgan, "Cyber Shock: New Ways of Thinking Must Be Developed for the Church to Keep Pace in the Coming Information Age," *Christianity Today*, 3 April 1995, 78–86.

138. Gustav Niebuhr, "Where Religion Gets a Big Dose of Shopping-Mall Culture," *New York Times*, 16 April 1995, A1, col. 1.

139. Bill Leonard, quoted in Niebuhr, "Shopping-Mall Culture," 14.

140. Gustav Niebuhr, "The High Energy Never Stops," *New York Times*, 16 April 1995, 14; Niebuhr, "Shopping-Mall Culture," 14; and Trip Gabriel, "MTV-Inspired Images, but the Message for Children Is a Moral One," *New York Times*, 16 April 1995, 14.

141. Niebuhr, "Shopping-Mall Culture," 1.

142. Slaven, "Lights! Camera! Religion!" 1, 4.

143. Dowling, "A Light in the Desert," 66–73.

144. See Ostwalt, "Conclusion."

145. See Moseley, *A Cultural History*, xv–xvi, 161. See also Edwin S. Gaustad, Darline Miller, and G. Allison Stokes, "Religion in America," *American Quarterly* 31, no. 3 (1979): 250.

146. See Gilkey, *Society and the Sacred*, x; Fowler, *Unconventional Partners*, 3; and Peter W. Williams, *Popular Religion in America: Symbolic Change and the Modernization Process in Historical Perspective* (Englewood Cliffs, N.J.: Prentice Hall, 1980, 1989).

147. See Moore, *Selling God*, 17, 221–22.

148. Nathanson, *Over the Rainbow*, xviii. See also Husband and Hayword, *The Secular Spirit*, 11.

149. Mark Twain, quoted in Moore, *Selling God*, 147.

150. See Smart, *Beyond Ideology*, 221–32 and W. Warren Wagar, "World's End: Secular Eschatologies in Modern Fiction," in Wagar, *The Secular Mind*, 239.

151. See John Lukacs, "It's the End of the Modern Age," *The Chronicle of Higher Education*, 26 April 2002, B9. Lukacs discusses the return to a "pictorial" orientation in contemporary society that mimics the Middle Ages.

PART I

1
SPACE/PLACE/PRE-TEXT

The spaces we inhabit become the places we construct, the places in which we move and live and love and worship. Human beings project meaning into the spaces they inhabit. Spaces tell stories, but they do so as pre-text, apart from text, and sometimes supplementary to text. In the Christian tradition, no space is more obviously enriched with metaphorical meaning than a church. From the grand cathedrals of Europe, to plain Puritan structures of the New World, to megachurch sports arenas in Los Angeles, these worship spaces enfold symbolic religious meaning and express fundamental values, beliefs, and desires. But specifically religious buildings are not the only spaces that express values and beliefs. Secular spaces such as patriotic monuments, memorials, and commercial icons sometimes become "holy" ground with deep meaning for a culture or society. Thus, with spaces we have a pre-text that enfolds metaphorical and symbolic meaning, and we have places that demonstrate the flexible and malleable boundaries that exist between the sacred and secular—our sacred places sometimes mimic our secular ones while our secular spaces often take on sacred functions. Part one illustrates the two directions of secularization through spatial arrangement by considering contemporary changes in church structures and functions in chapter two and by examining a secular political institution in chapter three that functions with sacred intent. Megachurches and Love Valley demonstrate the secularization and sacralization of American space.

THE SECULARIZATION OF TRADITION: MEGACHURCHES AND THE MARKETING OF CHRISTIANITY

Zurich, Switzerland: heart of the sixteenth-century Swiss Reformation. Huldrych Zwingli led the reform with a brand of zealous Christianity designed in part to drive worldly and Catholic characteristics out of Christian worship. In Zwingli's church, if the Bible did not prescribe a certain act or ritual, such an act was disallowed. Thus, there would be no organ music in worship or icons to adorn the ritual space. These were fine for the Catholic Church but too worldly for Zwingli. His complaint centered on the secularity issue. For Zwingli, both the Catholic Church and many of his Protestant allies were too embroiled in worldly cares and practices. Yet Zwingli allied himself with civil authorities in order to carry out his reforms. Thus, we see the problematic nature of dealing with the relationship of religion and secularity.[1]

Contemporary Zurich is marked by wealth and by the high living that accompanies being the banking capital of the world. The city is characterized by a vibrant youth culture that stands in stark contrast to Zwingli's austere religion. Old Town Zurich teems with swarms of young people streaming in and out of bars, cabarets, sex shops, and X-rated movie theaters. On centuries-old streets, where Zwingli walked and preached a faith of austerity, the ambience is now high energy to appeal to youth, to members of Generation X in search of entertainment and immediate gratification. If Zwingli were alive in Zurich today, his fiery sermons would likely take on a new zeal and fervency.

This scene plays itself out in the narrow streets of medieval Old Town to create a strange setting for what some hope to be a new kind of church reformation. In stark contrast to Zwingli's attempt to drive out worldly and secular elements from the church, the International Christian Fellowship (ICF) is promoting a reformation for the twenty-first century—the megachurch movement. Some three and a half centuries after Zwingli, Zurich has once again become a center for church reform, and this time, rather than leading a Swiss reform movement, the ICF is attempting to use Zurich as a European spearhead for the megachurch movement. Rather than battle worldly characteristics that make their way into the church, the ICF embraces secular ways to capture the attention of what they see as a restless twenty-something generation that is largely unchurched but in search of spiritual peace. The ICF uses secular enticements to attract these young people to church by filling their services with a Christianized version of high-energy, entertainment-oriented activities in worship that tend to mimic what one might find on the streets of Old Town. Visiting an ICF worship service, one gets the impression that this church is in competition with the secular attractions in this thriving city and that it is using or borrowing secular activities from popular youth culture to compete with those elements attracting Xers.[2]

A service that employs movie clips, MTV-style entertainment, and pop music with Christian lyrics in order to draw the unchurched to worship seems strangely out of place anywhere in Europe, let alone in Zurich. But it seems to be working as the church continues to experience success and growth. With a heavy emphasis on outreach and evangelism, the goal is to recapture a lost generation. The strategy is to use the culture of that generation to shape a liturgy and, to some extent, a theology. The church is very forthright and conscious concerning its target audience, Xers; its motivation, outreach; and its strategy, use of popular culture.[3]

The first Sunday of each month at the ICF is set aside for special services to attract new young people to the church. It is during these services that the megachurch philosophy is most visible. In particular, the philosophy embraces using elements of popular culture that will make going to church relevant and attractive, and necessarily adopts secular culture as its baseline standard. In contrast to Zwingli's sixteenth-century reform to drive secular elements out of the church, the megachurches and the ICF's contemporary reformation embrace parts of popular and secular culture to make Christianity relevant for a generation searching for some meaningful guiding philosophical or ethical perspective. Will this movement, which became popular first in the United States, prosper in Europe? A strong history of state religion makes the scenario improbable. But in Switzerland, a country historically proud of its independence, the movement seems to be gathering steam. And some six years after I first encountered the ICF movement in Zurich, the church has grown and spread and seems to be experiencing success. Certainly, Switzerland would be the logical place for any such movement to begin and take root in Europe, if in fact it does. The outcome of the Zurich experiment will tell us much about the state of American and European society and the extent to which each has been secularized in the contemporary world.

CHRISTIANITY AND SECULARIZATION

Many theologians critique the megachurch movement and decry the state of the contemporary church for allowing itself to become secularized. Much of what critics term secularization arises from a comparison of current practices to what religion used to be—a debate between innovation and tradition. But the suggestion that the secularization of Christianity is a contemporary or Protestant phenomenon ignores the history and development of the church from its inception. When we witness concessions religion makes to secular science, no matter how delayed, such as Pope John Paul II's recognition of the theory of evolution or the Catholic Church's 1992 reversal of its condemnation of Galileo's theories about a heliocentric solar system,[4] it is easy to forget that the Christian tradition has been secularizing since its beginning. Many of the prescriptions outlined by Paul and other early Christian writings arise from the complexities stemming from the church's contact with secular society. One might even argue that one of the church's early defining moments, the Council of Jerusalem, occurred in response to secularization. In the first century, the struggling new religion was still as much a Jewish sect as it was a separate religion. The tradition's first crisis came when Paul and others began to make "concessions" to Hellenistic culture in order to spread the religion and to make the religion relevant on a larger scale. These concessions to secular culture allowed Christianity to survive and spread, but the tradition was changed by these secularizing trends.

Alongside these secularizing trends in early Christianity, a pattern of anti-secularism developed during times of crisis and hardship in the Christian community. The Book of John's Revelation urges the persecuted faithful to remain steadfast in light of the dawning apocalypse. According to John's vision, the final judgment would separate the faithful from the worldly, the sacred from the secular; for these reasons, Christians were urged to abstain from secular ways (Roman ways), even if it meant death. This same anti-secular attitude was echoed by Montanus, a second-century prophet who warned of doom and urged the church to return to its pure state, or to the way things were in the early days before the church had been tainted by worldly concessions. Prophets and reformers invariably take up the call to reform the church by returning it to its pristine and primitive condition. Whether Paul, Montanus, St. Francis, Zwingli, or Alexander Campbell and Barton Stone, the message represents a reaction to the same enduring secularizing tendencies that have been part of Christian history from the beginning.

So a pattern established itself early on: the tradition institutionalized and necessarily made concessions to secular society, and some leaders/prophets spoke out against such concessions in favor of a pure, untainted religion. But not all reaction was negatively disposed against secularizing tendencies. Some in and outside the church were able to use secularization to great political and ecclesiastical advantage. For example, Christianity experienced a wholesale period of secularization when the emperor Constantine recognized Christianity as a legitimate religion. Until this point in its history, the Christian story often had been told through martyrs' blood and struggle with the empire as the sect struggled in a hostile culture. Worship was simple, if not secret. Worship places, if they existed as such, were more often than not someone's home or the catacombs. Hierarchy was at a minimum. Then suddenly, in one swift move in the early fourth century, Constantine revolutionized Christianity. He recognized the persecuted religion, granted it tolerance, and perhaps even adopted it. For the first time in history, Christians were free to worship with imperial sanction. The church changed rapidly: rituals were formalized and became more elaborate as befitting an imperial religion; creeds took on a greater and more political role; rich and impressive worship houses were constructed; artwork flooded churches as an aid to worship; clergy took on greater prestige in society. In short, the church became more institutionalized, more political, wealthier, and took on a more prestigious and culturally central role in society. Christianity became more secular and worldly than ever before, but once again, secularization allowed the church to thrive. With its newfound wealth and respect, the costs of being Christian were greatly diminished.

Because of these changes, one would expect a protest against such secularization, and of course it happened. The Donatists believed the church had been corrupted and created a noisy schism. Some priests viewed imperial sanction as a worldly apostasy and protested quietly by retreating into seclusion where they could escape the worldly entrapments of the new church. The monastic movement began to organize seriously and gain momentum in a rejection of Constantine's new Christianity in which membership was easy and fashionable. "Too worldly" was the complaint of the first Christian hermits, and they sought seclusion away from the secularized aspects of the church. But the protest was small, and the church entered a new era of its history.

Constantine's legitimization of Christianity led to a new and energized church, a church that would grow to enjoy power and prestige in the secular realm. In the East, the Byzantine Church quickly became the imperial church and was intimately involved with the imperial dynasty. In the West, Augustine wrote about the relationship of the Christian to the secular powers. In his classic work, *The City of God,* he asserted that Christians, who must for a time live in the secular world, are ultimately citizens of the heavenly city, a higher authority. While Augustine's treatise was meant to direct the Christian's ultimate allegiance, later interpreters read him as establishing a hierarchy of sorts that justified their assertions of ecclesiastical authority in secular matters. And by the collapse of the Roman Empire in the fifth century, the church in Rome was poised and ready to step into the power vacuum created by a crumbling secular governing structure. Armed by later interpretations of Augustine's *City of God* and led by opportunistic and able popes like Gregory the Great, secular power was virtually thrust upon and readily accepted by the medieval sacred institution. The church of the Middle Ages became the power broker in medieval Europe, manipulating secular rulers and secular events and culminating with the symbolic coronation of Charlemagne as Holy Roman Emperor in 800. With this event, the Holy Roman Empire, an intimate marriage of church and state in medieval Europe, was formalized, and the secular involvement of Western Christendom was actual as well as expedient.

The Middle Ages saw the rise and fall of a succession of popes, some who used their secular powers very effectively to build an empire for the Christian church. Incredible wealth and extensive political clout transformed the papacy into an administrative and governmental quagmire requiring skilled and able leadership and diplomacy. The secular powers of the church were never greater, and state Christianity became the norm throughout Europe. Popes manipulated rulers and controlled events. Their power is perhaps best illustrated by the well-known and famed story of Hildebrand (Pope Gregory VII) and German King Henry IV. During the eleventh century, the two found themselves at odds over the issue of lay investiture. Hildebrand, a reforming pope, sought to discontinue the practice of lay investiture as a means of centralizing authority and maintaining stricter control. The temptation of secular princes to settle favors and debts by handing out attractive bishoprics as a means of political expediency was simply too great in Hildebrand's eyes. Henry, however, balked at this restriction of his power and made an appointment in direct disobedience of papal decree. The crisis came to a head when Hildebrand excommunicated Henry and the German nobles pressured their leader to make amends with Rome. The two sides scheduled a summit at Augsburg to settle the issue. While Hildebrand made his way north to embarrass Henry on his own turf, Henry headed south in hopes of spoiling Hildebrand's staging. Hildebrand fortified himself in a castle at Canossa in northern Italy because he feared Henry came to meet him with the sword. But Henry appeared before the pope at Canossa barefoot, dressed as a penitent, eventually able to wring a reluctant absolution from Hildebrand. This clash between sacred and secular forces represents the degree to which ecclesiastical and secular authority had become intermeshed and interwoven. The church, a sacred institution, had secularized to a tremendous degree during the height of the Middle Ages. Likewise, secular authority in this case was undergirded, if only symbolically, by sacred sponsorship.

Medieval Catholicism was not alone in its ecclesiastical involvement with secular and worldly authority. The Protestant reform movements of the sixteenth century were as much interested in ecclesiastical/institutional reform as they were in theological reform. Luther's protest started as disgust over clerical abuse, and he sparked a revolution against ecclesiastical authority structures. But Luther's reform did little to undo the extent to which secularization had affected the institutional church. Luther found himself an ally of the civil authorities when he was appalled by the peasant revolt. And neither Luther nor Calvin would hear of dismantling the church-state partnership that medieval Catholicism had so meticulously constructed. In fact, Calvin's Geneva experiment in theocracy represents the claim of a church with unquestioned secular reach. Henry VIII's state church in England did nothing to challenge a secularized ecclesia. Of the Protestant reform movements, only the radical wing of reformers, the Anabaptists and their offshoots, tried to sever the church-state tie and undo the effects of a secularized ecclesia. Even today, the descendants of these reformers hold staunchly to the principle of separation and normally maintain strict provisions against worldly involvement. Perhaps in contemporary America, the Amish groups in Ohio and Pennsylvania best represent this protest movement against a secularized religion.

While secularization of Christianity is best expressed in Europe through its history of state religion, this is not the case in the United States, which has attempted through civil law to keep church and state separate. Does this mean that the United States is less secularized than Europe? Although many scholars claim it is so, it is not necessarily the case. The church in North America since the Revolutionary period has not enjoyed state support as in Europe, so the sacred-secular entanglement is not established as the rule. Nevertheless, Christianity in the United States has secularized in different ways, including voluntarily adopting and competing with popular culture and secular models of entertainment.[5] In the absence of compulsion, the church had to attract, and in many cases it attracted by conforming to popular trends. As noted earlier in this book, traditions such as the Social Gospel movement of the nineteenth century provide an excellent example. Unable to compete with popular culture with a radically different worldview, the Social Gospel proponents attempted to compete by adopting and revising the popular, secular worldview and thus competing with secular culture bolstered by sacred foundations.

Religion in the United States has always operated on a voluntary basis; however, this concept is relatively new and developing in Europe. Therefore, in Europe, with church participation no longer compulsory or even expedient, it often appears that European society is more secular (less religious) because European churches have not operated on the basis of competition. Although church attendance is not an adequate indicator of religiosity by itself, the statistics are telling. According to Ronald Inglehart of the Institute for Social Research, the United States boasts 30 to 32 percent of the population attending church on any one Sunday, while countries in northern Europe only cite a 5 to 15 percent church attendance.[6]

More than church attendance, however, we can look at the history of the entanglement of the sacred and secular in Europe and America to assess the extent of secularization. Whereas in medieval Europe, secularization appears to have occurred under what Peter Berger has termed a "sacred canopy,"[7] where the church's sacred authority included secular society, in modern America, the opposite appears to be occurring. The church in the United States appears to be operating under a "secular canopy," where secular and popular trends often dictate ecclesiastical strategy. The level of authority for religion in these two paradigms is drastically different, but in both models, secular involvement is a given and secularization is a foregone conclusion. If secularization means that a religious tradition loses authority to control society's ways, then perhaps Europe is more secular; however, if secularization means entanglement with secular and popular culture, then the church in the United States seems to be more defined by secular society. We should not make this an either-or definition of secularization but adopt a definition broad enough to include both trends of secularization.

This brief survey of Christian secularization is neither exhaustive nor representative in intent or effect. It is meant simply to point out that from its inception, the Christian religion began institutionalizing and interacting with the secular world. This interaction led to secularization—the church in Western society has never been a purely sacred entity. And despite the title Holy Roman Empire, Western society has never been a completely sacred culture. The process of secularization has differed in its extent and effect at various points in the church's history, but the process has been a consistent and ongoing part of the Christian institution. Secularization is different in Europe than in America, not as much in degree as in kind. It is probably fruitless to argue that one culture is more secularized than another, as many do in the case of Europe or in comparing the great diversity of cultures that make up Europe and the United States.

In addition, this survey sets the stage for a discussion about the megachurch movement. The movement is a purposeful attempt to incorporate secular and popular culture in the life of the church; therefore, it presents in concentrated form trends that take place anyway. A description of the movement will reveal much not only about how Christianity might be secularizing but also about how American and European communities will respond to such a movement. Will American Christians respond more readily to the megachurches because they are already more in tune to popular and secular culture? This seems to be the case at least initially, as we will explore later. At least in part, the ready acceptance of the megachurch movement in the United States has developed as an American trend during the last twenty to forty years.

The megachurch movement in some ways grew out of the rise of media evangelism in the 1970s and 1980s, a movement that enjoyed much more momentum in the United States than in Europe. Fundamentalist Christian leaders discovered a mass market for their evangelical form of Christianity through various forms of mass media. After pioneering efforts in radio and television, evangelists wholeheartedly embraced these worldly media as a way of spreading the gospel. Their entanglement with secular culture is symbolized perhaps most clearly by Jim and Tammy Bakker's Heritage, U.S.A., theme park. The Bakker's managed to market Christianity by nostalgically depicting secular America through a sacred lens—or was it sacred religion through a secular lens?

At its height of popularity, Heritage featured Main Street, U.S.A., a mock street of yesteryear depicting small-town America and values associated with an ideal and nostalgic appropriation of the past. Social and religious conservatives rely on such a view of America to resurrect a vision of a lost golden age of America—an age that can and must be recaptured through revival and return to God. The message of Main Street was clear: America was blessed by God, but it was the America of the past that had been so blessed. Contemporary America had lost its spiritual moorings, and short of a return to the nostalgically centered values of yesterday, America would be doomed. Just when this golden age was supposed to have occurred is unclear, but it was definitely before the dramatic social changes that marked the 1960s. Vestiges of this and of the social agenda of the conservative Right appeared on Main Street of Heritage's mock village. Toy stores sold "pro-life" dolls and Christian storybooks. Main Street advocated nothing less than John Winthrop's "city upon a hill," where America was envisioned as a sacred society blessed by God and Americans were considered God's people. This civil religion was not so much the vision of a sacred society as it was a secularized religion, because the main vehicle of its expression (Main Street) was an American and contemporary secular icon.

These secularized themes and a gospel based on cultural and material prosperity were marketed and communicated using technology and media, methods evangelicals have been experimenting with throughout the twentieth century. Even before twentieth-century advances in technology, as Mark Noll demonstrates, evangelicals had long since effectively learned to communicate and evangelize by shaping their message to appeal to their audience. Thus, we see in George Whitefield's preaching to "plain people in plain language"[8] the nascent philosophy that would spark later attempts to catch people where they are in life. And in nineteenth-century evangelical tract societies, we see evangelicals using the technology of the day to evangelize beyond the evangelical community.[9] These two tendencies, to identify with the audience and to use technology to communicate, form the backbone of the secularization of the evangelical message in the twentieth century.

Evangelicals learned early on to use mass media in the attempt to reach a large audience beyond the evangelical community.[10] Realizing that periodicals, magazines, and printed material in general might galvanize a community within the evangelical culture but were largely unsuccessful as evangelizing tools,[11] evangelicals turned to new technologies as a way of overcoming the cultural and sometimes geographical space between them and their targeted audience. At first, the telephone seemed to be a promising tool for reaching large numbers of people easily and was often used to start new churches.[12] Creative churchmen recognized radio as a medium for reaching the masses and began to use radio ministries to overcome geographical barriers.[13] Radio evangelism experienced remarkable growth during the 1970s and 1980s in the United States in terms of the number of broadcasts, but there is little evidence that actual audiences increased dramatically.[14] Thus, evangelicals went in search for a more effective medium for spreading the Christian message. They found it in television, which gave evangelical preachers "access to millions of living rooms"[15] and to mainstream America.

Claims by televangelists about audience size via television vary and stretch as high as forty million during the height of televangelism in the mid-1980s. However, many question these estimates and the effectiveness of television when it came to actually gaining new converts, the goal of the evangelical ministry.[16] Others question whether television really closes the cultural gap between evangelicalism and broader American culture.[17] Nevertheless, it is certain that the use of media, particularly television, connected evangelical culture to secular popular culture in a way that was new and novel, and this experience provided evangelicalism and evangelicals a sense of relevance and power through participation in a popular secular medium.[18] This sense of relevance and inclusion in the mainstream culture eventually became one of the cornerstones to the megachurch movement and provides the best example yet of the secularization of the evangelical message.

In the end, televangelism reached its peak and declined not because it was a failed method but because bad press and scandals affected the ministries of the Bakkers and Jimmy Swaggert. While the methods seemed to be effective, regardless of whether they were proper, the managers and messengers of the movement transgressed and televangelism lost its momentum. Nevertheless, the acceptance of secular values to market religion did not disappear and has reemerged with a vengeance in the megachurch movement.

At the same time evangelicals were experimenting with technology, they also discovered the power of large churches. The 1970s witnessed the rise of super churches in America that developed alongside of, in conjunction with, and sometimes in competition with radio and television. As Joel Gregory points out, these churches often exert tremendous "religious and secular power"[19] and attempt to influence popular culture, political processes, media, education, and other secular institutions. By involving themselves in secular matters and institutions, these churches are perhaps the best example in America of the secularization of the traditional Christian institution.[20] For example, First Baptist Church in Dallas, Texas, called by Gregory the "mother church of all the super churches,"[21] operates radio and television outlets, a newspaper, and a college.[22] The church has attempted to create a society within its doors and to control the flow of knowledge by creating its own institutions that function in competition with secular institutions. However, in doing so, it has adopted secular models and methods and has become secularized in the process. Coral Ridge Presbyterian Church, according to Scott Thumma, offered a concert series including country music stars and the music of Andrew Lloyd Webber.[23] A final example includes Robert Schuller's Crystal Cathedral, which operates with the philosophy of marketing that mimics secular marketing and advertising. In the attempt to meet the modern needs of his constituency, Schuller attempts "to throw the kind of bait out that they would like."[24] Critics suggest this baiting allows the concerns of the secular world to determine the agenda of the church.

NOTES

1. See G. R. Potter, *Zwingli* (Cambridge: Cambridge University Press, 1976).

2. The descriptions of the ICF worship service and of contemporary Zurich are based on my visit to Zurich during September 1996. Additional information about the ICF came from the organization's promotional literature and Web site (www.icf.ch).

3. Leo Biggers, pastor of the ICF, interview with author, 15 August 1996.

4. See "Pope Accepts Theory of Evolution," *Raleigh News and Observer,* 25 October 1996, 1A, 16A.

5. See R. Laurence Moore, *Selling God: American Religion in the Marketplace of Culture* (New York: Oxford University Press, 1994).

6. Cathy Lynn Grossman, "Charting the Unchurched in America," *USA Today,* 7 March 2002, 4 (www.usatoday.com). Grossman quotes Ronald Inglehart for these statistics.

7. Peter Berger, *The Sacred Canopy: Elements of a Sociological Theory of Religion* (Garden City, N.Y.: Doubleday, 1967).

8. Mark Noll, *A History of Christianity in the United States and Canada* (Grand Rapids, Mich.: Eerdmans, 1992), 92–93.

9. See Noll, *History of Christianity,* 227.

10. For an examination of the history of evangelical use of media, see Bill Jarrett, "The Lively Experiment: American Evangelicalism and Twentieth-Century Technology" (paper presented at the North Carolina Religious Studies Association, Boone, North Carolina, October 1993).

11. Stephen Board, "Moving the World with Magazines: A Survey of Evangelical Periodicals," in *American Evangelicals and the Mass Media: Perspectives on the Relationship between American Evangelicals and the Mass Media,* ed. Quentin J. Schultze (Grand Rapids, Mich.: Zondervan, 1990), 137.

12. See Harold E. Metcalf, *The Magic of Telephone Evangelism* (Atlanta: Southern Union Conference of Seventh-Day Adventists, 1967); and Richard N. Ostling, "Many Are Called: Dialing for Jesus," *Time,* 27 February 1989, 79.

13. See Everett C. Parker, Elinor Inman, and Ross Snyder, *Religious Radio: What to Do and How* (New York: Harper & Brothers, 1948); and Dennis Benson, *Electric Evangelism* (Nashville: Abingdon, 1973).

14. Quentin J. Schultze, "The Invisible Medium: Evangelical Radio," in Schultze, *American Evangelicals and the Mass Media,* 171–72.

15. Merrill McCloughlin, "From Revival Tent to Mainstream," *U.S. News & World Report,* 19 December 1988, 52–57.

16. See Stewart Hoover, "The Meaning of Religious Television: The '700 Club' in the Lives of Its Viewers," in Schultze, *American Evangelicalism and the Mass Media,* 234.

17. Peter G. Horsfield, *Religious Television: The American Experience* (New York: Longman, 1987).

18. See Stewart M. Hoover, *Mass Media Religion: The Social Sources of the Electronic Church* (Newbury Park, Calif.: SAGE Publications, 1988).

19. Joel Gregory, *Too Great a Temptation: The Seductive Power of America's Super Church* (Fort Worth: Summit Group, 1994), xiii.

20. See Lyle E. Schaller, *The Seven-Day-a-Week Church* (Nashville: Abingdon, 1992); and John N. Vaughan, *The Large Church: A Twentieth-Century Expression of the First-Century Church* (Grand Rapids, Mich.: Baker, 1985).

21. Gregory, *Too Great a Temptation,* xiv.

22. Ibid., xiii.

23. Scott Thumma, "Exploring the Megachurch Phenomena: Their Characteristics and Cultural Context," Hartford Institute for Religion Research (hirr.hartsem.edu), 12.

24. Robert Schuller, interview by G. A. Pritchard, in *Willow Creek Seeker Services: Evaluating a New Way of Doing Church* (Grand Rapids: Baker, 1996), 50.

2
MEGACHURCHES

They are known by several aliases: megachurches, super churches, the next church, "full-service churches, seven-day-a-week churches, shopping-mall churches, and pastoral churches."[1] Some are huge, while others have visions of grandeur and growth. However, what binds these "megachurches" together is not so much their size but their philosophy of evangelism: a way of conceiving church that focuses not on the churched but on the unchurched, that ministers not so much to the believer as it pitches to the nonbeliever. The megachurches bring the unchurched into the sacred walls with a seven-day-a-week approach to the needs and worries of contemporary life. The philosophy is working well in America, not so well in Europe. At a time when mainline denominations are hurting and small churches are failing, some boast the megachurches are the fastest growing segment of the religious population in the United States.[2] Others claim that the megachurch movement represents the future of the church in America and will lead to a major reform of American Christianity. At the same time, the movement is carving out a shaky foothold in Western Europe.

The megachurches represent the secularization of traditional religion—not its failure, disappearance, or loss of authority but its conformity to secular life and to popular culture. These churches are thriving, growing, spreading, and exerting influence over the lives of their parishioners. So traditional theories that view secularization in terms of loss of authority or the gradual disappearance of religion do not stand up in light of this contemporary church phenomenon. However, these churches are secularized because they represent a molding of tradition to the exigencies of secular culture. In these "next churches," Christian tradition has been altered by mass media, geographical mobility, democratization, and the rapid social change characterizing contemporary life.[3] These secular developments in the twentieth century have provided challenges to the Christian community; in the case of the megachurches, they have provided opportunities and an avenue for reform.

Except for fundamentalist groups or groups that define themselves over against popular culture, the contemporary church in America is a solid part of the popular culture mainstream. As R. Laurence Moore has persuasively argued, the church in America competes in the marketplace for loyalty and attention and, as a result, has had to market its product in order to compete.[4] The church in Europe, with its history of state support, might not be required to adopt the same market mentality, but it shares an intimate history with secular power structures. Thus, even though the church's connection to secular society traces a different history in America than in Europe, in both places Christianity has secularized to the extent that it has taken on the characteristics of secular culture, either to compete or to satisfy its secular benefactors. In this way, Christianity in the contemporary world is reactionary to secular culture,[5] and the megachurches, wanting to compete not only with other churches but with secular enticements as well, are perhaps the most reactionary of all. Particularly in America, if these churches are to compete with secular entertainment and enticements, they must create and offer an attractive lure.[6]

How do the megachurches produce a lure that will entice contemporary, restless, overstimulated nonbelievers to attend their services? How do the megachurches convince their parishioners that they would be better served attending church than pursuing other activities on Sunday morning and during the week? They compete by giving their parishioners the same product, by providing and peddling popular culture in sacred clothing. These churches use television, drama, movies, games, technology, and other brands of secular entertainment to explore the supernatural,[7] to attract those who might otherwise not attend church. Some of this entertainment might be purely secular, such as aerobics classes, counseling centers, and church-sanctioned dependency groups,[8] but they contain a Christian prefix, such as "Christian aerobics."[9]

Many scholars have produced important work on the megachurch movement. I am indebted to Scott Thumma's work on megachurches in general and to a full-length study by G. A. Pritchard on the megachurch history and philosophy.[10] The megachurch movement embraces communities across the world, but one church stands out as the unquestioned leader in this reform movement: Willow Creek Community Church in the suburbs of Chicago. Willow Creek is huge—it has attracted twenty-seven thousand people for special Easter services[11] and recently boasted a weekend attendance of twenty thousand. In the year 2000, regular weekend attendance was around seventeen thousand, representing a 20 percent increase during the previous five years.[12] Willow Creek has taken a philosophy of church growth and developed it more than any other contemporary church community; the church is leading a worldwide movement under the leadership of Bill Hybels, a huge staff, and the Willow Creek Association, the organization that oversees the vast network of churches modeled after the Willow Creek philosophy. The more than one million people who attend Willow Creek functions annually represent only a fraction of those who are influenced by the church through the association, books, and tapes.[13] This phenomenal church began as a youth group that Hybels helped lead called "Son City." Hybels and the other leaders of the group stumbled onto the discovery that young people responded to their ministry when they used youth culture, popular music, and "hip" language to communicate. The successful strategy provided the prototype for the method employed at Willow Creek and its associated churches—using the language of the unchurched, a language that is necessarily secular, to attract them to church.[14]

At least one proponent refers to Willow Creek's approach as "the 'apostolic' church," because it models the early church as the church spread into the Hellenistic world.[15] The "apostolic" designation implies that acculturation and secularization have characterized the church from the beginning and even account for much of its evangelical success. The strategy of acculturation or adaptation shows the strong influence of Robert Schuller on Hybels. Schuller's highly successful ministry in California, symbolized famously in his Crystal Cathedral, played an important role in forming Hybels's own approach to church growth and outreach. Hybels was influenced by Schuller's book, *Your Church Has Real Possibilities!,* and in 1975, before the birth of Willow Creek, Hybels attended the Robert Schuller Institute for Successful Church Leadership. What Hybels learned from Schuller was how to respond to the needs of the unchurched, epitomized by Schuller's famous "drive-in" church.[16]

Schuller inspired the dominant and key concept in the megachurch movement, "relevance." Relevance is the key, and relevance is voiced over and over again by ministers of megachurches as the one goal they seek to attain—the most crucial characteristic that separates their churches from the traditional denominational churches. In the attempt to be relevant to their targeted audience, one minister boasts, "We give them what they want, and we give them what they didn't know they wanted—a life change."[17] Another describes relevance in commercial terms: the new way of doing church is "one-stop shopping for your social, educational and spiritual needs." By contrast, "Some churches are stuck. They're still doing church the way it was done in the '50s. It's boring, and people will not attend."[18] The "one-stop shopping" metaphor for relevance recalls Bill Leonard's phrase for the megachurch movement, the "Wal-Martization of American religion."[19] Bishop Charles Blake, the leader of the eighteen thousand–member West Angeles Church of God and Christ, likened his church to a "shopping center" in an interview with National Public Radio's Duncan Moon. Blake said, "I feel that a large church should be something like a shopping center, so that individuals in the community can come to a church institution for whatever need or whatever goal or objective they may have at that given moment."[20] Bishop Blake's assessment demonstrates the megachurch need to be everything to everybody, or at least to meet the needs of the church's targeted audience. In Bishop Blake's church, the congregation in the community of South Central Los Angeles is African American and the church supports some eighty ministries, many with a focus on social and urban renewal.[21] Another megachurch minister connects relevance with technology: "Archaic terminology doesn't resonate with the younger generation because they've been brought up with technology. If the church doesn't use the language they're familiar with, then we're perceived as having no relevance in their lives."[22] Some church leaders adopt the language of business, of corporate America;[23] others use the language of youth culture or popular culture. The message from these ministers is clear: in order to survive, in order to grow, in order to reach a lost world, they must address the existential concerns of a secular society by adopting its language and customs to appear relevant to such a society.[24]

Most of these churches adopt secular standards in subtle ways, perhaps by organizing church around secular, cultural holidays rather than around the liturgical calendar.[25] Others deliberately and publicly abandon "centuries of European tradition and Christian habit,"[26] as if habit is synonymous with irrelevance. Regardless, as Pritchard reveals, the desire to be relevant moves the ministries and methods of these churches "toward the language and priorities of popular culture . . . [and] affirms the surrounding culture."[27] The concern of some critics is that if its goal is to affirm society, such a church compromises its ability to speak prophetically to society. The desire of these churches to be relevant replaces denominational loyalty and erodes theological and creedal importance.[28] Without the standards of creedal guidance, secular culture threatens to provide the creeds and beliefs governing these congregations. If there is such a secular creed, it is the creed of relevance.

Obviously, the megachurches' purposeful abandonment of "European tradition" would not work as well in a society that is heavily traditional in its religious institutions. In America, religion has always been innovative and mutable, changing to meet competitive demands in a society where the success of religion depends on its ability to attract adherents.[29] As one might imagine, the megachurch philosophy seems to work best in this free-church environment. On the other hand, in Europe, where tradition rather than innovation has defined the church in the modern era, the megachurch movement is catching on very slowly, despite a concentrated effort by the Willow Creek Association. Willow Creek Association staff attribute this slow growth to Europe's history of state religion and a cultural suspicion of large institutions with popular appeal.[30] This points out some interesting differences in the European and American situations when it comes to the secularization of tradition. Europe, a much more traditional society than the United States in religious matters, is less prone to secularize its religious traditions when secularization is defined as it is here.

In subsequent pages I will be drawing upon information and trends gleaned from two megachurches in particular: the Willow Creek Church (the paradigmatic megachurch in America), and a pioneering and relatively successful megachurch venture in Zurich, Switzerland (the International Christian Fellowship or ICF). Featured in chapter 1, the ICF is one of the most successful megachurches in Europe. In 1996 it boasted 600 to 1,000 in attendance at its larger services and held a variety of services, some targeting the unchurched in the best Willow Creek fashion and others—charismatic-style services—geared to believers.[31] The ICF targets young adults, the Xers, and incorporates plenty of music and video technology into its services.[32] The service is certainly unconventional and seems out of place in a European city like Zurich. In addition, it is very different from the Willow Creek service and will provide some interesting contrast in the pages that follow.

HOW MEGACHURCHES SECULARIZE TRADITION

Christianity has witnessed and participated in secularization since its inception, but the megachurches represent an exaggerated example of this dynamic in the contemporary church scene. In the next few pages, I will briefly examine ways that megachurches secularize Christian tradition, focusing on what Bryan Wilson and others call "internal secularization," a process that leads to the "evacuation" of sacred orientations within the church.[33] Internal secularization occurs when churches purposefully use "elements of the broader culture" to eliminate a perceived cultural gap between the Christian message and the unchurched.[34] Churches might employ many strategies to bridge the gap, but in the final analysis, the results are the introduction of secular elements, categories, and standards into Christian worship and theology. With this introduction of secular culture, the process of secularization is initiated or continued. My understanding of how megachurches secularize tradition has been profoundly shaped by the descriptive and interpretive work of two authors in particular. The writings of G. A. Pritchard and of Scott Thumma provide invaluable information on the megachurches' unique philosophy, methods, and characteristics. From their work and from my own exposure to the megachurch movement, I have isolated at least six areas that demonstrate the secularization of Christianity in the megachurch movement:

1. *Packaging.* The megachurches "package" and market Christianity to a secular audience through a secular lens. They use market research and secular marketing methods to determine how to present their product to the public in a nonthreatening and attractive package. This consumerism approach works well in the United States because of the free-market mentality when it comes to religion. The result of this marketing scheme is a secularized package.

2. *Organization.* Since many of these megachurches are huge, organization and structure can be a nightmare. In the attempt to manage the shear magnitude of the undertakings of these churches, secular models of organization are borrowed from the business world.

3. *Programming.* The megachurches place a premium on interesting and engaging programming, and the predominant model comes from the secular entertainment world.

4. *Ideology.* For the most part, the megachurches have incorporated a secularized theology into their sermons and evangelization in order to make the message more palatable. This secularized theology is based in large part on insights from secular psychology as well as from biblical and systematic teachings.

5. *Function.* The megachurches have in practice taken over the roles generally associated with the secular sphere. Self-help groups, exercise groups, education, child care, and other "secular" functions can

be found within the walls of the church as a means of attempting to meet the needs and fulfill the desires of parishioners.

6. *Space*. The megachurch movement represents a secularization of sacred space, whereby meetings might take place in or mimic the space of secular institutions.

Packaging

When megachurch ministers talk about evangelism, it is difficult to distinguish between their discussion and a presentation on effective advertising. Phrases like "product loyalty," "target audience," "consumer orientation," "client needs," and the like dominate the discussion. This marketing phraseology has replaced theological terms like sin, the lost, and even repentance. The megachurches bring in tons of people because they have developed an effective method to reach the unreached and to convince them they should come to church. When Bill Hybels talks about marketing strategy, he speaks about Christianity as if it were a product and about those he evangelizes as clients or consumers. "The 45-and-under generation has a consumer-oriented mindset. They patronize the restaurants and stores they like, and they'll attend a church for the same reason."[35] Ministers who have modeled their churches after Willow Creek echo the same sentiment.[36]

Armed with this understanding of the lost as consumers, ministers strike out on aggressive church-growth campaigns using market research to understand the needs of the unchurched and to meet them by understanding their culture and mimicking it in the worship setting. In order to accomplish this, they often rely on secular models for marketing.[37] When Pastor James Emery White started a Willow Creek-styled church in Charlotte, North Carolina, he first commissioned a survey of unchurched people in the area, tallied the results of the survey about their needs and wants, and set out to build a church designed to meet those needs.[38] The results? The successful Mecklenburg Community Church in Charlotte and White's book on church growth, *Opening the Front Door: Worship and Church Growth*. This marketing approach is typical of Willow Creek-type churches and, according to David Luecke, represents the "most important innovation" of the megachurch movement.[39]

Once the survey is done, ministers then develop a strategy for meeting the needs that are highlighted by the needs analysis. In general, these churches develop "seeker services" designed exclusively to attract the unchurched. They are not designed to meet the needs of believers but to ensure that visitors—who are primarily unchurched—return. Seeker services are designed to "identify" with the unbeliever by being relevant

and by responding to the needs expressed through the survey and market analyses.[40] In order to better identify with their target audience, staff
members and ministers at Willow Creek are encouraged to maintain
active lives "in a totally secular realm," and market research teams might
attend secular plays and rock-and-roll concerts to get a better understanding of popular culture.[41] Early on, Willow Creek developed a seven-
step strategy for reaching the unchurched individual: 1) church members
and leaders befriend the unchurched, 2) church members and leaders
invite the unchurched to attend services, 3) unchurched individuals then
visit services designed specifically for them, 4) unchurched individuals
begin attending, 5) they join a small group, 6) they become involved in
a service role, and 7) they become good stewards.[42] This and similar
strategies characterize the megachurch philosophy of evangelism and
church growth.[43]

Who are these folks targeted by megachurch evangelists? They are
baby boomers[44] and, to some extent, the Generation Xers as the first-
generation participants in the movement begin to age out. The
megachurches are trying to tap into that very large group of people who
are also very affluent. According to Pritchard, Willow Creek is very clear
about whom they are trying to attract to their church. The target audience is made up of unchurched baby boomers, especially the male heads
of households, with a typical client profile being a professional who is
25 to 45 years old, college educated, white-collar employed, and married with children.[45] With this kind of strategy, it should be no surprise
that these churches produce homogenous congregations[46] and that they
are located in affluent suburbs. But there are exceptions to this typical profile, one being the ICF in Zurich. Zurich has targeted a different client,
the Xer generation, the baby busters rather than the boomers. Early
market surveys indicated that the urban environment in Zurich lent
itself better to reaching that audience, a group less likely to be tied to
traditional religious groups, so the Zurich congregation set out to reach
a different target audience. As a result, their worship patterns are different and are designed to appeal to a younger, single, and more restless
crowd. In fact, the music resembles MTV-style music, accompanied by
multimedia presentations, and crosses over to embrace popular contemporary Christian music.[47]

The marketing approach works, at least for targeting groups and
designing programs for them. However, as some critics point out, it is
not necessarily a good trend for the church. For some, megachurch
growth strategy is too market oriented[48]—a secularized and marketed
kingdom of God.

Organization

As you might imagine, these large churches with growing numbers, huge staffs, fluctuating budgets, and fluid and ever-changing attendees provide special challenges for church leaders. Since these churches represent a secularized institutional form, one would expect them to adopt secularized methods for organizational structure. This seems to be the case. Bryan Wilson notes that secularization in general leads to the ecclesiastical tendency to organize along the lines of business corporations.[49] This tendency can clearly be seen in the comments of leaders in megachurches in the Los Angeles area, who emphasize the commercial and business nature of the religious mission of these huge churches.[50] The tendency is modeled in Robert Schuller's writings and refined in the practices of Willow Creek Community Church. In addition, churches in the Willow Creek Association learn and often adopt this secular management style to run growing institutions.

As Pritchard details, the Schullerian approach can best be seen in Schuller's influential book, *Your Church Has Real Possibilities!* (1974). In the chapter "Principles of Successful Retailing," Schuller outlines several principles of management and planning that help to direct church growth. The reader is initially surprised to see "surplus parking" as one of the priorities for ensuring church growth. However, when you consider the target audience, affluent corporate heads of households in the suburbs, the parking requirement and the need for general "accessibility" make perfect sense. Schuller also writes about the necessity for "inventory," a retailing phrase that for Schuller means understanding what the target audience wants and making it available. Third, Schuller outlines "service" as a requirement for success. Like any good pep talk from a CEO of a corporation, satisfying the customer becomes the cornerstone of a growing church. It is not surprising that critics point to this ideology as destructive to Christianity. After all, how can a church maintain a prophetic role in society if its priority is to satisfy the client? Schuller also describes the importance of "visibility" through advertising and, finally, the importance of positive "cash flow." The language, if not the priorities, are those of the corporate world and represent the marketing of Christianity in a consumer-oriented world.[51]

Willow Creek has adopted this management approach and implements it very effectively. From the supervision of staff and volunteers to the managing of budgets, the language and methods of corporate America predominate. In fact, according to Pritchard, staff members at Willow Creek early on began to read and model the concepts from Kenneth Blanchard's *Leadership and the One-Minute Manager,*[52] a secular business bible for corporate executives. This management style creates very efficient and well-managed organizations and seems to work well in the megachurch setting, at least in terms of organization.

The secular corporate style of managing churches is particularly well suited for the megachurch movement in the United States because of the strong free-market economic machine driven by corporate America. The management style appeals to the target audience of these mega-churches as well, since the client is about as likely as not to be a corporate manager of some sort. The style resonates well with the audience. Whether or not this corporate management style catches on in Europe is yet to be seen, as the megachurch movement in Europe has not really emerged as a recognizable entity. The Zurich ICF has adopted some of the Schullerian techniques described above. For example, the ICF does a particularly good job of advertising using eye-catching flyers, a slick German-English newsletter to promote church activities,[53] and a professionally constructed Web site.[54] Yet other corporate techniques are understated at the ICF, which might be a reflection of the different target audience as much as anything. In any case, the European megachurch movement has not yet demonstrated the commitment to corporate-style management that has worked so well in the United States.

Programming

Bryan Wilson has noted that the secular entertainment industry makes traditional church services appear bland and uninteresting, and that this is one of the motivations behind revivalism, that is, to revive interest as much as anything.[55] In fact, as R. Laurence Moore points out, from the preaching of George Whitefield during the Great Awakening and the camp meeting revivals of the nineteenth century, interest and entertainment have always been a part of the revivalism movement. According to some, this has shaped American religion in a society that promotes competition of religions.[56] So American religion, at least, has a built-in entertainment quotient that in the minds of many is related to the successful luring of congregants. Willow Creek Community Church and megachurches in general take this observation to heart. Although insisting that they do not entertain as much as teach in an engaging manner, the programming or entertainment component in seeker-style services is perhaps the most important part of the service. Scores of hours from dozens of volunteers go into each week's programming. The result is a worship service that resembles secular entertainment in form with the use of contemporary-style music, video clips, and other visual aids to engage the worshipers.[57]

The Willow Creek philosophy hinges on the assumption that affluent baby boomers, its target audience, were weaned on television and, therefore, cannot respond to an argument without visual and auditory stimulation. So in order to capture the short attention spans of contemporary churchgoers molded by sound bites, commercials, and half-hour TV spots, megachurches use the arts and contemporary programming and entertainment styles to reach the seeker.[58] There is some evidence that Willow Creek's assumptions about auditory and visual stimulation are accurate;[59] although mainly anecdotal evidence supports the effectiveness of this programming on religious education, it does at least seem to pique the interest of churchgoers and keep them engaged for a short period of time.

The megachurches are very careful to offer professional quality entertainment, and they expend energy and money to ensure quality equipment and performers. They are also concerned that the entertainment be interesting. The death knell for a weekend service seems to be boredom, and the megachurch philosophy tries to stamp out uninteresting programs. Multimedia drama is a main component of their services and includes twelve-foot-tall video screens and computer-generated graphics. One service even included a rappelling Rambo character to illustrate a Father's Day lesson.[60] While some megachurches often incorporate Hollywood images, the focus in the ICF church in Zurich seems to be music, popular music. The ICF even creates its own CDs with worship music.[61] This focus on music probably reflects the interest of the ICF's Xer target audience. One church mounted an "anti-boring" advertising campaign to attract the disinterested-unchurched crowd. The church's flyers confidently proclaimed, "Lots of people are coming because they're fed up with boring sermons, ritual that doesn't mean anything . . . and music that nobody likes."[62] A church newsletter printed the headline DULL, BORING, DEAD ON ARRIVAL: SOUND LIKE THE LAST CHURCH SERVICE YOU WENT TO? The newsletter then continued to describe how "to create a definitely fun and totally non-boring service."[63]

The programming of the megachurches focuses on keeping seekers engaged and keeping them from being bored, and the methods they employ seem to work.[64] But church ministers insist that the focus is not on entertaining but on communicating the gospel message.[65] So the entertainment value of the programming energies in megachurches is of secondary importance to the theology communicated through them. And it is to this theology, to a secularized theology, that I now turn.

Ideology

One of the ecclesiastical tendencies that accompanies secularization is ecumenicalism, the attempt to break down differences between groups and to remove boundaries for greater cooperation. This was a practice early on in the church's history and remains a predominant strategy in the mission field,[66] resulting in greater acceptance of church teaching by a wider audience because the sharp edges of theology are muted. However, ecumenicalism also results in an erosion of theology or a watering down of the theological standards that make groups distinctive. So it is not surprising that many, if not most, megachurches are nondenominational.[67] Even more importantly, this loss of distinctiveness seems to promote the emergence of a secular theology purposefully designed to attract those who are immersed in secular culture. The ideology becomes secular, as does the language. This has happened with much of the theology in many of the megachurches, representing a danger to some critics because success depends on a large degree of accommodation to the secular.[68]

This secularization of theology is unavoidable once megachurches target their audience and then adopt methods to identify with that audience. Rather than trying to mold their audience to a foreign way of viewing reality, these churches adopt the worldview of their target audience. According to G. A. Pritchard, historian of the Willow Creek Church, the worldview adopted by and promulgated by megachurches is none other than "the psychological worldview of the American culture"[69] and represents a secular measuring stick for the church's theology.

Pritchard argues persuasively that the origin of this secularized theology is Robert Schuller's "self-esteem" approach to theology, in which a theocentric approach is replaced by a "human needs approach."[70] When theocentric theology is replaced by anthropocentric ideology, the secularization of theology has taken place and the theology has become an anthropology. The result is a theology based on secular psychology that replaces God's will with personal fulfillment and that uses psychological principles to exegete Scripture and communicate theological principles.[71]

According to Pritchard, this emphasis on personal fulfillment can be seen quite clearly in the content of weekend messages at Willow Creek. Psychological categories and topics such as self-esteem, addiction, conflict resolution, self-identity, self-awareness, and family history tend to direct, if not dominate, the preaching and teaching of the seeker services. In addition, secular psychology books are recommended, referred to, and sold in the church bookstore.[72] This pop-psychology approach is predictable given the megachurch philosophy of relevance and identification. In its most primitive form, it panders to the needs of baby-boomer angst over personal fulfillment. Of course, not everyone agrees. For example, George Hunter calls the movement apostolic because it mimics the early church in its techniques for reaching converts. He suggests it is the method and not the message that sets megachurches apart.[73]

Function

Bryan Wilson has pointed out that with secularization, religious content in church is reduced; therefore, churches must take on other functions in order to remain relevant. Wilson writes, "With its reduced religious content, the act of church-going in the United States may fulfill other functions."[74] This is a predictable development with the megachurches—they have taken on the functions of everyday life, attempting to fulfill the mandate the earlier Social Gospel movement failed to complete. The irony is that at the same time churches are taking on secular roles of everyday life, trained professionals are taking on some of the traditional roles of the priest and clergy (for example, secular marriage counseling).[75] The result is that the boundaries between sacred and secular functions are disappearing, and this seems particularly true with the megachurches' purposeful openness to secular society.

The same strategy that allows the megachurches to grow, as Charles Trueheart suggests, also threatens to turn these churches into "the Welcome Wagon, the USO, the Rotary, the quilting bee, the book club, the coffee shop . . ."[76] or any number of other secular clubs and organizations. The ever-present and unmistakable presence at the megachurches of secular-style and sometimes secular-sponsored groups demonstrates the ever-increasing secular functioning of the megachurches. Trueheart describes the programs at one church, but this generic scene could easily be transferred to any number of megachurches. At one megachurch there is "a seminar on effective single parenting; 12-step recovery meetings by category (alcohol, drugs, abuse), . . . a parents-of-adolescents meeting, . . . and a women in the workplace brunch."[77] The secularization of function begins with the megachurch philosophy of relevance. Because the churches allow the client to set the agenda, it becomes necessarily a secular agenda.

As these churches grow and expand into suburban areas, they often do so with considerable controversy, in part because their existence as religious bodies offers them some protection in development issues. In large part, religious institutions do not have to abide by the same zoning restrictions as private businesses. Therefore, these "meet-all-your-needs" institutions can sponsor any number of services and conveniences in areas where private enterprises cannot compete.[78] There will certainly be legal wrangling on the rights of megachurches to set up shop in ways that otherwise might be forbidden by local zoning, and this comes as a direct result of the purposeful function of these churches.

Space

Finally, a more recognizable but less definable characteristic of the church that is subject to secularization through the megachurch movement is the secularization of space. The contemporary church has responded to secularization by trying to lessen the physical and psychological distance between the clergy and the laity. This has resulted in a shift away from formalism in all parts of worship, including the appearance and structure of buildings.[79] The great cathedrals that at one time were designed to instill awe, to demonstrate the magnificence of the Almighty, and to strike worshipers with a sense of otherness have been replaced in many instances by nondescript buildings that seek to make people comfortable. The megachurches do not want to confront their clients with a sense of otherness. Rather, they want the seeker to feel at home.

This change in worship space philosophy is reflected in the meeting places of the megachurches. Many of them are corporate and hotel-like, with atriums, food courts, and fountains.[80] Willow Creek's grounds resemble and are modeled after a four-star hotel or corporate headquarters.[81] Other churches begin by meeting in large urban hotels (the ICF in Zurich) or in school buildings. Regardless of whether the megachurch meets in a church building that looks like a secular building or in a secular building that houses the church, the space philosophy is the same—meet in a place that is informal, familiar, nonthreatening, casual, and immediate. Oftentimes spaces that enhance or make possible multimedia events are necessary for the contemporary-style worship that is so characteristic of megachurches.

Sometimes this philosophy of space creates strange scenes that bring elements of the amusement park or ballpark into the confines of the church. One Los Angeles megachurch, the Faithful Central Bible Church, meets in Great Western Forum, where the L.A. Lakers at one time played basketball.[82] Fast-food stands, coffee stands, and in Trueheart's phraseology, "a cappuccino cart with parasol . . . dispensing the secular sacrament"[83] conspire to secularize religious and holy space. Sacred ground is modeled on the profane; transcendent space on the mundane—all done to remain relevant to the unchurched rather than to provide contact with the sacred. This physical transition once again produces an irony. Whereas in the past, secular buildings (banks and colleges) used architecture to remind its clients of great cathedrals, now the sacred institutions are adopting architectural styles to resemble secular institutions.[84]

RESULTS AND CONCLUSIONS OF THE SECULARIZATION OF TRADITION

My focus in this chapter on the megachurch movement should not be taken as a suggestion that the megachurches are the only contemporary churches to be secularized or secularizing. Christianity is experiencing secularization and has since its inception. In fact, the whole Christian continuum could be viewed in terms of relative position on a secular scale, with some traditions more accommodating to secular culture than others and none static on the scale but changing in relation to acculturation and other factors. My focus on the megachurch phenomenon is to highlight some of the more obvious effects of secularization in concentrated form. The characteristics discussed above could be used to describe any number of Christian traditions to some extent—some more, some less.

Secularization is definitely taking place in the Christian community, but it will not result in the disappearance of Christianity or in the complete absorption of the church into the social context. There will always be sects in the tradition that define themselves against the establishment and against culture. Even if these sects secularize and accommodate, others will take their place.[85] Nor will secularization necessarily result in a loss of power for religion, because groups exist that so identify with secular culture that they draw vibrancy from it. Rather, secularization is a measure of the degree to which traditions accommodate themselves to popular culture, which in turn results in subtle changes to the tradition. While secularization certainly changes the face of Christianity, it does not necessarily spell its decline. In fact, secularization, by popularizing the religion, might make Christianity more viable, more resistant to decline, more widespread throughout the culture—even if it is less recognizable as a counterculture movement.

Those who caution against secularization in megachurches are not so worried about the disappearance of Christianity as they are about the wholesale changes that occur when involvement with popular culture becomes the standard. Many are concerned about the "gimmicky" approach to attracting parishioners or about the dilution or distortion of the Christian message to make it palatable for a wide audience.[86] Certainly, when the tradition acculturates, it risks its prophetic voice because it can no longer speak out against the culture it has adopted.

This accommodation and compromise with society and culture, which many see as a compromise of eternal truths for relative cultural standards, is what worries most critics.[87] Marketing makes the audience sovereign rather than God, according to the critics, and the gospel message becomes simply relative to time, place, and opinion.[88] Church leaders insist they never compromise the truth but simply make it relevant. Certainly there is a fine line that leaders and critics alike must balance.

Regardless of whether or not Christianity is capitulating to relative cultural standards, it is certain that secularization is changing an evolving tradition. Whether or not this is a positive or a heretical move often depends on the individual making the value judgment. I make no such attempt to judge, but rather recognize that secularization is changing the tradition in significant ways and that secularization is a powerful force, perhaps a strengthening force that will allow Christianity to grow and thrive or perhaps a weakening force that will destroy Christianity as a distinctive voice in the cultural landscape. One could also draw parallels with other religious traditions and their relationships to culture. However, by focusing on the Christian tradition, and one part of that tradition, we can see how the interaction between religion and culture involves an ongoing, evolving relationship that can change either culture or religion or both.

Secularization involves a disappearing or at least a malleable boundary between religion and culture, a boundary that can either make religion more relevant (as the megachurches seek to do) or completely irrelevant (by becoming indistinguishable from the rest of the culture).[89] When churches secularize and accommodate—for whatever reason—they not only evangelize the unchurched to Christianity, but as Pritchard articulates, they are "also evangelizing Christians toward the world."[90] This is the dialectical relationship that secularization brings to the religion–and–culture question—the dialectic is as old as the tradition and will continue both to strengthen and to corrupt the church, to shape the tradition in significant ways. Whether the megachurch movement will continue to participate in this dialectic perhaps hinges on how well it continues to uphold the tension between religion and culture. If the accommodation to secular culture becomes complete, then the dialectic will disappear and the megachurch movement will become an inconsequential footnote in the annals of church history. If, on the other hand, the movement can maintain a creative tension with popular and secular culture without capitulating, then the megachurch movement might realize its goal of leading a significant church reform movement. Perhaps even Willow Creek and its association of churches will define the American church for the near future, as proponents suggest.[91]

The ability of the movement to adapt to Europe might determine its future. If the megachurch movement can make significant inroads into European Christianity, then it stands a chance of creating significant reform. If, on the other hand, it remains tied to American Christianity as it is now, the Zurich congregation and a few others notwithstanding, then the movement is likely to become simply one of many in the diverse and freely evolving landscape of American religion.

NOTES

1. Charles Trueheart, "The Megachurch," *The Sunday Oregonian: Forum*, 22 September 1996, E1. See also Scott Thumma, "Exploring the Megachurch Phenomena: Their Characteristics and Cultural Context," Hartford Institute for Religion Research (hirr.hartsem.edu); and Scott Thumma, *The Kingdom, the Power, and the Glory: Megachurches in Modern American Society* (Ph.D. diss., Emory University, 1996).

2. Trueheart, "The Megachurch."

3. Bryan Wilson, "New Images of Christian Community," in *The Oxford History of Christianity*, ed. John McManners (Oxford: Oxford University Press, 1993), 617, 587–89.

4. R. Laurence Moore, *Selling God: American Religion in the Marketplace of Culture* (New York: Oxford University Press, 1994), 5.

5. Bernard Eugene Meland, *The Secularization of Modern Cultures* (New York: Oxford University Press, 1966), 145–46. See also William Lloyd Newell, *The Secular Magi: Marx, Freud, and Nietzsche on Religion* (New York: Pilgrim Press, 1986), xiv.

6. See Mark Hulsether, "Interpreting the 'Popular' in Popular Religion," *American Studies* 36, no. 2 (fall 1995): 133.

7. Paul Nathanson, *Over the Rainbow: The Wizard of Oz as a Secular Myth of America* (Albany: State University of New York Press, 1991), 17. See also Julie Slaven, "Lights! Camera! Religion!" *The Charlotte Observer*, 1 June 1996, G1, G4. See also Thumma, "Exploring the Megachurch Phenomena."

8. Gustav Niebuhr, "Where Religion Gets a Big Dose of Shopping-Mall Culture," *The New York Times*, 16 April 1995, 1, 14.

9. Steve Johnson, Chicago Tribune critic, quoted in James Wall, "Viewing the Megachurch: Between a Gush and a Smirk," *Christian Century* 112, no. 10 (22 March 1995): 315–16.

10. See Thumma, "Exploring the Megachurch Phenomena;" Thumma, *The Kingdom, the Power, and the Glory;* and G. A. Pritchard, *Willow Creek Seeker Services: Evaluating a New Way of Doing Church* (Grand Rapids, Mich.: Baker, 1996).

11. Niebuhr, "Shopping-Mall Culture," 1.

12. Eric Reed, "Willow Creek Church Readies for Megagrowth," *Christianity Today*, 24 April 2000, 21–24.

13. Pritchard, *Willow Creek Seeker Services*, 11–12. See also Pritchard's dissertation, a comprehensive study of Willow Creek Community Church that numbers

over 800 pages. The dissertation is rich with citations and is available through Communication Institute, Washington, Illinois.

14. For the history of Willow Creek from its roots in Son City, see Pritchard, *Willow Creek Seeker Services,* 31–49.

15. George G. Hunter III, *Church for the Unchurched* (Nashville: Abingdon, 1996), 26–34. See also James L. Kidd, "Megachurch Methods," Christian Century 114, no. 16 (14 May 1997): 482–85. Kidd quotes Hunter in his review of the book.

16. Pritchard, *Willow Creek Seeker Services,* 49–50, 52.

17. Trueheart, "The Megachurch," E7, quoting Kenton Beshore, senior pastor at Mariners Church, Newport Beach, California.

18. Mark O'Keefe, "The Megachurch: Oregon," *Portland Sunday Oregonian: Forum,* 22 September 1996, sec. E-1, p. 7, quoting the Reverend Marilyn Sewell of First Unitarian Church in Portland, Oregon.

19. Niebuhr, "Shopping-Mall Culture," 14.

20. Bishop Charles Blake, interview by Duncan Moon, *Morning Edition,* National Public Radio, 20 April 2001, transcript, hour 2, p. 15.

21. Ibid.

22. Slaven, "Lights! Camera! Religion!" G1, quoting Jacqulyn Weekly.

23. Blake, interview by Moon, 16.

24. See Rodney Stark and William Sims Bainbridge, *The Future of Religion: Secularization, Revival and Cult Formation* (Berkeley: University of California Press, 1985), 436; and Moore, *Selling God,* 65, 209–18.

25. Pritchard, *Willow Creek Seeker Services,* 123.

26. Trueheart, "The Megachurch," E1.

27. Pritchard, *Willow Creek Seeker Services,* 223.

28. See Pritchard, *Willow Creek Seeker Services,* 138; and Lee Strobel, *Inside the Mind of Unchurched Harry and Mary: How to Reach Friends and Family Who Avoid God and the Church* (Grand Rapids, Mich.: Zondervan, 1993), 66. See also Blake, interview by Moon, 16–17.

29. See Moore, *Selling God.*

30. Staffers at the Willow Creek Association, interview by the author, 13 August 1996.

31. Leo Bigger, leader of the ICF, interview by the author, 2 October 1996.

32. Leo Bigger, interview by the author, 15 August 1996.

33. Wilson, "New Images of Christian Community," 593.

34. Pritchard, *Willow Creek Seeker Services,* 206, 128–29.

35. Bill Hybels, quoted in Pritchard, *Willow Creek Seeker Services,* 73.

36. Trueheart, "The Megachurch," and O'Keefe, "The Megachurch: Oregon."

37. The marketing theory followed at Willow Creek is based on Philip Kotler, *Marketing Management: Analysis, Planning, Implementation, and Control,* 6th ed. (Englewood Cliffs, N.J.: Prentice Hall, 1988). See also Pritchard, *Willow Creek Seeker Services,* 68–70.

38. See James Emery White, "Churches, Listen to the Unchurched," *The Charlotte Observer,* 27 March 1995, 7A.

39. David S. Luecke, "Is Willow Creek the Way of the Future?" *Christian Century* 114, no. 16 (14 May 1997): 479–83.

40. Pritchard, *Willow Creek Seeker Services*, 25–29. See also Thumma, "Exploring the Megachurch Phenomena."

41. Pritchard, *Willow Creek Seeker Services*, 64–65.

42. Ibid., 23–24.

43. See Luecke, "Is Willow Creek the Way of the Future?"

44. Trueheart, "The Megachurch," E7.

45. Pritchard, *Willow Creek Seeker Services*, 59.

46. Trueheart, "The Megachurch," E7.

47. Leo Bigger, interview by the author, 15 August 1996 and 2 October 1996. This impression is also based on the September 1, 1996, seeker service at the ICF.

48. Trueheart, "The Megachurch," E7.

49. Wilson, "New Images of Christian Community," 596–97.

50. Peggy Hill and Bishop Kenneth Ulmer, interview by Duncan Moon, *Morning Edition,* National Public Radio, 20 April 2001, transcript, hour 2, p.16.

51. See Pritchard, *Willow Creek Seeker Services*, 51ff., for an assessment of the Schullerian approach.

52. Ibid., 42.

53. *ICF Church News* 4 (1996).

54. www.icf.ch.

55. Wilson, "New Images of Christian Community," 606.

56. See Moore, *Selling God.*

57. See Pritchard, *Willow Creek Seeker Services*, 81–82.

58. Ibid., 89–91.

59. See Neil Postman, *Amusing Ourselves to Death* (New York: Viking Penguin, 1985); David Wells, *Turning to God* (Grand Rapids, Mich.: Baker, 1989); and Strobel, *Inside the Mind of Unchurched Harry and Mary.*

60. See O'Keefe, "The Megachurch: Oregon," E1. See also Trueheart, "The Megachurch," E7; and Pritchard, *Willow Creek Seeker Services*, 89.

61. Leo Bigger, interview, 15 August 1996, and *ICF Church News* 4 (1996): 4.

62. Mailer, Mecklenburg Community Church.

63. *In Touch,* Mecklenburg Community Church's newsletter, November 1993.

64. There are dozens of testimonials from seekers about the services they attend; descriptions like "fun," "entertaining," "relevant," and "engaging" abound. See Ken Garfield, "Nontraditional Church Appealing to Many," *Charlotte Observer,* 24 May 1993.

65. Pritchard, *Willow Creek Seeker Services*, 33–36. See also Thumma, "Exploring the Megachurch Phenomena."

66. Wilson, "New Images of Christian Community," 596.

67. See Thumma, "Exploring the Megachurch Phenomena," 5ff.

68. See Wall, "Viewing the Megachurch," 315–16.

69. Pritchard, *Willow Creek Seeker Services*, 153.

70. Ibid., 53.

71. Ibid., 57–58, 154–56.

72. See Ibid., 154–56, 227. Examples of psychology self–help books widely read at Willow Creek are Melody Beattie, *Codependent No More;* David Keirsey and Marilyn Bates, *Please Understand Me;* and Henry Cloud, *When Your World Makes No Sense.*

73. See Kidd, "Megachurch Methods," 482–84. See also Hunter, *Church for the Unchurched.*

74. Wilson, "New Images of Christian Community," 593.

75. Ibid., 608.

76. Trueheart, "The Megachurch," E7.

77. Ibid.

78. Haya El Nasser, "Giant Churches Irk Some Neighbors," *USA Today* online, 23 September 2002.

79. Wilson, "New Images of Christian Community," 595.

80. Trueheart, "The Megachurch," E7.

81. Pritchard, *Willow Creek Seeker Services,* 81–82.

82. Moon, interview, transcript, 16.

83. Trueheart, "The Megachurch," E7.

84. Ibid.

85. See Stark and Bainbridge, *The Future of Religion.*

86. See Slaven, "Lights! Camera! Religion!" G1, and Pritchard, *Willow Creek Seeker Services,* 192–94.

87. See Peter Berger, *The Sacred Canopy: Elements of a Sociological Theory of Religion* (Garden City, N.Y.: Doubleday, 1967), 156, for the "accommodation and resistance" roles of the church. Pritchard raises this concern focusing on the tendency to compromise eternal truth to relative cultural standards. See Pritchard, *Willow Creek Seeker Services,* 192–94.

88. Pritchard, *Willow Creek Seeker Services,* 244–49. See also Wall, "Viewing the Megachurch."

89. James D. Hunter and Stephen C. Ainlay, eds., *Making Sense of Modern Times: Peter L. Berger and the Vision of Interpretive Sociology* (New York: Routledge & Kegan Paul, 1986), 151–52. See also Pritchard, *Willow Creek Seeker Services,* 249.

90. Pritchard, *Willow Creek Seeker Services,* 239.

91. See Luecke, "Is Willow Creek the Way of the Future?" for his quote of Lyle Schaller.

3
LOVE VALLEY:
The Sacralization of
Secular Space

As the megachurch movement results in the secularization of sacred space, function, and intent, other cultural movements attempt to sacralize what would normally be considered secular or profane. They try to locate transcendent possibility in the mundane, to allow sacred import and sanction of some secular means to perfect society, to allow the kingdom of God to exist in and through human social organization. This spreading out of sacred possibility through secular forms represents the second direction of secularization. We see it in religious utopian movements, whose attempts to organize social and natural space to perfect secular society provide the basis of sacred experiments—whereby the "City upon a Hill"[1] is rooted in secular soil but is given life by sacred water.

Creating a sense of place is a human tendency, done to grant legitimacy to the places we inhabit and to places where something special has happened or happens. We see the sacralization of place everywhere, in our civil religious monuments, in our utopian spaces, in our veneration of pilgrimage sites such as Graceland or the Grand Canyon. I hope to demonstrate how we sacralize space by positing a template of sorts—a categorization of spatial attributes that characterize sacred space. The template can be superimposed on a place to gauge its intentions toward the sacred and arises out of the following portrait of a unique, eccentric experiment in the sacralization of American space—the North Carolina utopian town, Love Valley. By bringing this town to light in the following pages, I hope to explain how to recognize the sacralization of space when it occurs.

LOVE VALLEY AND SACRED PLACE[2]

Like the Congo in Joseph Conrad's *Heart of Darkness,* the Midwestern landscapes of Willa Cather's fiction, and the confining cityscapes of Theodore Dreiser, Love Valley represents the way humans (authors, readers, filmmakers, architects, and others) have shaped their spaces to create a "spirit of place." Whether these spaces come alive on the page, the screen, or the town's main street, organizing spaces into meaningful places is a sacred, creative act, much akin to the Genesis act of organizing chaos. The creative act of organizing sacred place describes the sacralization of secular spaces like the town of Love Valley.

To demonstrate this meaningful attempt to create sacred place, I will discuss the spirit of place as containing both sacred space and time and suggest some elements that give places sacred qualities. Second, I will describe Love Valley as a contemporary utopian experiment, built on the notion of sacred place, wherein the "spirit of place"—including both sacred space and time—functions at both the physical and ideological levels as a utopian text for the town. In the process, I am suggesting that a "community text" exists in Love Valley. This community text is made up of oral history, the character of the town and its inhabitants, and the story of the town as reported in newspapers and promotional material. The crucial element in this community text is how the town and community are perceived by its founders and inhabitants. The community text may differ and probably does differ significantly from how others perceive the town; it may even differ from an objective history of the town. But the community text tells us how Love Valleyites understand their town, its history, and its utopian impulse.[3] The community text validates the idealism upon which the town was built in part by defining the town of Love Valley as a sacred place.

In talking about Love Valley as a sacred site, I am using a definition of sacred place that is clearly recognizable in religious studies and could be used to describe traditional types of sacred spaces such as buildings erected for worship or natural areas where rituals take place. However, it is my feeling that places can constitute sacred space through their functions, not just through their proposed or planned purpose. Therefore, I define sacred place functionally and have isolated a few characteristics I will discuss before continuing with the community text of Love Valley. First, definition:

Sacred Place includes notions of "space" and "time," geography and temporality—sacred places can be located on a map and on a time-line or temporal circle. Sacred Place must be "uncrowded," if not empty, in order to allow for projection of fantasy and the evolution of myth. A Sacred Place acts as a void into which myth comes into being.[4]

So for the purpose of this discussion, a sacred place is located in space and time and functions religiously to bring about a crucial myth. This definition suggests seven characteristics of sacred places that allow them to function religiously and mythically.

1. Premodern Western worldviews, for example, a biblical worldview, defined sacred place as a site that mediated the divine Other and allowed otherness, God, access into profane reality. However, a postmodern Western worldview no longer places God in opposition to humanity; rather, place itself works in opposition to human being and thus becomes otherness itself. So rather than mediating the divine Other, sacred places are the "other"—holiness is not contained within a sacred place, holiness is the otherness of place—powerful, seductive, and challenging to human being.

2. This otherness of place comes about in part when place is dangerous and provocative.[5] These characteristics of spaces and times carry the ability to inspire awe and fear. It is not fear of the Lord that makes a place sacred as much as it is the fear produced by the implied threat of place—the dense forests of Appalachia, the sheer height of the Alps, the shrouded depths of oceans. And while not necessarily inducing fear, even medieval cathedrals continue to create awe and wonder based on an illustration of power. The awe produced from threat can elevate place to otherness.

3. Sacred places carry a utopian element. Be it a temporal utopia or a spatial one, sacred places tend to attract like-minded individuals who, to varying degrees, imbue a place with a sense of utopian perfection, social reformation, or individual transformation. For this reason, one's sacred place might be another's mundane world. A utopian element—function, purpose, or agenda—can make a place sacred; examples include Eden, Jerusalem, Mecca, Puritan New England, Love Valley.

4. Sacred place is foundational—it provides the place (space and time) wherein enlightenment takes place. Sacred places not only construct paradigmatic space but also set the space in an era beyond time, some time other than the present. The Eucharist altar transports one

to the first-century upper room; the Buddhist temple offers transcendental possibility that lifts one beyond location and time;
Jerusalem provides spatial as well as temporal connection to sacred
events in Jewish, Christian, and Islamic history; U. S. civil-religious
shrines in and around Washington, D.C., transport us to the times
and places important to our nation's founding and early years—
Mount Vernon, the Lincoln and Jefferson Memorials, the
Washington Monument. In every instance, sacred time and sacred
space are invoked in sacred places.

5. Sacred places assume and promote a participatory element, as
   Robin Sylvan points out in his work with the Burning Man
   Ceremony[6]—in other words, tourists do not sacralize a cathedral,
   communicants do. Sometimes pilgrimage functions as a sacralizing
   act, but so too do dance, music, and other ritualistic acts of faith that
   are integral to the character of the space. Furthermore, the act must
   be an appropriate participation. For example, a priestly sacrifice
   constituted a sacred participatory act in the Jerusalem Temple;
   Antiochus IV's sacrifice to Zeus was a desecration.

6. As in other areas of contemporary American life, secularization
   affects how we define and treat sacred places. An understanding of
   sacred space is shifting dramatically in the Western world. We no
   longer need saints, relics, or the association with sacramental grace
   for a space to appear sacred, although these things are often present.
   Secularization in the West witnesses the continuing disintegration
   of boundaries between sacred and profane—we have no problem
   sacralizing the formerly secular or desacralizing the sacred. Thus,
   our civil religion declares the Tomb of the Unknown Soldier
   sacred, while our popular religion does the same with Graceland,
   the Grand Ole Opry, or in this case, Love Valley. At the same time,
   we can turn religious buildings into art museums or homeless
   shelters—we can desacralize.

7. Finally, I think in America we are obsessed with sacralizing natural
   or wild space. Whereas medieval Europe built its sacred places, its
   grand cathedrals, Americans humanize their wild places. This has
   been part of the American appropriation of sacred place and part of
   the American religious psyche since the founding and colonization
   of a vast continent that yielded a country stretching from sea to sea.
   Sacralizing natural space was a new idea for Western Christianity,
   not European at all, and it is characteristically American. We see it
   in our reverence for our national parks; in our once real and now
   romantic obsession with the West, an untamed frontier beckoning a

nation to it; in Thoreau's sojourn in the woods; in John Muir's rhap-
sodies about Yosemite Valley;[7] with the environmentalist's sermons
about preservation and conservation.

LOVE VALLEY AND THE SACRED SPIRIT OF PLACE AS A UTOPIAN COMMUNITY TEXT

With these seven elements defining sacred place, I would like to introduce to you Love Valley, a utopian community that functions as sacred
place through community text and metaphor, which were established by
the founder and by the inhabitants of the town. In short, Love Valley is
an intentional community established as a sacralized secular space (an
incorporated town), which is expressed primarily through metaphor
based on rural agrarianism and western myth.[8]

A lone cowboy reined in his Chickasaw stallion and clipped slowly
down the dusty street. Once outside the general store, Dakota hopped
off his mount, threw his reins over the hitching post, dusted off his long
riding coat, and started toward the store. He stopped long enough to
consider cooling his parched throat before buying supplies and decided
against the saloon. The café sounded good, though, and he decided to
stop in there before returning to the trail. As he sauntered toward the
store, the old planks of the boardwalk creaked under the weight of his
boots. He shouted a greeting and tipped his hat to a couple of friends
who had just returned from hunting game in the surrounding mountain
passes, and the sight of their rifles brought a smile to his face as he
remembered and patted the six-shooter at his side. Once inside the store,
the cowboy bought a few camping supplies. As he browsed among the
leather goods, he remembered he must stop at the saddle shop before
leaving town. The cowboy cast a long glance down Main Street, looking for the mayor of the town: he had some business with the mayor, but
that could wait until later. Dakota decided against the café, mounted his
horse, and through the dust of an early fall afternoon, they cantered out
of town and returned to the trail.[9]

Dakota and his mount do not constitute the opening scene of a
Western movie. Rather, this is a fictionalized account of what you might
encounter on the dusty streets of Love Valley, North Carolina. Andy
Barker, the founder and longtime patriarch of Love Valley, harbored a
childhood dream not so different from that of many of his playmates—

he dreamed of horses, cowboys, and the West he saw immortalized in classic Westerns. His religious conversion on a French battlefield during World War II was added to this vision of playing cowboy. From a foxhole promise made to God, Barker fashioned a plan for his return home and outlined his idea to his mother in a letter: "My part of the bargain (with the Lord) is to build a town, a Christian Community with clean recreation and strive to help people know more about God and His outdoors. I know I'd never make a preacher, but can build a church and help out personally in many ways. We can keep young boys occupied and out of trouble by letting them help run the place."[10]

Nine years later, Barker bought a large parcel of land in a rural section of northern Iredell County in the hills of the Brushy Mountains, quit his lucrative contracting business, moved out of an elegant Charlotte, North Carolina, home, and moved into a tent on his newly acquired land. From makeshift headquarters, he began building, by himself, a cabin and a "cowboy town." His wife and children eventually joined him in the cabin, and they began to gather a community of eccentric individuals attracted to living in an intentional community that looked like the set of a Western movie, complete with dirt streets where no cars are allowed, hitching posts for the only approved form of transportation, wooden sidewalks, a saloon, a dance hall, a jail, and a general store—all conforming to the principle (and later law) that all buildings look at least one hundred years old and mimic simple clapboard buildings.

Why? Barker harbored goals of transforming and reforming society. He wanted to restore what he perceived to be a lost sense of morality and sanity. He harbored a romantic vision of an American golden age based on western nobility. The myth of the West Barker wanted to reconstruct in Love Valley was the West of the silver screen, where ambiguity concerning right and wrong did not exist; where independence, courage, and chivalry were regarded as primary virtues; where young people mastered the art of outdoor living to counter other less savory teenage activities; where "wholesome" activities corresponded to godly living and advanced the cause of Christianity.[11] A Christian cowboy town—this was the community text of Love Valley that has been written and revised through almost five decades of struggle and turmoil. But the town still exists, the cowboy persona still prevails, country-and-western music provides the anthem, and Love Valley still functions, at least in the mind of Barker and some old-timers, as a paradigmatic place—a sacred place that offers an antidote to some of the problems of society. And this antidote comes in the form of a reconstructed place and time—the

American West of the nineteenth century—the American West symbolized by Gene Autry and Roy Rogers.

According to my functional definition of sacred place as a time and
place that allows the production of a crucial myth, Love Valley qualifies.
Love Valley's history reflects a community text based on strong oral traditions and consistent community self-understanding. This utopian text
includes the functioning of the town as a sacred place that reflects the
seven characteristics listed above.

First, Love Valley constructs a place that functions as otherness itself—
Love Valley is the thing—it does not mediate otherness; in other words,
it is not a church or a synagogue. Rather it is key itself. A visit to Love
Valley, according to early promoters of the village, could produce escape
from the demands of everyday life and lead to spiritual and moral renewal
and regeneration. To live there would help create a holy community that
would in time lead to the regeneration of the larger society. That Love
Valley has generated tremendous controversy, suspicion, and even hatred
during its history hints at the power generated by its alien status.

In part, the otherness of Love Valley establishes the utopian village as
a sacred place because the town itself is tinged with danger and menace.
This is the Wild West, after all, and Love Valley's community text is filled
with stories mimicking the best of the untamed western myth. The text
includes stories of lawbreakers, fights on Main Street, rodeo heroics, and
the martial imposition of law by the justice of the peace and his deputies
(Barker served as justice of the peace as well as mayor for much of the
town's history). A municipal law requires that if visitors and residents of
Love Valley carry guns (guns were commonplace at one time and are not
uncommon at present), the guns must be loaded. So if you walk the
streets of Love Valley and see a cowboy with a six-shooter strapped to his
hip or a rifle on his horse, you can be assured that the weapon is loaded.
A tinge of menace fills the community text of Love Valley—as it must to
fulfill its character as sacred place.

Love Valley as otherness also gives us a clue to Barker's vision of the
utopian element of Love Valley. Part of what set Love Valley apart was his
promise that to live in Love Valley was to separate from the larger society, if only to establish a smaller society that would be reforming in
nature. Love Valley was begun as an intentional community and was
meant to maintain a transformative relationship with the larger society.
Love Valley was not conceived to be merely a weekend retreat. In fact,
Barker spent much energy in the early years discounting the characterization of his community as a dude ranch. Rather, Love Valley was
designed to be a self-supporting, permanent community that would aid

in the spiritual renewal of its inhabitants to equip them to spread reform to the larger community. This utopian purpose is most clearly expressed through Barker's attempts to use the town as a base for social reform projects, including at various times providing low-income housing, job training, and relocation; rehabilitative camps for troubled youth; educational reform proposals designed to help rural and impoverished school districts; activities and programs designed to promote racial tolerance; and other similar socially progressive initiatives. Barker sponsored some of the projects; the town sponsored more. Barker also envisioned using Love Valley as a political base to spread his vision of social reform to a statewide level. He launched state senate campaigns and ran for governor of North Carolina twice on a strong populist platform. Alas, he has been elected to nothing but the mayoral post of Love Valley, a position he has held for most of the town's history. Still, in its intentional character to reform not only its inhabitants but also the larger society, Love Valley exists as a utopian town. Not surprisingly, the community text of Love Valley thrives on stories extolling acts of altruism and self-sacrifice by Love Valley's leaders and its citizens. These range from extraordinary kindness to strangers and opponents to self-sacrificing behavior for animals. In every case, the community defines itself by a community creed based on the Golden Rule, and the community text, its collection of stories and tales, tie back into the magnanimous character of the town's leaders.

Love Valley promotes enlightenment for participants and for the larger society by recreating a sacred time and space—the western, pre-industrial, rural-agrarian town—and by suggesting at least implicitly that many societal ills can be traced to industrialization, urbanization, and the breakdown of families. For Barker and Love Valley, the "Old West" is the golden age, paradigmatic, and Love Valley functions to transcend time and space to give its idealistic inhabitants access to this sacred place. The West carries mythic weight—undoubtedly, the West that Barker has recreated resembles the real West little, but it does recreate the West of our popular culture—the mythic West of B movies. It is a myth based on tough-minded independence, unambiguous morality, and peaceful coexistence with nature.

In this West, Love Valley requires or at least encourages a participatory element. The western theme is pervasive—virtually everyone rides horses and dresses in western garb; the music of Nashville is preferred everywhere except for the Barker household, where strains of classical music from the Barker radio are heard during the day. The rodeo persists as the principal entertainment. The cowboy persona is ubiquitous and infectious—it even attracted and affected a countercultural element that settled in Love Valley in the early 1970s. In 1970 Love Valley and Barker hosted a music festival that attracted over seventy thousand hippies and counterculture drifters to hear the Allman Brothers Band. The festival was a public relations and logistical nightmare for Barker and the towns-people of Love Valley because of the huge crowds, drugs, nudity, and countless problems any town of seventy would encounter if its popula-tion surged to seventy thousand in a weekend. After the festival, a few of the hippies stayed on in the town to clean up the place or because they had nowhere else to go. Soon they were riding horses and playing cow-boy right along with the most clean-cut and conservative cowboy Christians of Love Valley. Even some of the Allman Brothers used Love Valley as a base for a short time.[12]

Love Valley blurs the distinction between sacred and secular at every point in its history: its political reform agenda is wrapped in Christian language; its genesis as a cowboy town is all confused with Barker's desire to seal a deal with God; and the rough-and-tumble association with guns, outlaws, and motorcycle gangs is balanced by the unofficial creed of the town, the Golden Rule (a rule Barker has stated publicly on more than one occasion). Love Valley's one-time association with popular, rock-and-roll, and country-and-western musicians inspired two songs about Love Valley that are filled with religious language. The first, by Loonis McGlohon, pictures Love Valley as a valley of peace and hope between mountains of hate, a place absent of intolerance.[13] The second was written by Don Berg and recorded by the rock group Flood. It tells the story of a young man who finds "the promised land" in Love Valley.[14] A world-famous strongman, Joe Ponder, who lives in Love Valley and holds a couple of Guinness world records, prepared for his strength feats (such as pulling tractor-trailer rigs with his teeth, a stunt he advertised with business cards that read "Pulling for Jesus Christ") in his sauna chapel, which is enclosed with stained-glass representations of religious scenes.[15] The first permanent building Barker erected is the little church that stands on a hill overlooking the town because of Barker's belief that any community should be built on the church. Here you have a cow-boy town, with a reputation as a hard-living, rough kind of place, over-seen by the church of the gentle Savior. The sacred-secular distinction in Love Valley is blurred.

Finally, Love Valley, as a self-styled representative of Americana, tends to elevate the natural world to sacred status. Barker's initial venture was predicated on the belief that communion with nature produced com-munion with the divine, that rural life produces this sort of closeness, and that natural space, or at least rural space, is somehow superior to urban space. It is simplicity, the type of simplicity lauded by the Transcendentalists of the nineteenth century rather than promulgated by the best-selling books of the twentieth, that Barker and the Love Valley residents are trying to produce through communion with nature. Perhaps a cowboy named Arizona, a longtime resident of Love Valley, said it best: "The simple life is better. . . . Why, even plumbing gives problems. I sometimes think we were better off before we had indoor plumbing and running water."[16] While building Love Valley, Andy and Ellenora Barker and their two children lived for two years in a cabin with no running water, not even an out-house, while cooking meals over an open fire.

Love Valley is an intentional community built on utopian idealism. Its fifty-year history has produced a community text that defines the experiment for those who know the story well. The setting of this story is a sacred place, a setting that transports one beyond space and time to a paradigmatic place, a place where the necessities of secular life give way spatially to sacred place.

NOTES

1. This biblical reference from Matthew 5:14 is used in a famous sermon by John Winthrop to characterize the New World religious and social experiment. Ronald Reagan also referenced the image in his farewell presidential address. The image of the City upon a Hill has a firm foundation in America's civil-religious understanding.

2. This chapter on Love Valley as sacred space is based in part on a paper I delivered at the annual meeting of the American Academy of Religion, November 2000, Nashville, and on a response to four papers presented at the annual meeting of the American Academy of Religion, November 1999, Boston. The papers and authors are as follows: Jay Blossom, "'An Ideal Summer Resort for Christian Families': Wholesome Entertainment in Early 20th-Century Winona Lake"; Thomas S. Bremer, "From Pilgrims' Sacred Topography to Tourists' Sacred Landscape: A Brief Tour of Western Religious Travel"; John Powers, "Shangri-la Comes to Hollywood, or Hollywood Comes to Shangri-la: Tibet and Popular Culture in the 1990s"; Robin Sylvan, "Burning Man and Rave Culture: A Pre-Millennial, Postmodern, Future Primitive Popular Religious Revival."

3. See Conrad Ostwalt, *Love Valley: An American Utopia* (Bowling Green, Ohio: Bowling Green State University Press, 1998), 2; David Kimbrough, *Taking Up Serpents: Snake Handlers of Eastern Kentucky* (Chapel Hill, N.C.: University of Chapel Hill Press, 1995), 7–8; William Lynwood Montell, *The Saga of Coe Ridge: A Study in Oral History* (Knoxville: University of Tennessee Press, 1970), viii, xviii.

4. These concepts reflect the work of Sylvan and Powers. Robin Sylvan writes about the landscape and human body as a "blank canvas" at the Burning Man

Ceremony ("Burning Man and Rave Culture"), while John Powers discusses the "myth-making process" in conjunction with popular images of Tibet ("Shangri-la Comes to Hollywood").

5. Powers writes about "otherness tinged with menace" in his paper on Tibet, "Shangri-la Comes to Hollywood." See also Bremer, "From Pilgrims' Sacred Topography to Tourists' Sacred Landscape."

6. Sylvan notes the unofficial creed at the Burning Man Ceremony is "no observers, only participants" in his paper, "Burning Man and Rave Culture." Also see Bremer, "From Pilgrims' Sacred Topography to Tourists' Sacred Landscape."

7. See Bremer, "From Pilgrims' Sacred Topography to Tourists' Sacred Landscape."

8. For a complete treatment of Love Valley, see Ostwalt, *Love Valley: An American Utopia,* and Conrad Ostwalt, "Love Valley: A Utopian Experiment in North Carolina," *North Carolina Humanities* 1, no. 1 (fall 1992): 101–8.

9. This vignette was previously published in Ostwalt, "Love Valley: A Utopian Experiment," 101, and is reprinted here by permission. The remainder of the chapter on Love Valley is based on that article and on Ostwalt, *Love Valley: An American Utopia,* copyright 1998, Popular Press. Reprinted by permission.

10. See Ostwalt, *Love Valley: An American Utopia,* 9. The letter was dated 1 February 1945 and was recorded by D. L. Morris in an unpublished manuscript housed in the Appalachian Collection at Appalachian State University, Boone, North Carolina. See Morris, ch. 1, p. 4.

11. Ostwalt, *Love Valley: An American Utopia,* 16. See also Jim Taylor, "Dude Ranch Shaping Up in North Iredell Valley, *Statesville Record and Landmark,* 4 June 1954, 1, 8.

12. See Ostwalt, *Love Valley: An American Utopia,* chs. 6 and 7.

13. See Ostwalt, *Love Valley: An American Utopia,* 11. Lyrics and music of "Love Valley" are by Loonis McGlohon.

14. See Ostwalt, *Love Valley: An American Utopia,* 113–14. Don Berg wrote the song "Love Valley, U.S.A."

15. See Ostwalt, *Love Valley: An American Utopia,* 142–46.

16. Ostwalt, quoting Arizona, in *Love Valley: An American Utopia,* 136.

PART II

4
NARRATIVE/TEXT

An Anglican priest kisses the text after the morning's reading; an observant Jew touches the mezuzah, a repository for sacred words; a grandmother gently, or not so, scolds a youngster for mistreating the family King James Version of the Bible; the U.S. Constitution and the Declaration of Independence are preserved in the National Archives building; Mao's little red book was once treated with devotional intensity. Texts carry sacred import, contain within their pages sacred power. We know this about religious texts, but it is also true, or can be, about secular texts. Any text that has the power to change lives or to open the portals of truth possesses sacred possibility, so that the phrase "religion and literature" is a given and self-logical turn of phrase—at least in Western culture since the Enlightenment, as the written word rose to supremacy as the truth-bearing entity within society and culture.

However, in our postmodern, contemporary context, we see a demystifying of text, a secularization that, like the trend affecting other parts of our culture, is proceeding in two directions: the secularization of sacred texts and the sacralization of secular texts. In order to see what is happening with the secularization of sacred texts, we need only focus on the treatment of the Bible in our culture during the last 150 years or so. I will do so only briefly in order to focus on the second direction of secularization within literature, the sacralization of secular texts. In the case of the sacralization of secular texts, the disciplinary approach to religious studies known as "religion and literature" gives us the best systematic approach to understanding secularization. In that context, I will consider what popular prose and classical literature have to offer a culture in search of religious landmarks.

THE SECULARIZATION OF THE BIBLE

What makes a text like the Bible sacred? If the mythic structure of story gives revelation validity, then we can issue the following postmodern dictum: the Bible is no longer a sacred text—at least not functionally so—at least not for the majority of readers. Contemporary Christians and biblical scholars have virtually rendered the Bible devoid of sacred function as a text that can open up transcendent truths through the mythological task. I have no statistics to prove this—I am simply reflecting on my own efforts at Bible reading and study, on my interactions with sincere Christians of all denominations, on my familiarity with serious and accomplished biblical scholars and exegesis methods, and on my teaching experience with undergraduate religion students. The postmodern Bible has been thoroughly secularized, and the project came from two sources: the scholarly community, whose approach was adopted by the Left, and the fundamentalist community in reaction to the intelligentsia. Both sides secularized the sacred in different ways, and the result is a barren Bible, stripped of its mythological power to reveal truth.

When Julius Wellhausen popularized the documentary hypothesis for explaining authorship of the Hebrew Bible, the result was a revolution in biblical reading. Wellhausen convincingly demonstrated that the religion of the Hebrews evolved through historical periods and that this evolution could be seen in the various historical and cultural patterns reflected in his progressive dating of the Pentateuch. Literary methods and historical and cultural considerations entered the conversation when readers attempted to understand biblical meaning. Wellhausen helped transform biblical scholarship, and from at least his time through much of the twentieth century, the attempt to employ literary, historical-critical, and cultural studies to understand the Bible has been motivated by the desire to add empirical validity to the textual study.[1] Others followed Wellhausen: many attempted to write biographies of Jesus in their "search" for the "historical Jesus"; others sought ways to use historical-critical methods to make the Bible more meaningful for contemporary Christians. Almost all ended with portraits of Jesus or the Bible that differed greatly from the sacred text because the approach tended to sidestep myth while still giving credence to the importance of myth.

Rudolf Bultmann, a German Form critic of the New Testament, proposed a program of demythologization of the New Testament so it would be more relevant and understandable for contemporary Christians. Bultmann's working thesis was that the culture and worldview of the New Testament period was so alien to the contemporary scientific worldview that mythological components in the Gospels needed to be excised or reworked so the message of the gospel could become preeminent. To his great credit, Bultmann reminded us that myth is a powerful religious element that is rightly understood metaphorically, not literally. Nevertheless, Bultmann has often been misunderstood and misused, and his program of demythologization has sometimes been used to strip away mythic elements in the New Testament rather than to bring them into symbolic focus. In the end, Bultmann's demythologizing stance submits mythological meaning to historical and cultural analysis, and once again, myth becomes subordinate to history and science, in method if not in hermeneutics. As myth props up historical interpretation, the sacred becomes secularized.

From Wellhausen to the most hardened Bultmannian demythologizer to the ardent Christians in search of the "historical Jesus," from Form critics to redaction critics to source-critical historians, the past 150 years or so of biblical scholarship have given us fresh insights into biblical texts. Historical perspectives and literary criticism have provided a wealth of information for better understanding biblical texts and traditions. Yet for all the indebtedness the Jewish and Christian worlds owe literary-critical methods for understanding biblical texts, what has this methodology cost us?

When such methods are used exclusively to study biblical texts, the result may be a "demythologized" text that has also been desacralized. While historical criticism promises to provide insight into the text by giving historical and cultural grounding, and literary criticism promises to reinvigorate the study of metaphor, these methods do not always deliver on their promises. Often the biblical text's meaning becomes secondary to reconstructing the historical circumstances or the literary structures so that the hermeneutical task becomes less crucial or falls away entirely. Or liturgical and doctrinal demands locate meaning in history or literary structure and cement it in place—freeze it in the past or in the text, so to speak, so that meaning becomes static, frozen to the intent of the author (as if we can know that), imbedded in the structure, unable to escape and transmute or evolve, and thus unable to become alive and meaningful for contemporary readers. In the effort to enliven the text, modern criticism, if taken alone, makes the Bible a sterile and barren literary landscape. If the biblical text stands for nothing more than any historical tome or poetic text, then the Bible has been secularized— the authority of historicism supersedes truth; the mandate of empiricism supersedes the yearning for revelation. When only historical and literary methods are used in the study of the Bible, the metaphorical power of myth is lost. Such approaches may be mandated in state universities to avoid separation issues; they may be required in seminaries in order to exegete texts effectively; but it must be remembered that these marvelous tools arose to provide scientific validity to biblical studies. The need to make the process scientifically verifiable provides us evidence of the secularizing process in the tools and methods of biblical scholarship.

However, the academic Left of biblical scholarship is not the only culprit when it comes to secularizing the Bible. Responses from the Right to scientific and historical criticism of the Bible also desacralize the Bible, perhaps unintentionally and even unwittingly. Christian fundamentalism, arising in the early part of the twentieth century partially in response to new critical methods that questioned some long-held truths of biblical narrative, equally destroys the metaphorical power of the Bible by insistence on an inerrant text. Requiring an inerrant text is another way of submitting the Bible to empirical mandate. The desire for an unambiguous Bible with a straightforward truth is not only misguided but exposes the need for "hard facts" rather than the more "substantive truths" of metaphor and myth. Fundamentalism desacralizes the Bible as much or perhaps more than historical-critical methodology because it submits the text to the test of empiricism and in doing so destroys the mythic element that makes a text sacred.

Christian fundamentalism simply cannot handle a sacred text, because fundamentalism confuses truth with fact, myth with history, metaphor with literalism. And in such confusion, fundamentalism destroys the integrity of the sacred text and renders it a secularized instruction manual, barren and frightening in the wrong hands. Both historical-critical methods and fundamentalist demands destroy the metaphorical use of the Bible through empirical readings—one relying on historicism, the other on the assumption of divine perfectionism. But both destroy the metaphorical authority of Scripture if misused and thus strip the Bible of its sacred import. What both approaches must uphold, a task easier for historical and literary methods than for fundamentalism, is that the sacred text's power lies in metaphor and myth. Both approaches need to rediscover what Tim O'Brien describes as the power of "story-truth," which can be "truer sometimes than happening truth."[2]

A personal example highlights the levels of textual power and myth. As an undergraduate religion major, I remember well being undisturbed by my first exposure to historical and literary methods for studying religious texts because they were applied to nonbiblical ancient texts—the myths I studied historically were not myths crucial to or related to my faith or beliefs. But when my teachers first asked me to use those same tools on biblical literature, I took it as a challenge to my ingrained notion of an inspired text. Likewise, I also distinctly remember having a very difficult time the first time I was exposed to an alternative myth or metaphor that challenged the one I had inherited from my biblical tutelage in conservative Christian churches. When I read and studied the gnostic myths, I experienced a crisis of sorts because the challenge of Gnosticism was at the mythic level, not at the literary or historical level. I worked through this challenge of an alternative myth based on the same text, but it required me to strip away the immature faith I had inherited from others and claim a faith of my own. This was the first time I began to understand the power of metaphor and myth in religious faith, the first time I discovered personally that developed faith requires the epistemological step of examining honestly, and sometimes jettisoning, your presuppositions. Sacred metaphor demands this philosophical step—doctrinalized religious story forbids it.

A last reference will give another example of how the biblical text has been secularized in recent time. The phenomenally successful Left Behind series by Tim LaHaye and Jerry B. Jenkins demonstrates how the religious right might secularize the Bible. In the attempt to make the apocalyptic message more relevant to contemporary readers, Tim LaHaye conceptualized the series and Jenkins fictionalized Christian and Hebrew apocalyptic texts in a brilliant bit of extrapolation. Asking the famous "What if?" question of science fiction, LaHaye and Jenkins explore how a premillennial conception of the apocalypse might play itself out in contemporary society. The interesting thing about this series is not the literature but the concept. This evangelical experiment is based on the notion that a fictionalized account is necessary to get the message across. So using a secular medium to impart a sacred message, LaHaye and Jenkins fictionalize, literalize, and secularize. If these Christian best-sellers and thrillers adopt the medium, the structure, the tone, and the method of secular literature, can the sacred stories be retold without destroying the metaphorical import of the original? Christian fiction like "Left Behind" witnesses another attempt at historicization (based on the belief that relevance is contingent upon contemporary location) and literalization (transferring biblical metaphor to actualized fact).

Left Behind, or any Christian fiction for that matter, represents contemporary secularization of sacred literature by adopting the forms and structures of secular literature to transmit an evangelical message. Like the megachurches, these fictions adopt secular cultural forms and infuse within them a Christian message. From outward appearances, they are successful—it is hard to argue with the huge numbers flocking to megachurches or to millions of books bought and read. Nevertheless, the numbers do not prove effectiveness. They do not even prove relevance. The question becomes: Will the success of Christian literature and institutions like the megachurches lead to relevance through the secular media or to irrelevance by sameness?

The really instructive element of the Left Behind novels is their perspective of a post-rapture situation. In the first novel, the book opens with the moral ruminations of a 747 pilot at about the time of the rapture, which in premillennialist lore includes the fantastic disappearance of true Christians. So the plot of the story takes place entirely in a post-rapture world as the main characters, the pilot, a newspaper reporter, an airline attendant, and the pilot's daughter, try to make sense of the chaos and fear following the disappearance of loved ones and a goodly portion of the world's population (including all children). The perspective is post-rapture, and the thinly veiled theological enterprise of the book is to prove biblical prophecy by placing it in the historical setting (prophecy, which is often seen as predictive, becomes past and thus verifiable). The perspective is subtle—by historicizing prophecy in the past, the authors lay claim to Truth and make their evangelical plea to those left behind. The urgency is palpable, energized by prophetic texts that have come true in the book. But the perspective changes the prophetic texts—it transfers the metaphorical to the literal, it takes the visionary experience of John's Revelation and other prophetic texts and cements it in historical concrete, and it sterilizes the potential richness and meaning of the apocalyptic myths by trying to literalize them in historical perspective. And all this is done through the secular medium of the novel. The secularization of the sacred apocalyptic myths has been completed in Left Behind. That these books are wildly popular gives us some clue to the extent that evangelical culture has adopted secular standards as the receptacle for the Christian message.

Just as the scholarly community has fixed the sacred texts in history, culture, and literary structure, conservative religion has hitched the Bible to doctrinal presuppositions. In both cases, the metaphorical power of the Bible has been lost, and with the loss of metaphor, we lose religion.[3] The rejection of the metaphorical stance is the destruction of the sacred, the secularization of the sacred, and the exchange of truth for fact. And this secularization comes not from secular powers nor from popular culture nor from enlightenment forces, but from the religious community itself. If religious texts have been so chained to liturgy and doctrine, if the sacred myths have been historicized so that symbolic meaning is lost, where does one turn to regain metaphor or myth? One must look to fiction that is not tied to or guided by religious doctrinal perspective or historical methodology; that is, one must turn to "secular" literature in the attempt to recover the sacred, and it is to the sacralization of the secular in literature that I now turn.

THE SACRALIZATION OF THE SECULAR: THE RELIGION AND LITERATURE MOVEMENT

The infamous megalomaniac of Herman Melville's *Moby Dick* finally appears in the novel some twenty-eight chapters into the narrative. Ahab's dramatic entrance provides a clue to how literature can participate in the secularization of religion through the sacralization of the secular. Ahab's presence not only demonstrates how Ishmael could experience the extraordinary, the Other, in the context of mundane experience, but it also suggests the power of literature to mediate an experience of the Other for the reader. As much as Ishmael had wondered about the mysterious Ahab, as much as he had anticipated meeting the man, when he does finally appear, the apparition is a revelation for Ishmael: "Reality outran apprehension," writes Melville.[4]

Reality does outrun apprehension—mundane experience outstrips the imaginings of even the most creative visionaries.[5] Our mundane experiences can lead to wondrous occasions filled with transcendent possibilities. For the reader, it can happen in the pages of a book;[6] for the character Ishmael, it happened on the deck of the Pequod. Many individuals claim it happens outside the confines of sacred institutions or rituals. When this happens, secularization of religious experience occurs because religious experience takes place outside the auspices of sacred organizations or sacred spaces. In such a case, the secular becomes sacralized.

The tendency in religious studies has been to dichotomize the concepts of sacred and secular based on the significant work of Rudolph Otto and Mircea Eliade in establishing the polarized concepts of sacred and profane. Thus, Eliade elaborates on Otto's terminology by suggesting that something becomes sacred when our mundane, profane world becomes a receptacle for "something of a wholly different order."[7] Too often Eliade's work is used to polarize different kinds of objects or different states, so that the contemporary world is often seen as emphasizing the secular or the profane rather than the sacred: in Lynn Ross Bryant's words, the "human rather than the transcendent."[8] But this polarization into types is not necessarily the logical conclusion to Eliade's categories. In fact, Eliade speaks of a confusion of types through the interaction of the mundane world and sacred reality. Thus, as Giles Gunn suggests, sacred and secular do not delineate "different kinds of objects" but "different ways of perceiving and then relating."[9] Perhaps we can step back from the polarization of sacred and secular and see them as part of a continuum rather than as different sorts of realities. This allows interdisciplinary approaches to religious studies, such as religion and literature, to flourish and to be effective. If sacred and secular are partners in a continuum of experience in approaching otherness, it certainly makes sense that religious experience can be expressed in either sacred or secular form; therefore, the study of sacred and secular culture and their intersections is appropriate.[10]

In the study of religion and culture, particularly when that study focuses on secular expressions of religious questions, the interdisciplinary field of religion and literature is perhaps the most developed subfield of its type in religious studies. In a sense, the modern study of Western religions, until recently at least, has been a project in religion and literature because these traditions are so heavily dependent on texts for their ritual and even for their institutional life. In addition, religious traditions often spawn devotional texts, such as *The Bhagavad Gita,* as a natural outgrowth and expression of religious feeling. Often these devotional texts tell us more about the practice of religion at a particular time than do official sacred texts of a religious tradition. Literature has and can provide an outlet for religious yearning just as it provides a medium for the expression of love, passion, horror, awe, and beauty. David Jasper has suggested that religion and art can teach truth in ways that overcome or outflank theological and doctrinal tyranny.[11] Thus, as a cultural form, literature will certainly overlap religion and religious expression because all cultural forms participate together in building meaning.

Nevertheless, in a broader sense, the study of religion and literature has grown into an interdisciplinary subfield that touches religious studies, literary theory, and cultural studies in general. This fact itself provides a good demonstration of the secularization of religion as the definitions of "religion," "the Other," and other sacred terminology have been broadened to function meaningfully in other secular forms of intellectual pursuit. Linking religion and literature in formal intellectual contexts has had a greater effect than simply recognizing the overlapping of two cultural forms. This linking has formalized within academia a secularization of religious studies because, at its heart, it seeks to find "the Other" not in the sacred sphere but in the secular realm of the literary imagination.

The study of religion and literature as a formal discipline traces a checkered history and development; its current vitality as a recognized, independent field of study has lagged in the past few years, particularly in America. One will find few formalized programs of study in religion and literature either in the United States or in Europe. Nevertheless, this interdisciplinary pursuit still exists in departments of English, theology, religious studies, interdisciplinary studies, and American studies. Theology courses are taught in seminaries using only "secular" literature. Literature courses are taught in universities using only "sacred" literature. And cultural studies courses are being taught everywhere that recognize the power of literature to carry and to communicate religious longing and belief. The religion and literature movement continues to build on a century of work by scholars from various disciplines. For a history of development of this interdisciplinary pursuit, one could hardly do better than chapter one of Giles Gunn's seminal work, *The Interpretation of Otherness: Literature, Religion, and the American Imagination*. Here, Gunn traces the movement through three phases beginning in the early twentieth century, helping us understand how the discipline has attempted to define itself. Eric Ziolkowski's more recent essay, "History of Religions and the Study of Religion and Literature: Grounds for Alliance," provides a type of history of the movement as well by placing it in the context of the development of the history of religions movement in religious studies.[12]

If religion and literature studies seem to be floundering at present, it is not because of lack of interest or participation. Rather, the field is undergoing redefinition as its initial momentum slowed after a "golden era." A generation of scholars built the discipline of religion and literature (Nathan Scott, Giles Gunn, Robert Detweiler, Wesley Kort, and others), and the one-time premier program in the field, the University of Chicago, constructed a rich and expansive approach to religious studies. Nevertheless, instead of producing a field of study with a unified goal and direction, religion and literature studies carry with them a variety of objectives and presuppositions, including testing the validity of formalism and New Criticism that dominated literary critical circles earlier in the twentieth century.[13] If the initial movement was reactionary, it ran its course without a unified vision of religion and literature. Now, a younger generation of scholars, some of them students of the above pioneers, are redefining the field, molding it in various ways to be even broader and more inclusive. Scholars like David Jasper, Carolyn Jones, Irena Makarushka, Mark Ledbetter, David Arnold, and Eric Ziolkowski are taking the study of religion and literature in various directions with equal lucidity and insight. Thus, the field's lack of a center or unifying force appears to be a weakness. This does not mean, however, that the field is faltering. Rather, it might be argued that the study of religion and literature is stronger than ever, more vital than ever, stronger and more vital through its presence and greater diversity across curricula and across scholarly interests than ever before. Whether the field will survive in recognizable form may depend on the emergence of strong leadership to focus its great diversity.

In the final analysis, the fact that religion and literature exists as a field at all demonstrates the secularization of religion, because it rests on the assumption that religious longing is expressed through secular cultural forms and that religious meaning can be gleaned through the study of secular writings. This is particularly true in the United States where the field developed in the context of New Criticism and tended to move away from theological reflection in the study of religion and literature.[14] Yet even in European circles, which seem to be much more open to religion and literature as a theological pursuit (indeed, David Jasper even calls for a "rediscovery of theology" in religion and culture pursuits),[15] the study of literature and religion, when undertaken outside the confines of sacred literature, represents essentially a secularization of religion. With this in mind, I will discuss some issues basic to the study of religion and literature before examining the work of four writers as a way of demonstrating how religion and literature as a field might incorporate various emphases.

As noted previously, the current state of the study of religion and literature is multidirectional, broad, and inclusive. It thereby embraces many different approaches, attitudes, assumptions, and methodologies. Yet with all the diversity in the field, work in religion and literature comes from two basic groups, religious studies scholars or literary theorists. For the most part, the work being done in the field comes not from "religion and literature" scholars per se but, as Giles Gunn has pointed out, from religion scholars with an interest in literature or literature scholars with an interest in religion or theology.[16] These two groups more often than not demonstrate vastly different approaches. Great diversity in terms of motivation and methodology is found even within the religious studies group. To demonstrate this diversity, I will discuss three different approaches to the study of religion and literature, recognizing that these general approaches do not exhaust the current complexity of the field.

The study of religion and literature proceeds as a literary pursuit, as a theological method, or as a religious studies tool. I will avoid considering religion and literature as it relates to "sacred" or devotional texts such as the Bible, the Qu'ran, or *The Bhagavad Gita*. Rather, I will focus and limit my attention to religion and literature as it occurs in relation to "secular" texts and authors: D. H. Lawrence, Toni Morrison, Willa Cather, James Agee, William Faulkner, Clyde Edgerton, or Amy Tan, for example.

Religion and literature scholars operating predominantly from a religious studies perspective generally fall into two broad and fluctuating categories: theological studies and religious studies. Although the distinction between these two categories might not be readily apparent, oftentimes the motivations and presuppositions of these scholars are vastly different. Those who proceed theologically sometimes begin with a set of assumptions, theological precepts, truth constructs, or accepted beliefs, and use or search literature to demonstrate or legitimize those beliefs. Literature becomes an extended metaphor that illustrates a belief already in hand. Carried to the extreme, this approach, of course, destroys the integrity of literature as literary works become little more than the handmaidens of preconceived truth constructs. In Noel Rowe's words, when this happens, "art is the servant of theology."[17]

In many ways, the field started with this approach of subverting literature to a theological perspective. The writer considered by many to be the father of religion and literature, T. S. Eliot, suggested that religion should dictate a standard for literature. In his famous essay "Religion and Literature," Eliot begins by asserting that "literary criticism" proceeds "from a definite ethical and theological standpoint."[18] While some would dispute that Eliot is making literature subservient to theology in his essay and instead creates ambiguity and uncertainty,[19] it seems to me that Eliot opens the possibility for a Christian moral standard that will judge literature suitable for Christian readers. This relationship between religion and literature exists for those who make religion, in this case, Christianity, the authority that judges aesthetic value from a particular theological stance.

Eliot's influence struck hard during the early and developing years of the religion and literature movement and produced scholars who were Christian apologists such as Gabriel Vahanian in *Wait without Idols*.[20] G. B. Tennyson suggests that literature found its origin in religion but was quickly divorced from it, becoming secular with no concern for religion. The implication is that literature arose to serve religious ends but later became deviant.[21] Making literature subservient to religious or orthodox standards may have found no greater expression than in Randall Stewart's *American Literature and Christian Doctrine*. As Giles Gunn and R. W. B. Lewis point out, Stewart reduces American religion to the concept of original sin and judges American literature by this single standard, effectively reducing literary criticism to a narrow doctrinal orthodoxy.[22]

Perhaps the most influential writer who falls into this apologetic category is Nathan Scott, a prolific and important scholar in the history of religion and literature who employs a muted and understated theological approach. Scott assumes that to have an adequate knowledge of Christian faith, one must study literature, because literature informs theology. Scott's writing is lucid, moving, and persuasive, giving apologetics an effective spokesperson for the literature and religion movement.[23]

Religious studies scholars, as opposed to theological apologists, might also fall into the trap of using literature to support or bolster a particular position, but at least in theory, they should approach literature as a product that might display the multitude of ways human beings have of expressing religious imagination. Religious studies scholars broaden the definition of religion so that it represents not one theological agenda but a host of religious problems that are common and basic to human beings as religious beings rather than to individuals committed to a particular religious sect or denominational affiliation. Thus, a religious studies approach to religion and literature might focus on issues of race and gender because they encompass the religious categories of liberation, equality, and humanness that extend beyond orthodox conceptions and prescriptions.

Beyond the numerous scholars who study religion and literature from a religious perspective, there is a whole host of scholars who pursue the study from a literary theorist's perspective. Just as a theologian might make literature a tool for religion, critics whose work in religion and literature is informed primarily by work in literary theory often make religion subservient to literature. David Jasper claims that theology became subservient to literature "as a part of a process of secularization which exalts the poet and artist as a kind of priest of the imagination, a modern prophet replacing ancient prophecy and its inspired utterance."[24] One example of this tendency to exalt the literary side of religion and literature can be seen in the critics who were heir to the New Criticism of the 1930s. These theorists tended to hail literary texts as supreme cultural forms unaffected by cultural settings, authors' beliefs, or audience sensibilities. Therefore, if religion is related to literature, it is only in the sense and to the extent that literature creates it. Literary texts and the critic's work must be unaffected by cultural forms such as religion and, in a sense, replace religion as cultural standard bearers. In their most extreme forms, art and literature as aesthetic forms function religiously and replace religion.[25] Religion is thus completely secularized as it is subsumed and swallowed up by art.

In previous descriptions of religion and literature studies, I have employed extremes in order to point out inherent dangers to this interdisciplinary pursuit; namely, that one discipline will overwhelm the other and that the legitimacy of religious studies, theology, or literary studies will be compromised. The dialogical nature of the religion and literature field has flowered into various approaches and emphases on author, text, or reader as methodological foci for study. Often defenders of one or the other position have argued for their approach as a way of politicizing the field. These arguments, while helpful perhaps for defining method, oversimplify the nature of literature by reducing it to authorial intent, objective text, or reader interaction. Likewise, scholars tend to oversimplify religion by reducing it to historical context, to objective truth or inerrant text, or to believer response. Literature and religion encompass at least these three corresponding movements, and when working between disciplines in the field, it is crucial to employ flexible methods to handle the complex nature of literature and religion.

Peter Berger's sociological view of religion is helpful in imagining the complex ways religion and literature might interact. In his classic text, *The Sacred Canopy,* Berger pictures religion and other cultural forms arising in three stages. The first is "externalization," the "outpouring" of human spirit and hopes in creative expression. The second is "objectivation," in which such outpouring results in a product that takes on an objective status of its own. The third is "internalization," the "reappropriation" of these cultural forms by human beings in meaningful ways, usually done in social contexts. For Berger, this is how society produces its cultural structures such as religion.[26]

Berger's paradigm is instructive for religion and literature because the three stages of development coincide with the three focal points of religion and literature. If these forces operate on the individual level as well as on the social level, then the literary process can be described using Berger's terminology. Externalization is the author's expression and outpouring of hopes, beliefs, and the creative spirit. Objectivation occurs when the author's creation becomes a "thing," a reified work that has objective status—a text. Internalization allows the text to be appropriated meaningfully by the reader. These stages are not independent occurrences but are interrelated and interdependent. A reader cannot appropriate meaning (internalize) from a nonexistent text or in the absence of any creative activity to produce such a text. Likewise, as David Jasper notes, "any piece of literature is finally created and complete only when it is received and responded to by the reader."[27] The reader is also sometimes influenced in this internalization process by a community. As obvious as this seems, we often proceed methodologically as if readers read in isolation and as if writers create without an audience. We need a hermeneutical approach that focuses not solely on one or the other but that is large enough to consider all three moments in the life of the literary experience.

The field of religion and literature, if it is to survive as a viable and fruitful discipline, must be truly interdisciplinary in nature without allowing the agenda of one field to overwhelm the other or without allowing one methodology to run roughshod over contributions from cognate fields. Because it is an interdisciplinary pursuit, religion and literature work is difficult, especially at the methodological level. However, looking at and recognizing these extreme methods also give us some idea of the great diversity of the field—precisely because it exists across disciplines. As examples, theologians might be more willing than others to be apologetic in their analyses, literary critics might be more interested in myth analysis, and feminist critics might be more inclined to find interest in the potential ideological components of literature. What is needed at the present is more constructive and less competitive dialogue—the field must be large enough and complex enough for all these approaches.

Religion and literature criticism must be done between the religious studies and the literary studies disciplines, with literature and religion interacting as implied long ago by R. W. B. Lewis.[28] Yet Lewis does not define the "between," and for years critics have been trying to pinpoint what has proven to be a shifting and flexible middle ground. Is the "between" Giles Gunn's "humanistic" and "hermeneutical" orientation to the common ground of culture and its symbols?[29] Or does the middle ground lie with Wesley Kort's narrative elements?[30] Or maybe the "between" lies in something more difficult to define, the ability of both religion and literature to challenge or critique culture.[31] Regardless, a great variety of approaches and procedures exists in the field of religion and literature, and we would be wise to practice what Giles Gunn long ago named "principled eclecticism."[32] In any event, we would do well to keep foremost in our minds the possibility of a dialectic existing between religion and literature—a dialectic so beautifully expressed by David Jasper: "For literature rescues religion from the dangers of dogmatism, blunt apologetic and crudely direct evangelism. While religion provides necessary ethical and theological standards to remind literature of the dangers of a beauty which serves evil or destructive ends."[33]

Methodological questions aside, if we embark on a study of religion and literature in the manner it has been practiced over the past fifty years, then we participate in the secularization process. A study of religion and secular literature assumes either that religious longing can be and is communicated through secular cultural forms or that secular cultural forms can be a prop for religion or theology. In either case, religion is found elsewhere besides sacred literature and sacred spaces. This should not be seen as a demise of or threat to traditional religion. Rather, this kind of secularizing tendency witnesses to the strength, vitality, and resourcefulness of human beings and their religious longings.

NOTES

1. See William G. Doty, *Contemporary New Testament Interpretation* (Englewood Cliffs, N.J.: Prentice Hall, 1972), 53.

2. Tim O'Brien, *The Things They Carried* (New York: Broadway Books, 1990), 179.

3. Writers as disparate as Joseph Campbell and Thomas Cahill recognize the centrality of metaphor to religious meaning. See Campbell, *Reflections on the Art of Living: A Joseph Campbell Companion,* ed. Diane K. Olson (New York: HarperCollins, 1991), 168–71. In this short essay we find Campbell distinguishing between metaphorical and historical readings of the Bible. See also Thomas Cahill, *The Gifts of the Jews: How a Tribe of Desert Nomads Changed the Way Everyone Thinks and Feels* (New York: Nan A. Talese/Doubleday, 1998), 49. In a few eloquent phrases, Cahill describes metaphor as the basis of "all language and all meaning" and, thus, "all religion."

4. Herman Melville, *Moby Dick* (New York: New American Library, 1961), 129. See also Conrad Ostwalt, *After Eden: The Secularization of American Space in the Fiction of Willa Cather and Theodore Dreiser* (Lewisburg, Pa.: Bucknell University Press, 1990), 118–25.

5. See Ostwalt, *After Eden.*

6. See Phyllis Carey, ed., *Wagering on Transcendence: The Search for Meaning in Literature* (Kansas City: Sheed & Ward, 1997), xv and xviii, for the possibility of finding "transcendence in literature."

7. Mircea Eliade, *The Sacred and the Profane: The Nature of Religion,* trans. Willard R. Trask (New York: Harcourt Brace Jovanovich, 1959), 4–14. See also Ostwalt, *After Eden,* 119.

8. See Lynn Ross-Bryant, *Imagination and the Life of the Spirit: An Introduction to the Study of Religion and Literature* (Chico, Calif.: Scholars Press, 1981), 16. See also Langdon Gilkey, *Naming the Whirlwind: The Renewal of God Language* (Indianapolis: Bobbs-Merrill, 1969); and Ostwalt, *After Eden,* 119.

9. Giles Gunn, *The Interpretation of Otherness: Literature, Religion, and the American Imagination* (New York: Oxford University Press, 1979), 171, 187. See also Ostwalt, *After Eden,* 118.

10. In a sense, sacred and secular exist only in relation to one another, so to separate them invalidates any sense of meaning they maintain as concepts. See Cesareo Bandera, *The Sacred Game: The Role of the Sacred in the Genesis of Modern Literary Fiction* (University Park: Pennsylvania State University Press, 1994), 16; and John Milbank, *Theology and Social History: Beyond Secular Reason* (Oxford: Basil Blackwell, 1990), 3.

11. David Jasper, "Art and the Biblical Canon" (keynote address, Religion, Literature and the Arts Conference, Australia, 1994), quoted in Michael Griffin, "Religion, Literature and the Arts (RLA) in Australia: An Introduction to This Special Issue of *Literature and Theology,*" *Literature and Theology: An International Journal of Theory, Criticism and Culture* 10, no. 3 (September 1996): 202–3.

12. See Gunn, *The Interpretation of Otherness;* and Eric Ziolkowski, "History of Religions and the Study of Religion and Literature: Grounds for Alliance," *Literature and Theology: An International Journal of Religion, Theory and Culture* 12, no. 3 (September 1998): 305–25.

13. David Jasper, *The Study of Literature and Religion: An Introduction* (Minneapolis: Fortress, 1989), 97.

14. Ibid., 4–5.

15. Ibid., 3.

16. See Gunn, *The Interpretation of Otherness,* 5–6, 13–23.

17. Noel Rowe, "The Choice of Nothing," *Literature and Theology: An International Journal of Theory, Criticism and Culture* 10, no. 3 (September 1996): 228.

18. T. S. Eliot, "Religion and Literature," in *Selected Essays* (Harcourt Brace Jovanovich, 1932), repr. in G. B. Tennyson and Edward E. Ericson Jr., eds., *Religion and Modern Literature: Essays in Theory and Criticism* (Grand Rapids, Mich.: Eerdmans, 1975), 21–30.

19. Jasper, *The Study of Literature and Religion,* 7–8. See also Gregory Saylor, "Introduction," in Gregory Saylor and Robert Detweiler, eds., *Literature and Theology at Century's End* (Atlanta: Scholars Press, 1995), 1; and David Hesla, "Religion and Literature: The Second Stage," *Journal of the American Academy of Religion* 46, no. 2 (summer 1978): 181–92.

20. See Gunn, *The Interpretation of Otherness,* 30ff.

21. G. B. Tennyson, "Introduction," in Tennyson and Ericson, *Religion and Modern Literature,* 11–12.

22. See Gunn, *The Interpretation of Otherness,* 21–22; and R. W. B. Lewis, "Hold on Hard to the Huckleberry Bushes," in Tennyson and Ericson, *Religion and Modern Literature,* 56–57.

23. For Scott's status as an apologist, see Gunn, *The Interpretation of Otherness,* 30–32.

24. Jasper, *The Study of Literature and Religion,* 6.

25. See Gunn, *The Interpretation of Otherness,* 34.

26. Peter Berger, *The Sacred Canopy: Elements of a Sociological Theory of Religion* (Garden City, N.Y.: Doubleday, 1969), 4.

27. Jasper, *The Study of Literature and Theology,* 63; Wesley Kort writes about "the three moments in the aesthetic circle," referring to author, text, and reader. Wesley Kort, *Narrative Elements and Religious Meaning* (Philadelphia: Fortress Press, 1975), 3.

28. R. W. B. Lewis, "Hold on Hard to the Huckleberry Bushes," *The Sewanee Review* 67, no. 3 (summer 1959).

29. Gunn, *The Interpretation of Otherness,* 5–6.

30. Kort, *Narrative Elements and Religious Meaning.*

31. See Irena Makarushka, "Framing the Text: A Reflection on Meanings and Methods" (paper written at Bowdoin College, Brunswick, Maine, October 1993). See also Cleanth Brooks, *Community, Religion and Literature* (Columbia: University of Missouri Press, 1995); and Alfred Kazin, *God and the American Writer* (New York: Knopf, 1997).

32. Gunn, *The Interpretation of Otherness,* 76.

33. Jasper, *The Study of Literature and Religion,* 8.

5
RELIGION AND "SECULAR" TEXTS

In the pages that follow, I will consider the works of four writers to demonstrate various emphases within the religion and literature field. I have chosen three southern U.S. writers to suggest that religion and culture are not monolithic entities even within regions that are often considered to lack diversity in religion and ideology. I have chosen an Asian American female and an African American male to demonstrate that the same diversity and the same "sameness" exist across ethnicities and gender, across cultural lines and tradition. A look at Clyde Edgerton's *Raney* suggests the power of secular literature to critique a culture's ideologies, religious institutions, and moral codes. Randall Kenan's *A Visitation of Spirits* shows us how a theology can grow out of the pages of secular literature and the cultural experience of southern African Americans. Amy Tan's *The Hundred Secret Senses* shows us how comfortable popular literature and culture can be with the dissolving boundaries between the sacred and secular. And Lee Smith's work demonstrates how secular fiction can operate as myth to offer insight into women's spiritual issues. While limiting my evaluations of Edgerton, Kenan, and Tan, I have chosen to provide a more comprehensive examination of Smith's body of work by way of contrast. By looking at these diverse works, I hope to show that these four novelists, in various ways, provide fruitful subjects for religion and literature work because each deals with the tension existing between religion and the secular world.

107

I have chosen these four writers for other reasons besides their demonstrating a religious and secular diversity within regional and ethnic literature. If we do live in a secular age, as many religious commentators suggest, then we can understand why our time is so characterized by various fundamentalisms. As I suggested previously, a society marked by the empirical quest for certainty, as a secular society ruled by rationalism might be, should not be surprised to witness the rise and flourishing of fundamentalisms in its religion, politics, and other cultural institutions. If fundamentalism is a characteristic of secular postmodern society, Edgerton, Smith, and Kenan offer stinging critiques of the fundamentalist quest for Truth. Rather than providing certainty, Christian fundamentalism in the works of these authors stifles and limits characters, sometimes with tragic results. Thus, they provide a critique of one of their culture's most enduring symbols: conservative southern religion. While Tan deals less with fundamentalism of the twentieth century, her novel pictures missionary religion of the nineteenth century in its conflict with foreign cultural traditions. Although not directly critical of missionary religion, the portrait of Christian missionaries exposes the shortcomings of the evangelical approach to Christianity. This literature challenges cultural and religious symbols, deconstructs and reconstructs cultural truths, and shares with religion the ability to make and grant meaning.

Finally, I have chosen these "regional" and "ethnic" writers in order to challenge preconceptions some readers bring to regional and ethnic literature. Regional and ethnic work is often seen to be exclusive, irrelevant for the large majority of readers outside the group. Nevertheless, it is my contention that such writing is as universal as any type of literature and can provide a particular kind of focus for the postmodernist context of religion and literature work. According to Wesley Kort, one of the problems of postmodern literature and criticism is its devaluation of a sense of space and place. Kort argues for religion and literature work that always includes narrative analysis of place and space.[1] Regional literature has always claimed a sense of place as its lifeblood and can provide a particular focus for literary work in a postmodern context. And the ethnic literature included here also focuses our attention on place in interesting ways: Kenan on the black community and Tan on China. In this way, literature is not simply about a particular place but about a sense of place—a sense of human beings struggling with universal problems in the context of the places where they live and function. So Kenan's and Tan's works demonstrate not only that universality can come from particularity but that universal concerns can exist across cultural dividers. And like Flannery O'Connor suggested years ago, regional writing—I would include ethnic writing as well—provides us the "possibility of reading a small history in a universal light,"[2] thus binding readers together through their shared humanness.

Therefore, I have chosen these four writers in order to view how diverse voices can critique sacred symbols in a way that speaks universally beyond the particularity of region, race, or gender. In this way, literature can establish a sense of place beyond the boundaries that create difference and separation and help us overcome our postmodern sense of dislocation in a challenging and secularizing world.

CLYDE EDGERTON, *RANEY*

Clyde Edgerton's delightfully funny first novel appears to be a harmless story about the inhabitants of a small southern town and the strong sense of place and community we like to imagine existing in such towns. The story follows the first year of marriage of Raney Bell, a sheltered and innocent Primitive Baptist from Listre, North Carolina, and Charles Shepherd, a more experienced and worldly city dweller from Atlanta. The story has predictable conflicts that provide much of the humor and promise to keep the reader entertained, if not laughing, throughout the entire novel. But beneath the charming story, beneath the hilarious antics of Edgerton's characters, lies a darker humor—a satirical look at the South, its beliefs, and its practices. Edgerton's satire critiques stereotypical views of religion, morality, and race in this book, and it is this power of his story to challenge and overturn dominant ideologies that highlights the role of place and community in the crises that define life. It is also this power of story that so frightened the administration of the Baptist college where Edgerton taught that it cost him his job. Edgerton's assessment of the episode is that the organization did not understand the satire and thus responded in fear to his novel.[3]

Edgerton's critique of southern evangelical religion begins with but does not stop with *Raney*. The same theme arises as a central problem in his second novel, *Walking Across Egypt,* as the eighty-six-year-old Mattie Rigsbee, one of the main characters of the novel, struggles with her Southern Baptist religious heritage throughout the story in her quest to do what is right and moral.[4] Mattie's religion permeates every aspect of her life and motivates her Christian benevolence and service;[5] it is because she takes her religion seriously that moral conflict arises. This conflict between religion and morality takes on an even more biting tone in *Killer Diller,* a story that continues with the characters from *Walking Across Egypt* and introduces the element of a Baptist university with a very strong need to control.[6] But *Raney* is where the most moving and soul-searching conflicts take place.

The novel represents an extended storytelling session for Edgerton, and the storytelling tradition in his art is an integral part of his work.[7] Like a good storyteller, Edgerton creates a sense of place that not only delineates the action of the story but grants possibilities for complex interactions between characters.[8] For example, even though the story is set in Listre, a small southern town in the 1970s, the setting is complicated by the introduction of Charles (from Atlanta), with his progressive ideas on race relations. The resulting interactions between Charles and native inhabitants of Listre suggest that race relations in Listre are more rooted in a pre–Civil Rights era than in a post-1960s setting. So the simple 1970s small southern town setting is made more complex by the introduction of alien elements that set the stage for change in the story. In many ways, the novel is about change and conflict in the South— conflict between old ideas and new, between rural and urban, between conservative fundamentalism and social progressivism, between bigotry and civil rights. These grand social challenges are played out in microcosm in the lives of Edgerton's characters, Raney, Charles, and their families, and it is with the development of these characters that Edgerton's storytelling and skills as a novelist emerge.

An examination of the novel's structure reveals the basic themes in Edgerton's satire. The story comes in three parts. In part one, "Blood Kin," the basic conflicts and issues of the story are presented through the introduction of the two families of Charles and Raney. With these two families, the reader learns that the central conflicts are cultural ones that embrace major items such as religion, morality, and racism but that even include smaller parts of life such as eating habits. In part two, "A Civil War," the tension between the newlyweds and their vastly different worldviews grows against the backdrop of the lingering remembrances of the Civil War, a conflict that set family against family, countryman against countryman. In this section, the cultural conflicts lead to the breakup and then partial reconciliation of Charles and Raney. Finally, in part three, "The Feed Room," the beginnings of resolution and reconciliation surface when the couple begin to compromise on some of the hard-line positions they hold concerning family and morality.[9]

The issues that provide the tension and then the occasion for reconciliation are cultural and nearly always revolve around religion in some way. Part one introduces the basic conflicts of the story. From the beginning, it is clear that Raney and Charles will have a hard go of it in their new marriage because of the vast differences in their backgrounds and upbringing. Raney is an uneducated, conservative Baptist who is narrow-minded in her acceptance and tolerance of differences. Despite her often acerbic nature, she is a likeable character because of her charming innocence. She is childlike and confuses words like "consummate" and "consumed" or "psychiatrist" and "psychiatric." Her childlike innocence is part of what attracts Charles and the reader but is also a source of tension in her marriage. By contrast, Charles is a college-educated, socially liberal Episcopalian with ideas that run directly counter to the conservative values Raney and her family hold so dear. These differences lay the groundwork for a battle of values deeply rooted in the respective families and backgrounds of the newly married couple.

Conflict surfaces in several areas of family and personal life for Charles and Raney. For example, while Raney and her conservative family abhor alcohol, Charles and his family view alcohol as an acceptable and necessary part of social life. Raney condemns drinking as less than Christian behavior on the part of "Episcopalians and Catholics and sometimes Methodists" (15). But drinking is not something good Christians do—alcohol is of the devil and drinking is a sin, and her alcoholic Uncle Nate symbolizes the disastrous effects of drinking for Raney's family. Imbibing is a litmus test of sincere Christianity for Raney, and it leads to conflict early on in the couple's relationship. When it becomes clear to Raney that Charles's father and Charles and his buddy have been drinking at the wedding rehearsal, she is outraged. Later, Raney and Charles experience a disastrous wedding night, Raney being repulsed by Charles's actions. She blames his offensive behavior on the champagne he was sipping—the champagne brought out "something corroded" in Charles (21). So for Raney and Charles (representing diverse cultural attitudes in the South), alcohol consumption is a source of conflict and negotiation.

Their attitudes toward alcohol highlight a deeper source of friction for the couple that comes to light in a delightfully funny passage describing the couple's wedding night from Raney's point of view (20). The honeymoon encounter is a disaster, and sexuality becomes a threat to the couple's happiness. Raney is repressed sexually, very innocent, and filled with notions (mainly gleaned from her mother) about how sexual encounters are to proceed. Raney views sex as her womanly duty, something to be endured grudgingly. Charles is more liberated and curious about sexuality.

The second night proceeded more smoothly when Raney "was able to explain to Charles" how he was "supposed to" consummate the relationship (21–22). Nevertheless, the problem with sex does not vanish on the second night of the couple's marriage and continues to plague the relationship through the middle part of the novel. Raney associates sex with prostitution (85–86), sees it as dirty (174ff.), and exposes her ambivalent attitudes toward sex when she discovers men's magazines for sale behind the counter of her daddy's country store (205–7, 212). She abhors the magazines but is curiously drawn to them and to images in her mind of naked men. When she discovers Charles is buying the magazines, her contempt for them overcomes her temporary curiosity. Raney's attitude toward sex becomes clear: desire is the problem. As long as sex is approached as a duty, a biblical duty, it is acceptable. But once desire enters in and sex becomes something you want to do, it becomes a sin. Raney's repression of sexual desire remains a sore spot in the relationship until a wonderful scene in part three.

Charles and Raney begin to overcome some of the turbulence in their relationship toward the end of the novel. The couple stops by Raney's daddy's store after closing and after Raney has had wine with dinner. Raney finds herself in the feed room, inundated by feelings of desire she cannot explain. She reasons that "there's nothing in the Bible about what married people can't do together" (226), and she and Charles end up sipping Southern Comfort and making love on the feed bags in the back of her daddy's store. Raney allows herself to feel sexual desire for the first time, she overcomes some of her inhibitions about alcohol and sexuality, and she begins to understand that sex can be more than a duty. While her maturation is occurring, Charles reciprocates with compromises of his own, and the two seem to be on the road to strengthening their turbulent relationship.

Other issues find at least partial resolution by the end of the story. For example, in the beginning of the novel, Raney maintains a very conservative view about the relationship of husband and wife. However, by the end of the novel, Raney has taken a job and has begun to question the preacher on some of the traditional attitudes about the subservient role of women in marriage. In addition, racial attitudes become a prime component of the couple's tense relationship. Charles's best friend is Johnny Dobbs, an African American army buddy. Charles's friendship with Johnny leads to ugly confrontations with Raney's family because of their racist attitudes. Raney eventually begins to mellow in her prejudices, and she consents to naming Johnny as the godfather of their baby; however, her openness to more liberal social attitudes is not complete. In a symbolic move, Johnny stays at a hotel rather than at the family's home when he visits. Nonetheless, by the end of the novel and the first year of the couple's marriage, the reader sees both Raney and Charles making concessions, compromises, and changes that bridge the cultural gap that separates them.

Finally, the friction points that make Raney's and Charles's first year of marriage difficult find clear expression in their differing allegiances to religion. Raney grew up Free Will Baptist and represents fundamentalist religion in the South, one of the South's enduring cultural symbols. Charles grew up Episcopalian, a tradition that symbolically represents a type of secularized and worldly religion for southerners. Fundamentalism is presented in this story as being narrowly focused on conversion, a personal relationship with Jesus, and a literal interpretation of the Bible, while it ignores some of the pressing problems of contemporary life, such as mental illness and alcoholism. On the other hand, Charles's Episcopalianism seems overly rational, formal, socially oriented, and insensitive to individual need. While his social orientation might tackle society's problems on the grand level, Charles is often blind to human need on the individual level, and Charles remains egotistical and aloof through much of the story.

For Edgerton, both types of religion are inadequate. Thus, Edgerton is able to critique religion in the South, a region that is known for its religiosity, in a sensitive and nondiscriminating way. Edgerton's novel addresses and critiques many moral, ethical, and social issues and traces them to roots in religious belief. In this way, he delves to the core of some of the South's most cherished notions, questions them by raising religious issues, and mounts this religious and value-laden critique not through religious literature but through a secular novel. This, of course, demonstrates the power of the secular medium of literature to raise religious questions and issues. Edgerton himself notes the connection between the religious and the mundane when questioned about religion and his writing. He claims that "the religious spirit" is reflected by "everyday life."[10] Edgerton's articulation of the relationship perfectly demonstrates how literature can represent a secularization of religion, theology is constructed in secular writings not about God but about human beings.[11]

LEE SMITH, "WITCHES AND JESUS"[12]

Rather than focusing on one of Lee Smith's works, I will consider several of her novels and short stories. The larger body of her work reflects a consistent concern for issues that are ethical and religious by nature if not by subject. Like Clyde Edgerton, Lee Smith is critical of southern religion, in particular the conservative fundamentalist variety, one of the

South's most enduring cultural symbols. Unlike Edgerton, Smith's fiction goes further to construct a competing religious mythology based in women's spirituality. Like Edgerton, Smith's fiction relies on a strong sense of place and in-depth character creations. Unlike Edgerton, Smith's place is the southern Appalachian mountains and her characters are the people of the southern highlands. Both Smith and Edgerton write about changes in the South in the last half of the twentieth century and point out the shifting boundaries between the sacred and secular in contemporary American and southern society.[13]

Spirits roam through the deep hollows of Sugar Fork; the rural country around Black Rock teems with the haunts of ghosts; witches glide through the forests across the hill boundaries of Hoot Owl Holler; the Spirit descends upon Grace Shepherd "like lightning" (*Saving Grace*, 271). At the same time, the revival preacher's drone rises from the tent into the night in the shadow of Black Mountain, calling poor sinners home; a young girl emerges from the baptismal waters of a plastic swimming pool "wet and saved" ("Tongues of Fire," 85); Ezekiel Bailey ponders the differences that split the Missionary Baptists from the Primitives; Travis Word falls to his knees to seek cleansing after love-making. Two sets of images permeate Lee Smith's Appalachian fiction to portray a dual religious consciousness: the first is characterized by an elemental, supernatural power bound up by nature and the mountains themselves; the second appears in the form of traditional religions that attempt to transcend the mountain peaks and valley floors.

Both sets of images abound in Lee Smith's Appalachian settings and are entangled in the rich stories about her mountain characters and communities. These stories reveal a complex religious consciousness that at once is bound up in nature yet transcends nature; that focuses on the mountain setting as sacred yet often denies that sacredness in favor of a heavenly home beyond the Appalachian sky. This dual consciousness more often than not depicts traditional religion as restrictive and often portrays its adherents, particularly its leaders, as hypocritical or repressed. Yet there is in Smith's fiction a spirituality that is available and empowering to her characters—a spirituality that is often found outside traditional religious institutions. This religious consciousness provides order and chaos for the lives of Smith's characters (for Crystal Spangler, for Richard Burlage, for Moses and Ezekiel Bailey, for Grace Shepherd), yet for all the importance of spirituality in Smith's fiction, in the end, traditional religion appears as mostly irrelevant and ineffectual in an Appalachia in the midst of change, modernization, and secularization.

Smith's fictional depiction of Appalachian religions relies heavily on generalizations and stereotypes. Even *Saving Grace,* which is the most religious of her works in terms of content, depends on stereotypical images of poor mountain preachers and people to portray the religious worldview of her characters. However, this in itself does not demean Appalachian religious traditions as long as the reader does not make the mistake of taking Smith's vignettes and generalizing them to all Appalachian religious traditions and faiths. These depictions do help set the context for her stories; her generalized representations determine what is possible and dictates the actions and feelings of her characters. Thus, while other types of writings are more helpful for understanding the intricacies and varieties within the Appalachian region, Smith's fiction gives insight into the religious condition in general and provides counterpoint to the study of Appalachian religious history and tradition.[14]

Smith's fiction represents the secularization of religion in two ways. Her depiction of traditional religion provides a kind of secular critique of religious faith by making value judgments concerning the relevance of religion to culture. Her portrayal of traditional religions symbolizes the extent of the secularization of sacred institutions through the construction of sacred stereotypes. The second set of religious images in Smith's work focuses on an elemental religion divorced from sacred institutions, and here we see secularization occurring differently. With these images, we see a sacralization of the secular as her mountain stereotypes and traditions rise to the level of myth.

Traditional Religion in Lee Smith's Fiction

Of the two images of religion and spirituality in Lee Smith's Appalachian fiction, those images surrounding traditional Appalachian religious movements are the most easily recognizable. Smith's work contains scenes and descriptions from the Free Will Baptists, the Primitive Baptists, the Missionary Baptists, the Holiness tradition, the tent revival, snake-handling evangelists, and Appalachian Methodists and Baptists. Most of these groups are barely represented outside Appalachia, some are dying out even in the high country, and Smith represents them in such a way to reinforce notions that Appalachia has a sense of otherness about it, an exotic element in all facets of its culture, including religion.[15] In her descriptions of these "exotic" faiths, it is clear that they are different from the mainstream churches outside Appalachia. Indeed, Smith's fiction provides a social hierarchy of churches that "primitivizes" some of these traditional churches.[16] Karen, the narrator in Smith's short story "Tongues of Fire," describes this exotic sense with her "social ranking of the churches," where the wildest of the congregations "were reputed to yell out, fall down in fits, and throw their babies"(64, 57).

In Karen's world and in Lee Smith's fiction, the more traditionally Appalachian the religion, the wilder and more uninhibited it appears and a greater sense of otherness accompanies it. Smith faithfully portrays some unusual worship practices of these Appalachian religious traditions, such as the peculiar preaching style found in some Appalachian Baptist denominations where the preacher punctuates his phrases with a characteristic "ah."[17] Sam Russell Sage uses this technique in *Fair and Tender Ladies* (93), as does the preacher, Mr. Looney, in "Tongues of Fire" (80). Smith also refers to the Primitive Baptist practice of "churching" its members in *The Devil's Dream* and in *Fair and Tender Ladies*. "Churching," according to Appalachian religion scholar Howard Dorgan, is an act of discipline where "an errant member is literally expelled from fellowship."[18] Reminiscent of frontier religions and revivals, in *Fair and Tender Ladies* Preacher Sage lines out hymns (93), and Oakley, Ivy's husband, dislikes Mister Blue because he "is one of these new kind of preachers that has gone to school for it, not just got the call" (264). This sense of otherness accompanying Appalachian religion is most obvious in *Saving Grace*, Smith's story of the daughter of a snake-handling evangelist who travels through North Carolina and Tennessee preaching in brush arbors and little independent Holiness churches. This novel depicts the bizarre rituals of handling snakes, drinking poison, handling fire, and raising the dead.

Smith's portrayal of these unusual practices from traditional Appalachian religions highlights the differences between them and mainstream faiths. In *Oral History*, Richard Burlage, a socialite from Richmond, makes this observation when he takes a pilgrimage to the wilds of Appalachia to teach school and refresh his soul. He draws a comparison between the "Catholic constraints imposed upon the spirit by the Episcopal Church" (135) and the free abandon in worship with the Freewill Followers at Grassy Creek. The Freewill Followers resemble the members of Karen's little Appalachian churches, have questionable social status, "let go" in church, speak in tongues, handle snakes, and rush the altar in a frenzy of emotion and fear for their eternal soul (138–39; 152–54). More often than not, when Smith portrays traditional Appalachian churches, they appear exotic, unrestrained, and oddly peculiar in terms of their relationship to other more socially acceptable religious faiths. Smith portrays these traditional religions as being less secularized (or at least less acculturated) and, thus, less relevant and more vulnerable than mainstream religious traditions.

Beyond this presentation of Appalachian religions as otherness, Lee Smith's fiction creates a type of generic Appalachian fundamentalism that is common in these traditional religions. Differences between the various groups and sects are present, and Smith's readers recognize an ongoing theological battle between groups concerning the role of grace, behavior, and the Holy Spirit. However, there is much more commonality between these various groups organized within one traditional religious worldview. This worldview is characterized by narrow and constrictive thinking, by the all-important conversion experience, by an overarching concern with the afterlife, and by an individualistic and self-centered religious concern.

For the most part, Smith's traditional religions are defined by a narrow and restrictive worldview that reduces religion to obsession with the afterlife. The traditional religious attitudes in *Saving Grace* are so restrictive they prevent Holiness women from wearing jewelry and Travis Word from going to college on a basketball scholarship. Such restrictions are meant to keep adherents of the faith separate from the world because of the belief that a heavenly home is their true world. This insular posturing promotes a method of dealing with secularization in a changing and modernizing Appalachia. In *Saving Grace,* Virgil Shepherd's proclamation, "These children may not have new clothes on their back nor new shoes on their feet, but they are going to Heaven with me," (9) demonstrates the belief that the saints should remain separate from this world in order to inherit the world to come.

This restrictive attitude toward the secular world and its accompanying focus on the afterlife is found and reinforced throughout Smith's fiction.[19] For example, in *The Devil's Dream,* Moses Bailey believes fiddle music is the "instrument of the Devil" and tries to keep his son from becoming interested in music (27) because it would lead to Satan instead of to heaven. In *Black Mountain Breakdown,* the main representative of religion in the book is the Reverend Garnett Sykes, Crystal Spangler's uncle. Garnett's main concern throughout the first portion of the novel is the eternal state of the souls of his family. Garnett expresses frustration that he "can't pray [Grant] into heaven" (49), and Crystal avoids Garnett "because she knows he will take her aside and tell her it's about time she accepted Jesus Christ as her personal Lord and Savior" (63). Later in the book, a tent revival works up participants' emotions over fear for their eternal souls, and the whole purpose of the revival meeting is to bring people to a state of contrition based on fear. As the hard sale affects

Crystal during the revival, "Fear shoots straight through the middle of her like a sweet sharp knife" (121). It is this fear that the revival preacher orchestrates, and it is this concern for the afterlife that drives traditional religions in Smith's work.

Fear for the eternal state of the soul is so strong in the presentation of these religious faiths that it eclipses the role religion plays in determining behavior. In other words, behaving morally is less a concern than getting saved, and all energy goes into salvation rather than morality. For example, Sam Russell Sage, the evangelist in *Fair and Tender Ladies,* cares only for saving souls and is known to sleep around when he is not preaching, and in *Saving Grace,* the charismatic Virgil Shepherd keeps mistresses in various locations and believes "a person could just go out and do whatsoever they damn well pleased, and then repent and get forgiven for it, over and over again" (164–65). In *Oral History,* Richard's journal describes this characteristic of traditional Appalachian religious faith when he writes, "Salvation . . . has nothing to do, apparently, with any notion of living a 'good life,' as I was brought up to believe a Christian ought to do"(139). Richard later proves his point when he walks the aisle on the fourth night of a revival meeting to receive salvation only to rush out of the church moments later to make love to Dory, the mountain girl who is the object of his obsession, even though he admits that to do so would go against everything that he knows to be right (152–54). The same loose connection between religious conviction and morality appears in *The Devil's Dream* as well. As Fred Chappell remarks, the Bailey family members have only three things in mind, "religion, music, and sexual love," and are quite willing to suspend their religion for sexual love.[20]

The most glaring example of Richard's observations about mountain religion's concept of salvation comes with the life and behavior of Crystal in *Black Mountain Breakdown.* Crystal experiences conversion at a tent meeting revival with such intensity that even her preacher uncle Garnett is envious. Crystal's mother's reaction is one of relief that Crystal has been saved, and for a time, Crystal becomes a religious dynamo, reveling in the intensity of her experience, reading and studying the Bible daily, singing hymns around the house, and helping her mother more than usual (129–30). However, Crystal's religious intensity fades quickly—she discontinues her daily Bible reading within a week of the end of the revival, and shortly thereafter she considers, with some degree of concern, her illicit love affair with Mack Stiltner. She quickly concludes, however, that even though her sexual relationship with Mack was a sin, it had very little to do with the state of her soul (136). Crystal decides that morality has nothing to do with salvation, that behavior is incidental to the Christian life, and proceeds to fill her life with a series of illicit and adulterous relationships. In Crystal's life, as with others in Smith's fiction, religion has little to do with how one acts in this life and everything to do with where one goes in the next, assuming a discontinuity between sacred and secular worlds.

The one obvious exception to this general depiction is Travis Word, Grace's preacher husband in *Saving Grace*. According to Grace's narration, "Travis Word was the first preacher I ever ran into that placed works above grace in order of importance" (164). Grace contrasts this to her father, who holds that believers can live life however they wish and receive forgiveness for their sins. Nevertheless, even though Travis emphasizes behavior, the goal is still the same—heaven. For Travis, the connection between morality and salvation is so strong that it drives him to his knees after he makes love to his wife, Grace. His long prayers seek cleansing, and his obsession with purity leads to a depressed and repressed life that eventually enslaves Grace and drives her away. But once again, with Travis, Crystal Spangler, and many of Smith's characters who get caught up in religion, the goal is otherworldly, the obsession is heaven. These traditional religions reject the secular world and its concerns in favor of the promise of heavenly paradise in contrast to religions that accommodate to the secular, a form of secularization. The danger, of course, is that if sacred institutions do not secularize and acculturate, they will become so otherworldly obsessed as to be irrelevant, anachronistic, and tragically comical.

Because this is the predominant religious attitude in Smith's traditional religions, it makes sense that the premier religious event is a radical and exemplary conversion experience. Ample scenes scattered throughout Lee Smith's writing chronicle this conversion experience: Richard Burlage's trip to the altar, the emotional experiences of those Richard is observing, the adolescent conversion of Karen in "Tongues of Fire," and the electrifying and sensuous crisis of Crystal herself. Crystal's conversion is the most detailed and will serve to illustrate the rest. Not long after the death of her father, Crystal becomes interested in religion and makes her way to a tent revival on the invitation of her childhood friend, Jubal Thacker, who eventually becomes a television evangelist. Crystal is a teenager with average adolescent anxieties at the time she visits the tent revival; however, she is burdened with extraordinary circumstances as well. She is trying to recover from the death of her father and has repressed the memory of being raped by her Uncle Devere. Thus, in addition to the normal adolescent uncertainties that often

make individuals susceptible to extreme emotion, Crystal is emotionally more fragile because of her unique circumstances. The reader is not
surprised, then, when she experiences powerful emotions during the
revival service.

Crystal's conversion is a crucial scene in *Black Mountain Breakdown*.
Crystal attends the big tent revival mostly out of a sense of loyalty to
Jubal, but once she is there, she quickly is taken in by the emotional
impact of the service. The service begins with the local Pentecostal
preacher exhorting the crowd (121). There is singing, prayer, testimony,
and the revival proceeds with a carnival-like atmosphere, complete with
a karate champion who uses his skill to demonstrate how God breaks
the barriers between God and humanity. The main event is the sermon
delivered by a visiting evangelist, Fred Lee Sampson. His sermon is traditional enough, emphasizing the impossibility of entering heaven by
good works and the necessity of accepting "the beautiful gift of salvation
through the blood of Jesus Christ" (126). All of this has a peculiar effect
on Crystal, and she slowly but powerfully responds to the emotional and
persuasive techniques of the evangelist.

As the service continues, Crystal "feels as if electricity is shooting
straight into her head and all down her body, crackling in every nerve"
(126). Fred Lee Sampson brings the service to a close by asking the congregation to sing "Just as I Am," "with every head bowed and every eye
closed" (126). Veterans of old-time revivals immediately recognize the
ritual, the hymn, and the technique as Sampson continues to plead over
the soft chords of the organ. The words, the hymn, the persuasion have
the desired effect—people begin to walk to the altar. And, of course,
Crystal walks the aisle, gives herself to Jesus Christ, is baptized in a plastic swimming pool, and "comes up sputtering, saved . . . dripping wet
and holy" (128).

This conversion scene is a typical one for Smith: a similar event plays
itself out in "Tongues of Fire," Richard's conversion in *Oral History* shares
some of these elements, and when Grace, in *Saving Grace*, finally experiences the Spirit, it "comes down on [her] hard like a blow to the top
of . . . [her] head and runs all over . . . [her] body like lightning" (271). This
general experience is reminiscent of the nineteenth-century camp meeting revivals and represents a generic Appalachian revival service for Smith's
fiction. The implication is clear—Lee Smith chronicles an Appalachia
where the old-time religious traditions have been preserved, at least
until fairly recently, but are giving way to intrusions of modernity and
the secular world, such as the plastic swimming pool and Jubal Thacker's
television ministry. And in this old-time generic religion, conversion

(getting saved) is much more crucial than good works for salvation and ultimately outweighs even moral action in terms of importance. The thoroughly anti-secular stance of such religion leads one inward and upward, not outward. Smith's fiction portrays Appalachian religion as individualistic and self-centered—it is all about what the individual gets out of the experience and not what the person gives. And what one gets is no less than the promise of eternal life. Lee Smith's stories depict these traditional religions as making little difference except to pacify the individual who has the experience.

This suggests an additional characteristic of Smith's generic traditional Appalachian religion—it arises from insecurity, if not psychosis, and afflicts mostly those who are marginal in some way. Ivy Rowe, in *Fair and Tender Ladies,* comments, "Life is so hard here that it leads many right to church" (157); Crystal gets religion shortly after her tragic rape and after her father dies; "Tongues of Fire" begins with the adolescent Karen "speaking in tongues" amid family tragedies and during emotionally charged times (56); Richard Burlage's religious experience comes at a time when he is struggling with his own sexual passions; *Saving Grace* depicts the exotic practice of snake handling that seems, in this book, to be the affliction and ritual of the perpetually poor. In almost every case, religion erupts during times of emotional distress or during times when religion provides some sort of release from difficult situations. Likewise, when times are good, when characters prosper, religion may be present, but it has little force in a person's life.

Elemental Religion in Lee Smith's Fiction

If Smith's depiction of traditional Appalachian religions represents the negative impact of sacred traditions resisting secularization, her portrait of a more elemental religious orientation suggests that authentic religion can arise outside so-called religious institutions, especially if those institutions are irrelevant. With her presentation of elemental religion, we see the sacralization of the profane, that which is extra-ecclesiastical.

Alongside traditional Appalachian religion, which erupts at various places in Lee Smith's narratives, is a second type of religious consciousness that pervades Smith's Appalachian fiction. This second form of religion is elemental, primal, closely associated with the landscape and nature, and often invokes a secret power that is disclosed to or available through female characters—a power that is sometimes revealed and symbolized through Smith's use of witches and her portrayal of women who are mystically connected to spirituality or nature.[21] This second type of religious consciousness is not as easily identifiable as the first because

it is not as obviously intrusive into the narrative. Nevertheless, it is perhaps more pervasive and ever present, and perhaps that too is why it is
not as easily recognizable.

This elemental religious consciousness is first recognized in the strong
sense of otherness in the profane world, often in connection to the natural environment.[22] In much of Smith's fiction, the landscape has a mystical quality and the setting takes on sacred characteristics. This is
particularly true in *Oral History,* which is concerned with the land and
physical changes brought to the mountains.[23] The novel is set in and
around Hoot Owl Holler, "the prettiest holler on God's green earth"
(22), and traces the history of the Cantrell family in order to explain the
Cantrell curse. The first significant Cantrell figure is Almarine, a man
who enjoys a special relationship with the land and with nature. Indeed,
in this story, as Rosalind Reilly has noted, the mountains themselves initiate longings that "propel the novel forward."[24] The mountains themselves cast spells because they constitute a sacred space where
"supernatural enchantment"[25] sways the actions of characters. Almarine
brings the curse on the family by getting involved with the witch Red
Emmy, and the curse is passed along through successive generations to
visit tragedy on the family. This family myth operates as all myth does,
to provide sacred explanations, and it takes place, as all myth does, in a
sacred setting. This sacred sense of setting is particularly strong in the first
section of *Oral History* where settings are mystical, often associated with
circle imagery that gives them sacred power, as Reilly suggests, and
where action sometimes takes place in "froze-time" (40), a sacred time
where time is suspended and events become surreal.[26]

This image of the mountains as sacred place is reinforced at the
beginning of section two of the novel when the reader is introduced to
Richard Burlage, who is a foreigner to the area and whose response to
the mountainous terrain is "Dear God!" (93). Richard, in his awe-
stricken state, means for his sojourn in the mountains to be "a pilgrimage . . . to the very roots of consciousness and belief" (93). Richard's
pilgrimage is to a sacred place and time rooted in the mystical bends and
crevices of the mountains and valley floors.

The elemental and primal sacred setting of Lee Smith's fiction is reinforced by the role of ghosts, witches, and superstition in the mountains.
The belief in spirits ranges from Crystal Spangler's naive belief in Ghost
King Clarence B. Oliver, who would protect her from all the other
ghosts who sometimes threatened her at night, to Granny Younger's
insistence that Red Emmy belonged to the Devil, was a witch, and was
responsible for the Cantrell curse. Perhaps this traditional connection to

superstition and its part in an Appalachian religious consciousness can best be seen in Granny Younger's role as healer and, therefore, life force in her traditional community. Granny Younger typifies the confusion of superstition with traditional Christianity by reciting a magical formula to stop bleeding. The formula is based on Ezekiel 16:6, "And when I passed by you, and saw you weltering in your blood, I said to you in your blood, 'Live ...,'"[27] but in Lee Smith's mystical, sacred Appalachian setting, it takes on magical and supernatural qualities (20). Granny Younger also suggests a magical incantation that includes the mark of the cross, ashes, and the recitation of the names of the Father, Son, and Holy Ghost in order to break the witch's spell (46). With Granny Younger, the traditionally Christian is fused with the primal, and the mystical element of Appalachian religion becomes clear. And with Granny Younger, one can see in Smith's female characters a mystical ability to harness a bewitching connection with the elemental powers of nature.

This connection between Smith's female characters and the elemental powers is sometimes evident in the context of traditional religious forms. If female characters in Smith's fiction are connected to and empowered by ghosts and the elemental spirits, this connection is extended to the relationship with the Holy Spirit in *Saving Grace*. There is an authentic, empowering experience of the Spirit in this novel, yet it seems to elude Grace's father, who handles snakes for show without anointing, and it is unavailable to Travis Word, whose restrictive religion makes him melancholy and sad. Rather, it is discovered by Grace's mother, who plunges her hands into hot coals without harm, because she was empowered by the Spirit and could handle fire as "a perfect pleasure in the Lord" (26). And later, near the end of the novel, Grace discovers this secret place in the soul through the Spirit and presumably handles the burning coals as "a joy in the Lord" (271) just like her mother.[28]

This elemental religion affords wholeness and connection, according to Rosalind Reilly, by "providing meaningful myths to empower the lives" of Smith's characters.[29] Personal, family, and communal myths provide meaning for the characters in Smith's narratives. This is seen most powerfully in Crystal Spangler's life. Crystal's breakdown occurs because she loses herself through the loss of her own story (she represses the memory of the rape by Devere and dissociates herself from that event) and through the loss of her father, whose relationship with his daughter was based on storytelling.[30] When Crystal loses her source of story and myth and forgets her own story through repression, she breaks her link to wholeness; she disengages herself from the elemental religious consciousness that provides connection; she loses herself through the loss of her mythic past. Crystal tries vainly to recapture that link to wholeness through her radical conversion experience at the revival, but the traditional Christian experience fails to make up for the loss—only the recovery of myth can do that—only the recovery of the elemental, mystical connection to sacredness can empower Crystal.

The importance of story, the power of myth, is also strong in the novel *Fair and Tender Ladies,* a story told entirely through a lifetime of letters written by Ivy Rowe. Ivy's letters, the most intimate to a dead sister, Silvaney, allow Ivy to remember and tell her story. At one point in the narrative, Ivy slips into "a great soft darkness"(193). Ivy's depression comes at a time when her oldest child leaves home, and she tries to recapture her past through the stories that provide connection to her father and to the eccentric Cline sisters who used to come to Ivy's house on Old Christmas Eve and tell stories. Ivy's depression also comes at a time when she discontinues her reading, her letter writing, and, thus, her connection to her own story. The cumulative effect is that Ivy loses her connection to the past through the loss of stories, and she loses herself in the process. Ivy is lifted from her depression when she once again connects to her past through story. Ivy leaves her family and home for a short time with Honey Breeding. The pair start on what was to be a short hike up the mountain. During the walk, Ivy feels so comfortable that she begins to tell Honey all about herself. She surprises herself by talking so openly to a stranger, but it feels like the first time she has really talked in a long time (223). They spend the afternoon telling stories and making love; Ivy is reminded of the stories she heard from her father during her childhood; they spend days in a cave; her depression is lifted—she feels young again.[31]

Nevertheless, Smith's characters learn that the past is not fully recoverable or knowable and that connection to the past, no matter how fulfilling, carries a price.[32] Ivy returns to her family to find her daughter dead and is faced with the ordeal of being forgiven by her husband and of forgiving herself. And Crystal slips into paralysis after the memory of her rape comes flooding back. So there is a paradox with Smith's depiction of recovering the past. On the one hand, it is, or should be, a source of strength. On the other hand, the past fails to fully integrate characters like Ivy and Crystal. The key to recovery is the *myth* of the past, perhaps what Lee Smith calls "the central mystery of the past."[33] Ivy recovers from her ordeal because she reconnects to her past through the stories of Honey Breeding and through the recovery of her own story. This recovery of myth is empowering and is a sacred act that takes place in a sacred setting, for Ivy near a mountain bald that she had never seen and in a mountain cave that provides shelter and nurture. Crystal does not recover because she loses the "mystery," the myth, when the past comes to her in all its reality.

Thus, Smith's Appalachian fiction is often characterized by the recovery of an elemental religious consciousness. And in Lee Smith's contemporary Appalachian settings, the connection to the elemental and the sacred, which depends on the connection to nature, the land, the spiritual, and the mythic past, becomes tenuous as the unspoiled, wild beauty of the land that captivated such characters as Almarine Cantrell and Richard Burlage slowly yields to strip mines, shopping malls, and towns and villages—to secularization and modernization. As concrete and pavement fill the mountain hollows, the witches disappear, superstition is replaced by religion, and Smith's female characters, who had enjoyed a mystical connection with the primal, search with fewer results for that secret power available through nature and spirit. Yet Smith's characters find ways to access that elemental spirit in a contemporary setting. Sometimes they attempt to reach the primal through traditional religions, yet the presence of the traditional impinges on the empowering capabilities of the primal.[34] Discovery of the primal through traditional religious experience can be seen in what Virginia Smith calls the "sexualizing of the spiritual"[35] (or the spiritualization of sexuality) and in Smith's depiction of women's connection to a primal force in nature.[36] The former can be seen in *Black Mountain Breakdown*, *Oral History*, and *Fair and Tender Ladies*, while the latter is best exemplified by "Tongues of Fire."

The spiritualization of sexuality (sacralization of the sexual), the connection of powerful religious experience with sexual desire and feeling, is a strong theme in much of Smith's fiction. In *Saving Grace*, Grace attends a homecoming revival, gets swept away by the emotionally charged event, and finds herself in the backseat of her father's car with Lamar, transferring the "butterflies" (102) in her stomach and "the general fever of that night" (106) into sexual passion. After making love, Grace finds herself prophesying while being "possessed of the Spirit" (107), and she discovers her spiritual gift of discernment. The connection between spiritual and sexual energy is clear.[37] Even a more mature Grace discovers this same connection after an afternoon of passionate love with Randy Newhouse. Energized rather than exhausted, "on fire" and "sizzling," Grace sings hymns all the way home and shouts, "Glory hallelujah!" In her words, "I thought I had been born again" (225).

The connection is even more pronounced elsewhere in Smith's fiction. In *Oral History*, Richard Burlage confuses his religious longings with his feelings for Dory. Richard attends a revival faithfully with the intention of meeting Dory there and is surprised to find that he is moved during the "invitational" on the fourth night of the revival. However, "whether the agitation . . . [he] began to experience at that moment had to do with a true religious impulse, or with . . . [his] anxiety over her" (153) is not at all clear. During his conversion experience, when he walks the aisle to the front of the church, Dory bursts into the back of the meetinghouse. Richard immediately leaves with Dory and they make love for the first time. The two lovers end up spending a passionate six weeks together. This period constitutes an epiphany for Richard, a period he describes as "a state of grace" (158). Richard's confusion of religious emotion with sexual desire ends with his finding grace in the latter rather than the former.

A similar confusion of feelings occurs in *Fair and Tender Ladies*. When Ivy Rowe, in Linda J. Byrd's description "the novel's sacred-sexual-maternal protagonist,"[38] attends a revival meeting, she is caught up in the emotionalism and is on the verge of responding to the preacher's pleas to "come right on up to Jesus." She feels "the firey hand of God clutching . . . [her] in the stomach" and is ready to respond to the altar call when her companion, Miss Torrington, encourages her to leave (94). The feeling is significant, and later Ivy associates her religious experience with her sexual desire. The "firey hand" she associates with God returns when Ivy feels sexual desire (97–98, 113).

The connection that Ivy makes between religious feeling and sexual desire is even more explicit in the experience of Crystal Spangler in *Black Mountain Breakdown*. As Anne Goodwyn Jones has suggested, Crystal "feels 'real' only when a man has shown sexual interest in her to which she responds, or when God enters her."[39] The sources of empowerment for Crystal are spirituality and sensuality. When Crystal visits the tent revival meeting and experiences intense religious feeling, she feels "electrified," as if "every part of her mind and body is on fire, flaming" (127), and she associates this feeling with her sexual relationship with Mack Stiltner. Smith writes: "She feels as if electricity is shooting straight into her head and all down her body, crackling in every nerve. . . . A current arcs through her body, making her feel like she felt when she was with Mack—alive, fully alive and fully real, more than real" (126). According to Jones, "Crystal trusts the sensual and spiritual voices inside her,"[40] and because she confuses these voices, she cannot unite them, and neither spirituality nor sensuality alone can empower Crystal—both are dead ends and neither can prevent Crystal's breakdown.

Smith's spiritualization of sexuality often happens in the lives of her women characters who are desperately seeking to unite body and spirit, as in "Tongues of Fire."[41] In this story, the adolescent Karen also confuses the spiritual with the sensual and feels "all wild and trembly inside" when young Johnny Rock Malone preaches (65). Later, she experiences the feeling familiar to Smith's characters, the "burning, stabbing sensation in . . . chest and stomach . . . like the hand of God" (84). But Karen goes a step further in her spiritual empowerment—she speaks in tongues. This is an exotic ritual that produces "a total thrill" for Karen the first time she hears of it (72). The first time Karen hears glossolalia, she knows she has discovered a source of power[42] when she goes to a Holiness church with her friend Tammy and discovers "a language" she "knew intimately" (81).

Virginia Smith suggests the description of Karen's experience demonstrates how "Smith confronts seriously women's need for a passionate language, an original voice that merges body and spirit."[43] Karen's finding that voice contrasts sharply with Crystal's paralysis and inability to speak at the end of *Black Mountain Breakdown*—Karen is empowered while Crystal is immobilized. This immobilization, in Smith's assessment, represents the "cautionary" element of the story concerning southern women's tendency toward passivity.[44] In any event, it is clear that this very sensuous religious experience has the effect of reaching a primal, elemental source of strength and freedom. Oddly enough, Karen discovers this liberation through a traditional Appalachian religion. It is here, through the empowering possibilities of religious feeling and through the spiritualization of sexuality, that the two types of religious consciousness in Smith's fiction, the traditional and the elemental, sometimes come together. Yet despite the occasional intersection of the two types of Appalachian religious consciousness, the two rarely work in concert. The traditional religious categories can intrude upon and upset the primal and vice versa because the former focuses on transcendence and the afterlife while the latter is firmly anchored in nature and the mountain settings, the mythic past, and in a spirituality expressed through physical, bodily experience. The two types of religious consciousness create a paradox—a conflict between the transcendent and imminent, the sacred and secular—a paradox that rarely allows Smith's characters to fully overcome their marginalization.

At least two sets of images surrounding spirituality give the reader a glimpse of Lee Smith's vision of an Appalachian religious consciousness. Religion appears in all its traditional denominational and ritual constraints and as a more primal and universal spirituality based on the natural world, the mythic past, and sensuality. Sometimes these types of religious expression collide, but when they do come together, it rarely leads to wholeness or empowerment. Instead, the sensual element leads the experience beyond social convention, the encounter is censored, and individuals lose any meaning because they suppress the experience rather than allowing it to free them. Richard returns to Richmond without Dory, Karen is jerked back into line and becomes socially acceptable again, and Crystal suffers a paralyzing emotional breakdown. The elemental experience of sensuality and spirituality is suppressed by social convention or by traditional religion, and results, according to Anne Goodwyn Jones, in a group of characters "who fail, who prefer intellectualizing to feeling, moralizing to sensuality, religiosity to spirituality."[45] As a result, in Smith's fiction, traditional religiosity becomes largely irrelevant.

This theme of change is consistent throughout Lee Smith's Appalachian fiction, and change affects religion as much as any other cultural attribute of Appalachian society. In Smith's Appalachian fiction, she most often chronicles an Appalachia that is losing its pristine and traditional past and that is rapidly losing its Appalachian distinctiveness.[46] Part of the reason for this dominant picture of change is that many of Smith's novels trace stories through generational changes—sometimes beginning in the late nineteenth or early twentieth century and following a family or story to the present or near present. The effect of these narratives is dramatic. *The Devil's Dream* follows a family legend through 150 years from 1833 in a little cabin on Cold Spring Holler to the glitz and glamour of the lobby of the Opryland Hotel at Christmas. *Oral History* chronicles a 100-year family history, and the dramatic change, modernization, and commercialization of Appalachia surface when the old family home becomes an attraction in the middle of a theme park, Ghostland.[47] In *Fair and Tender Ladies,* the nostalgic scene of the eccentric Cline sisters trudging through snow on Old Christmas Eve to share stories with their neighbors is replaced by the end of the novel with retrieving toys from layaway at a department store on December 23. Old Christmas is a thing of the past, and Ivy comments: "I was just thinking about the way Christmas used to be and how it has changed now and is more storebought, that is progress! Still and all, I miss the Cline sisters, and all the storytelling on Old Christmas Eve" (251). In *Saving Grace,* "a huge Food Lion supermarket" with a "drive-thru pick-up" replaces the old Duty's Grocery, a community crossroads store that used to sell home-made cakes (254). Finally, economic prosperity changes everything in *Black Mountain Breakdown* and even affects religious representatives in the book. In the space of a few short years, religion moves out from the dusty floors of a tent revival to the electronic, televised, healing evangelism of Jubal Thacker. These changes result in the transition of a sacred, mystical Appalachia to a modernized world stripped of its sacred power in part because traditional religions reject change and secularization. In other words, the result is a secular Appalachia stripped of the sacred rather than a mythic one.

Religion is pervasive in Lee Smith's Appalachian fiction—sometimes in the traditional settings of Primitive Baptist or Holiness congregations, sometimes in the mists of the hollows and hills of her settings, sometimes in the spiritual and sensual intersections experienced by her characters. But it is always present, always disruptive, sometimes empowering, sometimes deceptive, and sometimes devastating. Religious feeling and spirituality are rarely neutral; rather, her portrayal of an Appalachian religious consciousness is as passionate and alive as the characters themselves.

In Lee Smith's fiction, as in Edgerton's, the southern setting allows the critique of southern religion, an enduring cultural symbol. However, Smith's fiction goes further in positing an alternative religious vision based on women's spirituality and on other strong cultural symbols particular to the Appalachian region. And finally, Smith mounts this critique and constructs an alternative spirituality in the context of a secularizing and changing society, relying on an ongoing dialectic between sacred and secular categories—between elemental spirits and shopping malls, between the myths of a region and the gradual disappearance of its distinctiveness. Once again, reading and interpreting Lee Smith's fiction chronicles the secularization of religious longing, myth, and experience and demonstrates the spreading out of religion through secular cultural forms and media—in this case, the novel.

What we see in Smith's fiction is a double meditation on secularization. The fact that sacred impulse arises through her secular art is representative of the second direction of secularization: the sacralization of the secular. In addition, there seems to be a form of critique in Smith's fiction: religious institutions that refuse to secularize become irrelevant, and when sacred bodies no longer allow authentic religious experience, such sacred impulse will arise elsewhere through secular or nonreligious elements of the culture.

AMY TAN: *THE HUNDRED SECRET SENSES*

Lee Smith explores the complex relations between men and women, modernity and tradition, the existential and the spiritual. While many peg her a regional writer, it is mistake to limit her in such a way because her fiction carries much more universal significance than is implied by the designation of regionalist. In like manner, Amy Tan's fiction has often been described as ethnic because of Tan's own ethnicity and the topics and characters of her stories. Victoria Chen talks about Tan's female characters and their "dual cultural enmeshment" as if they represent Asian American women.[48] Some have even implied that Tan's novels can become a source for understanding Asian religion because of the focus in works like *The Kitchen God's Wife* on ancestors, deities, luck, rituals, and the like. In *Asian Religions in America: A Documentary History,* the editors refer to *The Kitchen God's Wife* as a text where Tan most clearly explores the religious landscape of Asia through her depiction of a Buddhist funeral.[49] And although Tan does give readers a glimpse of Asian traditions, especially as they have been appropriated in America, it would be a mistake to limit Tan's fiction to its helpfulness in understanding Asian Americans' struggles with a foreign culture. Tan's fiction far exceeds the parameters of Asian culture and embraces such universal concerns and topics as death and rebirth and relativity of time. My interest in Tan's fiction concerns not what she represents or reveals about Asian religion or culture. Rather, Tan is important to this book because her fiction develops characters who live and function in a secular world while easily moving between this world and the spirit world. Tan's characters often negotiate an easy intrusion of the sacred, the supernatural, into the secular world. Like Smith's fiction, Tan's is populated with ghosts and spirits, and because it works, Tan and Smith demonstrate the extent of sacralization of the secular in American popular culture. So Tan's fiction represents not so much cultural conflict as the sacred–secular tension in our society. What appears to be traditional Chinese culture in Tan's fiction is often little more than a sacred approach to the world—the conflict arises from the sacred encroaching on the secular, not from the East encroaching on the West.

This intrusion of the sacred into the secular is most clearly seen in *The Hundred Secret Senses.* Tan spoke in an interview about her emphasis on the spirit world and her fear that this emphasis would be seen as simply "Chinese superstition." Her perspective in the book comes through Kwan's (a main character) "Yin eyes"—the unusual vision that allows her to communicate with spirit people in the world of yin, people who have died and whose presence can be sensed all around us.[50] This is not a ghost story but a story that takes place between worlds, drawing heavily upon the spirit world. That she can write so convincingly about the world between worlds gives us some clue to the extent that our secular society is open to the sacred. Through Tan's creation and use of "Yin eyes" and "the World of Yin," her fiction opens the postmodern reader to a premodern concept—another world accessible through the agencies of this-world senses.[51]

Kwan's ability to see with yin eyes transports the reader across time and geography to nineteenth-century China, and part of the plot revolves around Christian missionaries in a Chinese village. The Christian message of the missionaries is ineffectual and the efforts of the godly are farcical. At the same time we see the failure of this traditional religious mission, the power of the spirit world is affirmed through nonreligious avenues. The reality of the yin world in the story brings the power of myth to play in a highly secularized San Francisco setting. So while traditional Christian missionary efforts are seen as misguided, the sacred through the power of myth receives new power and life.

In her full-length critical work on Amy Tan's fiction, E. D. Huntley devotes a chapter to *The Hundred Secret Senses* and a portion of that chapter to a Jungian archetypal reading of the novel.[52] This perspective is appropriate and helpful because it highlights the mythic component and structure of the novel to reveal the universal elements ascribed to Jungian theory, allowing the reader to negotiate the spirit world, the dream world, and the shift in plot perspective across two centuries. The story's setting also shifts from modern, secular, multicultural California to a "Yin world" based in China, and this jarring transition allows the intrusion of the sacred into the secular. It allows the spirit world to enter this world through memory and the senses, an intrusion that is related to spiritual and psychological wholeness in Tan's fiction. This spiritual perspective stands in stark contrast to the element of the supernatural in Lee Smith's fiction, which is anachronistic and superstitious, and the supernatural in Randall Kenan's fiction (to be examined next), which is related to pathology. Tan's perspective, seen through the Jungian lens, demands that the spiritual reside within the natural for human wholeness.

Perhaps even more importantly, such a Jungian approach allows the easy transition from the world of yin to this world without having to sacrifice credibility. Tan allows us to reconnect with the world of myth and gives us an example of how secular literature can do what sacred literature once did and perhaps can no longer do in the age of religious literalism. When we can learn from secular literature what once was the purview of sacred texts, the secularization process advances.

RANDALL KENAN: *A VISITATION OF SPIRITS*

I will end this chapter with a short review of a remarkable novel written by a talented young writer, Randall Kenan. Kenan published *A
Visitation of Spirits* when he was but twenty-six years old, a young age to
be able to produce such a dark vision of a world populated by ghosts and
spirits and to expose the tormented feelings of a young African
American boy. In Kenan's vision, we learn the story of Horace, a black
teenager who struggles with his homosexuality in a conservative religious community unequipped to help him deal with his feelings. The
inability of Horace to seek and find appropriate guidance in a world
where everybody and everything tells him he is a freak ultimately leads
him to suicide. Trapped in a world where his community fails him,
Horace leads the reader on an adventure that explores the prospects of
being gay, black, and southern.[53]

Kenan's story, like Edgerton's and Smith's works, highlights and critiques the ability of fundamentalist religion to deal adequately with the
complexity of the contemporary world. But with Kenan's work, the reader
is introduced to a different South. Whereas Edgerton's work provides
glimpses of rural and urban white middle-class existence and Smith's work
portrays Appalachian life, which is mostly white, Kenan's novel takes us
into the world of black southerners and reflects the community values and
religious beliefs dominant in a southern African American community.
Like the aforementioned authors, Kenan uses his story to reflect on the
values and morals promoted in the community through cultural religion
and beliefs. Yet unlike Edgerton and Smith, Kenan's work demonstrates a
conflict of cultural values within the black community.

Two dominant worldviews inform Kenan's novel: that of conservative, Calvinistic traditions, which Kenan likens to existentialist philosophy,[54] and a metaphysical vision based on an African American cultural
history steeped in a belief in demons and spirits. Here again, the sacred
and the secular collide in fiction, and Kenan uses these two worldviews
to create the crisis that Horace faces. Horace gets no help from his
preacher cousin Jimmy, no understanding from the staunch Christians
among his elders, and nothing but censure from a religious ethic that
condemns him as a sinner. Rejected by his family and by his religion,
Horace ends his life after being tormented by a demon during a hellish
night battling the spiritual underworld.

Horace enters his hell when he attempts a transformation, a conjure
common in the shamanistic practices of African traditions. Unable to live
with himself the way he is, unable to deal with the rejection and pain

caused by his homosexuality, Horace attempts to change his essence with the conjure. However, the experiment goes awry, and Horace finds himself trapped in the spiritual world and goes insane. Horace's insanity and his subsequent suicide raise important questions about the relationship between religion and insanity, homosexuality and spirituality, and the ability of traditional religious responses to deal with the complexities of contemporary problems.

Kenan's novel represents a secular theology at work. Matthew Guinn argues convincingly that Kenan's literature is a literature of revision that rejects "the dominant ideology." Drawing upon Henry Louis Gates Jr.'s concept of "signifyin(g)," Guinn points out that Kenan's rejection comes from his double marginalization as black and gay. He is not only marginalized as a black man but is also marginalized within the black community as a homosexual.[55] Kenan's signifyin(g) ideology points out that not all enemies of black culture are external—that the black church has in some sense failed the African American community.[56] Religion has failed Horace not because it is unable to deal with his secular challenges but because it is not large and expansive enough to deal with his spirit, his internal torment, his vision of beyond. Thus, religion fails him on a sacred level because legalism has replaced grace.

This cynicism about the church is reflected in Kenan's own agnosticism, which he openly discusses and which he claims evolved from influences that shaped his religious worldview. An early experience with the death of a close uncle led him to a fear of ghosts and spirits and to a worldview where visitations were possible. This African metaphysical worldview dovetailed with his early Calvinistic upbringing and with what he describes as an existential enlightenment during his college years. Kenan asserts, "Existentialism actually dovetails with Calvinism— how bleak the world is."[57] What emerges is a dark world defined by sin and depravity, as well as helplessness, looked over and populated by spirits and ghosts. In *A Visitation of Spirits,* the result is a frightening and upsetting vision that provides the backdrop for Horace's struggle with his tortured thoughts and insanity. Such a setting and background provide the stage for intense scrutiny of the human situation, of sin and forgiveness, producing a theology worked out in an arena that is expanded beyond the boundaries of orthodoxy—a philosophy that is secular but not necessarily atheistic.

Kenan's book is tragic and moving and represents a secular expression of religious themes perhaps exceeding those of Edgerton, Smith, or Tan. Because of his controversial subject matter that includes both race and sexual preference, Kenan finds no outlet in his traditional religion or in

his community—the subjects, at least homosexuality, are taboo or con-
demned. Therefore, he addresses homosexuality and spirituality through
a secular medium, the novel, since traditional religion avoids a meaningful discussion of the status of homosexuals in the church. Kenan's
explorations of race and sexuality are beyond the reaches of the traditional conservative church in the black community; finding no other
outlet, Kenan raises these issues in secular literature. But because this literature is certainly dealing with important moral and value-laden issues,
as well as with a spiritual world beyond the mundane, it carries a certain religious import.

SUMMARY

The idea that religious longings and beliefs can be expressed through
secular literature is nothing new. In fact, the idea establishes a well-
accepted basis for many studies and classes in universities and colleges.
The acknowledgment that religious meaning can be gleaned from this
secular cultural form indicates that secularization of religion is occurring
in the second direction, the sacralization of the secular. This is not secularization in the sense that religion is disappearing or that it is becoming unimportant in contemporary society. On the contrary, this is
secularization in the sense that the religious imagination has a persistence about it that allows it to spread out into society and to be expressed
in secular cultural forms. When formal religious organizations become
too narrowly focused, religious questioning, moral instruction, and discussions of values find their way into the cultural landscape in secular
forms like literature. Academicians acknowledge this movement toward
secularization. When we are willing to study religion through a secular
lens, then secularization is fairly well advanced.

We have seen how four authors fall back on their art to raise existential and religious questions, to seek religious answers, and to pose religious solutions. They are theologians in their own right, posing many of
the same questions theologians have posed throughout history. At the
same time, these writers contextualize such questions in a dialectic that
juxtaposes sacred and secular characteristics in an ambiguous world. And
this takes place not in sacred literature or in writing located within a religious tradition. Rather, this religious process takes place through cultural
products other than religion, through the secular form of literature. The
study of religion and literature represents more than an overlapping of
separate disciplines and categories; rather, the intersection of religion and

literature represents the extent to which secular forms can supplement, or even replace, religious structures as vehicles for religious longings and conversations.

NOTES

1. Wesley Kort, "'Religion and Literature' in Postmodernist Contexts," *Journal of the American Academy of Religion* 58, no. 4 (winter 1990): 582–83.

2. Flannery O'Connor, *Mystery and Manners: Occasional Prose*, ed. Sally and Robert Fitzgerald (New York: Farrar, Straus, & Giroux, 1957), 58. See also Michael McFee, "'Reading a Small History in a Universal Light': Doris Betts, Clyde Edgerton, and the Triumph of True Regionalism," *Pembroke Magazine* 23 (1991): 59.

3. Clyde Edgerton, interview by W. Dale Brown, in *Of Fiction and Faith: Twelve American Writers Talk about Their Vision and Work* (Grand Rapids, Mich.: Eerdmans, 1997), 122, 124.

4. Kenn Robbins, "Clyde Edgerton's *Killer Diller*," *Southern Quarterly* 30, no. 1 (fall 1991): 67.

5. Angeline Godwin Dvorak, "Cooking as Mission and Ministry in Southern Culture: The Nurturers of Clyde Edgerton's *Walking Across Egypt*, Fannie Flagg's *Fried Green Tomatoes at the Whistle Stop Café*, and Anne Tyler's *Dinner at the Homesick Restaurant*," *Southern Quarterly* 30, nos. 2–3 (winter/spring 1992): 90–92.

6. Robbins, "*Killer Diller*," 67. See also Edgerton, Brown interview, 120–21, on the influence of Edgerton's Southern Baptist upbringing on his writing.

7. Kenn Robbins, "A Conversation with Clyde Edgerton," *Southern Quarterly* 30, no. 1 (fall 1991): 60–61.

8. See Kort, *Narrative Elements and Religious Meaning*, 20–39. Among the narrative elements, atmosphere not only limits and provides boundaries but also allows for possibilities. This characteristic of atmosphere lends narratives a religious quality.

9. Allen Kromer examines *Raney* in light of Northrop Frye's category of romantic comedy with a particular focus on "resolution." See Allen Kromer, "Clyde Edgerton's Comic Vision" (master's thesis, Baylor University, 1992).

10. Clyde Edgerton, quoted in Susan Ketchin, *The Christ-Haunted Landscape: Faith and Doubt in Southern Fiction* (Jackson: University Press of Mississippi, 1994), 368.

11. Ibid., 353–54.

12. The material on Lee Smith was published previously in Conrad Ostwalt, "Witches and Jesus: Lee Smith's Appalachian Religion," *The Southern Literary Journal* 31, no. 1 (fall 1998): 98–118. Copyright 1998 by *The Southern Literary Journal* and the University of North Carolina at Chapel Hill Department of English. Reprinted with permission.

13. See Lisa Cade Wieland, "Old Times Not Forgotten: Family and Storytelling in Twentieth-Century Southern Literature" (Ph.D. diss., Marquette University, 1998), 23, and chs. 3 and 4.

14. There are many recent good books for studying the history, variety, and beliefs of Appalachian religious traditions. The best comprehensive study is Deborah

Vansau McCauley's *Appalachian Mountain Religion: A History*. Other recent studies that are helpful but more limited in scope include Thomas Burton, *Serpent-Handling Believers;* Howard Dorgan, *The Airwaves of Zion: Radio and Religion in Appalachia, Giving Glory to God in Appalachia: Worship Practices of Six Baptist Subdenominations,* and *The Old Regular Baptists of Central Appalachia: Brothers and Sisters in Hope;* David Kimbrough, *Taking Up Serpents: Snake Handlers of Eastern Kentucky;* James L. Peacock and Ruel W. Tyson Jr., *Pilgrims of Paradox: Calvinism and Experience among the Primitive Baptists of the Blue Ridge;* and Jeff Todd Titon, *Powerhouse for God: Speech, Chant, and Song in an Appalachian Baptist Church.*

15. According to Lee Smith, her regional fiction particularizes and, thus, stands out in "a world that's changing so fast and becoming so same." Her characterization of Appalachian religion is a case in point. See "Lee Smith: Interviewed by Nancy Parrish," *Appalachian Journal* 19 (summer 1992): 398.

16. In an interview with Susan Ketchin, Smith suggests that in Appalahchia, church affiliation partially determines social identity. See "Lee Smith Interview," in Ketchin, *The Christ-Haunted Landscape,* 52. See also William M. Teem, IV, "Let Us Now Praise the Other: Women in Lee Smith's Short Fiction," *Studies in the Literary Imagination* 27, no. 2 (fall 1994): 63–73.

17. For an examination of this technique, see Howard Dorgan, *Giving Glory to God in Appalachia: Worship Practices of Six Baptist Subdenominations* (Knoxville: University of Tennessee Press, 1987), 55–85.

18. Ibid., 18.

19. Smith's fiction demonstrates an irreverence for traditional religion that can be traced to newspaper articles she wrote as a student at Hollins. Nancy Parrish points out that many of her articles challenged traditional religious and social codes. See Nancy C. Parrish, *Lee Smith, Annie Dillard, and the Hollins Group: A Genesis of Writers* (Baton Rouge: Louisiana State University Press, 1998): 177, 179–81.

20. Fred Chappell, "Family Time," *The Southern Review* 28 (October 1992): 941.

21. See Rebecca Godwin Smith, "Gender Dynamics in the Fiction of Lee Smith: Examining Language and Narrative Strategies" (diss., University of North Carolina at Chapel Hill, 1993), 88–93. Smith argues that the sexual and spiritual power embodied by Red Emmy is that of the archetypal sibyl figure and that this mythic goddess symbolism is suppressed by society. Tanya Long Bennett argues that Ivy's letters in *Fair and Tender Ladies* undermine traditional Christian theology but suggest the existence of a profound spiritual life associated with nature. See Tanya Long Bennett, "The Protean Ivy in Lee Smith's *Fair and Tender Ladies*," *Southern Literary Journal* 30, no. 2 (spring 1998): 76–78, 80–81. See also Dorothy Combs Hill, *Lee Smith* (New York: Twayne Publishers, 1992).

22. See "Lee Smith Interview," in Ketchin, *The Christ-Haunted Landscape,* 46–48.

23. See Elisabeth Herion-Sarafidis, "Interview with Lee Smith," *The Southern Quarterly* 32 (winter 1994): 7–18.

24. Rosalind B. Reilly, "*Oral History:* The Enchanted Circle of Narrative and Dream," *Southern Literary Journal* 23 (fall 1990): 79–92.

25. Ibid., 82.

26. For a discussion of the circle imagery, sacred place, and sacred time in *Oral History,* see ibid., 79–92.

27. This passage is from the Revised Standard Version of the Bible.

28. See Elke Worley Payne, "In Search of the Female Voice: Religious Experience in the Fiction of Lee Smith," (M.A. thesis, Western Carolina University, 1997): iv, 1, 4; see also Bennett, "The Protean Ivy," 76–78, 80, 86.

29. Reilly, "*Oral History:* The Enchanted Circle," 80.

30. Gloria Jan Underwood has pointed out that memory is a key to understanding wholeness in Lee Smith's novels. Crystal, in *Black Mountain Breakdown*, loses herself because she loses her history. Likewise, Ivy does not because she accepts her memories. See Gloria Jan Underwood, "Blessings and Burdens: Memory in the Novels of Lee Smith (diss., University of South Carolina, 1991), 28ff., 110, 140.

31. Underwood, "Blessings and Burdens," 28ff., 110, 140.

32. See Edwin T. Arnold, "An Interview with Lee Smith," *Appalachian Journal* 11 (spring 1984): 244–46.

33. Ibid., 246.

34. "Lee Smith Interview," in Ketchin, *The Christ-Haunted Landscape*, 47, 53.

35. Virginia A. Smith, "Luminous Halos and Lawn Chairs: Lee Smith's *Me and My Baby View the Eclipse*," *The Southern Review* 27 (April 1991): 484. See also Virginia A. Smith, "Between the Lines: Contemporary Southern Women Writers Gail Godwin, Bobbie Ann Mason, Lisa Alther, and Lee Smith" (diss., Pennsylvania State University, 1989).

36. Rebecca Smith examines the role of the "strong, sacred, sexual female" and its accompanying spirituality as opposed to patriarchal religion as it appears in *The Devil's Dream*. See Rebecca Smith, "Writing, Singing, and Hearing a New Voice: Lee Smith's *The Devil's Dream*," *The Southern Quarterly* 32 (winter 1994): 48–62. Dorothy Combs Hill characterizes this as a "redemptive quest." See Hill, *Lee Smith*, 18–19.

37. See "Lee Smith Interview," in Ketchin, *The Christ-Haunted Landscape*, 45–46, in which Smith speaks of the inseparability of "religion and sex." See also Lee Smith interview with Claudia Loewenstein, "Unshackling the Patriarchy: An Interview with Lee Smith," *Southwest Review* 78 (autumn 1993): 486–505, for the connection between spirituality and sexual awakening.

38. See Linda J. Byrd, "The Reclamation of the Feminine Divine: 'Walking in My Body Like a Queen' in Lee Smith's *Fair and Tender Ladies*," in *He Said, She Says: An RSVP to the Male Text*, ed. Mica Howe and Sarah Appleton Aguiar (London: Fairleigh Dickinson University Press, 2001).

39. Anne Goodwyn Jones, "The World of Lee Smith," *The Southern Quarterly* 22 (fall 1983): 120.

40. Ibid., 129.

41. Debbie Wesley points to Smith's strong female characters who bring meaning through a creative connection to their bodies. See Debbie Wesley, "A New Way of Looking at an Old Story: Lee Smith's Portrait of Female Creativity," *Southern Literary Journal* 30, no. 1 (fall 1997): 88–90.

42. See Smith, "Gender Dynamics" and "Writing, Singing, and Hearing," and Teem, "Let Us Now Praise the Other."

43. Virginia A. Smith, "Luminous Halos and Lawn Chairs," 484.

44. Lee Smith, interview by William Walsh, in Linda Tate, ed., *Conversations with Lee Smith* (Jackson: University of Mississippi Press, 2001).

45. Jones, "The World of Lee Smith," 121.

46. See Arnold, "An Interview with Lee Smith," 244. Lee Smith discusses her fiction as a way of chronicling a time and place.

47. "This image of Ghostland is Lee Smith's contemporary portrait of Appalachia"—an Appalachia that has lost its pristine nature and has become commercialized. See Nancy D. Parrish, "'Ghostland': Tourism in Lee Smith's *Oral History*," *The Southern Quarterly* 32 (winter 1994): 37–47.

48. Victoria Chen, "Chinese American Women, Language, and Moving Subjectivity," in Harold Bloom, ed., *Amy Tan* (Philadelphia, Chelsea House, 2000), 83–92. The quote is from p. 83.

49. See Thomas Tweed and Stephen Prothero, *Asian Religion in America: A Documentary History* (New York: Oxford, 1999), 357ff.

50. "The Spirit Within," *The Salon Interview: Amy Tan*; available from http://www.salon.com/12nov1995/feature/tan.html.

51. See E. D. Huntley, *Amy Tan: A Critical Companion* (Westport, Conn.: Greenwood, 1998), 114.

52. See ibid., 142–49.

53. Randall Kenan, interview by V. Hunt, in "A Conversation with Randall Kenan," *African American Review* 29, no. 3 (fall 1995): 413–16.

54. Randall Kenan, quoted in Ketchin, *The Christ-Haunted Landscape*, 296.

55. Matthew Guinn, *After Southern Modernism: Fiction of the Contemporary South* (Jackson: University Press of Mississippi, 2000), 138, 139.

56. Ibid., 158.

57. Kenan, quoted in Ketchin, *The Christ–Haunted Landscape*, 296. For Kenan's recounting of his experience with the death of his uncle, see ibid, 281–14.

PART III

6
IMAGE/POST-TEXT

On weekend nights across America, young people and old flock to movie theaters or rent videotapes and DVDs to participate in one of popular culture's most pervasive sources of entertainment. The variety of available films is mind-boggling: from classic to experimental, adult to children's, suspense to comedy, emotionally draining to cheerful and lighthearted. Communal or solitary, film watching has become a staple of modern American culture, and it reflects how substantially we contemporary Westerners are drawn to audiovisual presentations that take us beyond textual storytelling. Images are everywhere in our new technologies: television, movie theaters, DVD players, Internet pages, and so on have inundated us with an image-rich culture. Certainly, the movie industry is a leader in this postmodern, image-rich, post-textual society. Because it is so omnipresent, it behooves us to consider seriously how this medium shapes, reflects, and otherwise dialogues with our cultural attitudes and beliefs. The American film industry is huge and influences the distribution of popular films and viewing habits in both America and Europe. Popular films constitute a significant portion of the fabric of popular culture and potentially exert powerful influence in society because of the mass market they reach. Popular films have the power to shape attitudes and to reflect beliefs. Film as a shaper of and reflection of our collective ideologies has sparked a contemporary interest in the intersection of religion and film.

As we have seen secularization marking our spaces and our texts in postmodern America, we see films marking a secularization of images and their accompanying sensations. Just as we see secularization proceeding in two directions with other cultural components of society, we also see this process happening at the intersection of religion and film. Films reflect the secularization of sacred image through movies devoted to presenting religious topics through a secular medium and the sacralization of secular image through films seemingly unrelated to religious topics yet religious or spiritual in their nature or functioning. The dual direction of secularization seen elsewhere in our culture arises in the film medium with such strong force and in such ubiquitous fashion that we may need to consider our culture post-textual in the sense that images have begun to supersede text,[1] thus reversing the effects of the rise of texts to supremacy since the Enlightenment.

Are we gathering at movie theaters for worship? Hardly. But some find in the experience uplift, community, sensation, value definition, and so forth, many of the things we search for in religion. So as the lights dim and sound comes up; as our minds are inundated with the sensations of light, color, and sound; as we hold hands, flinch, cry, and laugh, we return to a primal place, an elemental place, a place where the gods are defined and die—a sacred landscape of the soul molded by the secular screen of the movie theater.

RELIGION AND FILM[2]

That images are replacing texts as a primary vehicle for entertainment, if not instruction, is obvious to anyone who has struggled to get students to read seriously as opposed to watching a film. Religion and film classes have become wildly popular in religion programs, not because they are easy or perceived as such but because many students relate more readily, more enthusiastically, more intuitively, and more meaningfully to films than to books. I have experienced this in my undergraduate religion classes and through intensive discussions with colleagues who use film to teach religion. The power of image is manifested in today's youth, who have been reared with a steady dose of manufactured image on television, the silver screen, and the computer screen.

Yet students are not the only ones embracing the power of image in myth making. Religion and film classes are being taught by professors from a variety of perspectives, and religion and film books are produced from a rich collection of methodological approaches, including religious studies, myth studies, psychological studies, film studies, and the like.

Scholarly approaches to religion and film range from exploring the ability of film to dialogue with and in some cases rewrite Scripture,[3] to studies of the importance of film in theological dialogue and to procedures for and reasons for watching films from a theological perspective,[4] to studies that focus more on values and film's power to reform society,[5] to studies that focus on religious aspects of movies that are not defined by traditional texts, theologies, or moralities.[6] The recent list goes on and the titles themselves often reveal the perspective: *Explorations in Theology and Film: Movies and Meaning,*[7] *New Image of Religious Film,*[8] *The Word Became Flesh: Catholicism and Conflict in the Films of Martin Scorsese.*[9] The great diversity of religion and film studies demonstrates how seriously scholars take the idea that images can be powerful purveyors of sacred reality, theology, and ideology.

This realization about the power of film extends beyond the walls of the college classroom. Christians of all persuasions have had a long-running debate with Hollywood concerning possible harmful influences of films. Robert Johnston has written about this relationship in his exceptional book, *Reel Spirituality.* By focusing on the relationship between church and theater, Johnston demonstrates the growing sense in which religion has attempted to act as conscience for the movie industry. This demonstrates both the cultural connection between the movies and the church and acknowledgment by the church of the potential efficacy of the theater in affecting ideologies and morality.[10] Beyond the ethical debate, there is even ongoing political concern, particularly in America, about the negative impact films might exert on societal values. That prominent public figures have used film in social commentary suggests at least the perception that movies can play an important role in shaping or influencing behavior and morals. For example, 1996 U.S. presidential candidate Bob Dole reflected publicly about the destructive potential of Hollywood morals. In the wake of the 1995 New York torching of a subway token booth, then-Senator Dole used the occasion to lash out at Hollywood during his campaign for the Republican presidential nomination. In his speech, Dole mirrored the sentiments of law enforcement officials who were calling the violent incident a copycat crime based on the film *Money Train.* Dole's insight and political rhetoric decrying violence in film renewed a public debate about the ability of film to influence public behavior.[11] Later, President Clinton picked up on the call for Hollywood to reform itself, reinforcing the notion that film has the ability to affect lives, to influence behaviors, and to propagate beliefs. If this is true, then it is important for both the makers of film and the consumers of culture to recognize that film is a powerful medium that has the ability to influence attitudes and actions. As Joel Martin points out, Michael Ryan and Douglas Kellner argue in *Camera Politica* that films "often foreshadow political developments" and can shape collective ideology, that stories given life in film provide a significant way to formulate and shape collective values.[12]

If society mirrors film in this way, if action and behavior are affected by Hollywood, then we need to consider carefully the context and the impact of films like *Natural Born Killers* and *Pulp Fiction*. Such films are considered dangerous by some because they create an atmosphere of conflict and lead to a desensitization to violence in society.[13] The slippery-slope theory holds that we see violence on the screen, we become immune to its horror, we accept it in the social context, and violence then perpetuates itself simply because the public no longer is outraged by it. A graphic example that supports this theory dates to 1998, when two teenagers killed their victim by enacting scenes from the movies *Scream* and *Scream 2*. One of the teenagers confessed, suggesting that repeated exposure to movie and TV violence not only desensitized him to violence but enticed him to be violent as well.[14] If this type of desensitization occurs as routinely as suggested, we might also be concerned about seemingly innocuous films or nonviolent films. Films might perpetuate all types of ideologies, not simply an ideology of violence.

Films also have the power to influence individuals and communities positively, not just negatively. So if we are to blame Hollywood for glorifying violent tendencies, we should also praise the movie industry for communicating hope in films like *The Shawshank Redemption,* forgiveness in *Places in the Heart,* grace in *The Fisher King,* redemption in *The Spitfire Grill.* Scores of films showcase human nature in its most flawed, most vulnerable, and consequently noblest state. These films appeal to our higher nature. Positive or negative, the scope and intensity of the debate shows that our culture recognizes the power of film to affect or at least reflect values and beliefs; therefore, film has the potential to act religiously.[15]

Many religion scholars who are interested in the role films play in values, ethics, religious beliefs, and attitudes tend to focus on the power of film to shape and change ideologies. Margaret Miles's *Seeing and Believing* focuses on the reformative role of films in society.[16] In addition, Robert Johnston eloquently shares a personal story about the power of film that helped transform his life by viewing film "as the occasion not only to know about God but to know God."[17] On the other hand, some commentators suggest that films do not influence attitudes so much as they reflect reality. Thus, films do not encourage violence; they simply reflect a violent society by choosing subject matter from the culture.[18] This argument fundamentally removes the movie industry from responsibility and fights off the censor's scalpel. It seems fair and reasonable to acknowledge that films both reflect and affect society's attitudes, beliefs, values, and hopes. Included in these beliefs are worldviews and religious attitudes. Religion and films are both cultural products. As such, they define and represent who we are and what we believe. Films and religion can show us where we fail yet applaud our nobler state. Rarely does either do only one. As a result, films constitute an important cultural medium for the study of the intersection of religion and cultural forms.

The interdisciplinary study of religion and film is a fairly new area and has yet to emerge as a truly interdisciplinary field. Like religion and literature, this study is best done between disciplines, and one of the goals of the exploration of religion and film is to encourage film studies, religious studies, and popular culture studies scholars to communicate better with one another. In the past, Joel Martin reminds us, religious studies scholars and film studies scholars have largely ignored one another as well as the content of the others' discipline.[19] When attempts have been made to study religion and film, the result more often than not has been disciplinary, coming from one discipline or another rather than from between the disciplines. Since I am trained in religious studies, my approach to religion and film tends to rely on methods from religious studies and religion and literature as they are applied to film. This approach is insufficient, because there is a long established tradition of film studies that needs to be incorporated into such analyses as these. Cooperative interdisciplinary work that draws upon the expertise of film studies scholars, religious studies scholars, and scholars from various religious traditions will yield insightful views on culture and religion.[20] Religion and film as a cultural studies project will mature into a discipline when this layering of expertise from across and between the disciplines and traditions coalesce. For example, from the film *The Matrix,* my students and other Christian interpreters are tempted to view the character Neo as a messiah figure and to invoke the all-too-familiar Christ-figure image. But many scholars warn us against this easy assumption. Alice Bach, for example, reminds us that not all victims need be Christ figures in her analysis of *one Flew over the Cuckoo's Nest.*[21] So if not every victim in film need be a crucified Christ, neither does every messianic figure need be a savior Christ. Neo, in *The Matrix,* might as easily or more so be construed a bodhisattva from the Buddhist tradition.[22] That so many of my students peg Neo as a Christ figure demonstrates how uninformed Americans can be about various religious traditions beyond

Christianity. But even if religious studies scholars begin dialoguing more across traditions, religion and film work is still too oriented to religious studies. In addition to realizing that religious imagery beyond Christian imagery might exist in popular movies, we also need to learn more from film studies about special effects or from psychologists about mind control. How would this knowledge change our view of Neo as a religious messiah in *The Matrix?* We also need to consider that Neo may not be representing any religious imagery at all—perhaps he is just Neo.

Such interdisciplinary, intercultural, and collaborative work continues to expand, but several questions must be addressed if the disciplines of religious studies and film studies are to work constructively together. As obvious as it might seem, a definition of religion must be agreed on. Outside religious studies, religion is often defined as a set of truth claims, as an institution that considers itself the guardian of an orthodoxy. A religious studies definition of religion will be more constructive for an interdisciplinary approach to the study of film. In short, rather than defining religion as a set of truth claims, we should define religion as a process of making and searching for meaning. Thus, instead of religion being the antithesis of heresy, it is the combatant of nihilism. This broad definition of religion will prevent a study of religion and film from being defined by one orthodoxy or another, thus allowing each discipline to work unhindered by ideological allegiance.

This functional definition will work for an interdisciplinary study of religion and film but can be misleading as well. Consider the distinction M. S. Mason makes between "what makes a film 'religious' as opposed to one that uses religious imagery or that is simply about religion as a cultural phenomenon—a backdrop for the story."[23] In a commentary for *The Christian Science Monitor,* Mason writes about contemporary film's use of the image of Jesus in movies like *The Last Temptation of Christ* or *Jesus of Montreal.* These films tend to "exploit the metaphors and symbols of Jesus' life as traditionally embodied in Catholicism but avoid dealing with the implications of those symbols and metaphors." The movies so "trivialize Jesus' whole life" that they cannot function religiously; that is, they cannot treat concepts like forgiveness and evil seriously for a contemporary audience.[24] So Mason's criticism suggests these films use religious imagery and rely on religion as a cultural phenomenon but might not be "religious" in the sense that they function religiously for contemporary audiences. In this case, these seemingly religious films (because of subject matter) might fail to function religiously and should not be considered religious in the sense of the above definition.

Contrast this to films like *Places in the Heart* or *The Fisher King*. *Places in the Heart* is full of religious images and portrays religion as a cultural phenomenon, but it also functions religiously in that it translates religious concepts such as forgiveness and evil for contemporary audiences. In addition, *The Fisher King* is based on the legend of the Holy Grail, so it occupies a prominent place in our religious cultural heritage. But it also functions religiously because it raises religious questions for the audience. Mason writes, "It is really about the hunger for redemption . . . the need to search for truth and to respond with love to those around us."[25] Mason quotes Richard LaGravenese, who wrote the screenplay; for LaGravenese, redemption is "the only subject" for a contemporary American movie.[26] So *The Fisher King* functions religiously because it challenges contemporary audiences to grapple with theological questions, not because its subject matter draws upon religious cultural symbols.

One can further see the complexity of looking at films like this by considering Joel Martin's discussion in *Screening the Sacred* of *Rocky*, a film that is not obviously religious in any way.[27] On one level, the film treats religion as a cultural phenomenon as Rocky Balboa's Catholicism becomes a backdrop for the story to contextualize Rocky's ethnicity. On another level, one could interpret rich religious imagery in the film, such as the opening scene of a close-up of the face of a Byzantine Christ in light of the Christ figure that Rocky embodies. On a third level, we might consider what makes the film religious; that is, how does the film function religiously for the audience? Does it represent some sort of faith in justice for the oppressed? Does this represent a religious ideology? It is this third level, the functional level, that is the trickiest but also the most rewarding. And although I will be concerned with these three ways of considering religion and film, the third consideration will attract most of the attention in this chapter.

With the assumptions that film provides a medium for studying the religious dimensions of culture, that films can function religiously for individuals and for society, that films can reflect as well as affect beliefs and behaviors, and that film is a powerful communicator of values, I turn to this exploration to better understand how such beliefs and values interact in the public sphere. First, we will consider briefly the state of the religion and film field (if it can be considered a field); second, we will look at the future of the field; third, we will focus on how contemporary culture and traditional religion interact by viewing religion in film in light of the secularization thesis of this book. I will illustrate the secularization thesis by looking at what the contemporary world has done with a traditional religious category—the idea of the apocalypse.

THE STATE OF RELIGION AND FILM AS A DISCIPLINE

To refer to religion and film as a discipline is probably premature. As noted above, the study is very new and is still being shaped and explored by scholars in religious studies and film studies. For the most part, there has been little dialogue between film studies and religious studies. As Joel Martin points out in *Screening the Sacred,* much of the early work done by religion scholars focused on classic or art films (this is particularly true in Europe), and much of the work by religious studies scholars has been theological in nature.[28] However, these generalities are beginning to change, and we have seen increased interest in popular films in books like *Screening the Sacred* and *Reel Spirituality.* And interest in the interdisciplinary nature of the topic, which is obvious from the exploration of religion and film at religious studies conferences, American studies conferences, and cultural studies conferences, is balancing the theological viewpoint and adding diverse perspectives. More and more emphasis is being placed on popular films because of their potential for reaching mass audiences and, thus, affecting popular ideology. These changes map out the predominant direction of this protodiscipline and suggest agenda items for the future of religion and film if it is to continue as a viable interdisciplinary project. If work in religion and film continues, and if this protofield continues to develop, methodology must come to the forefront of discussion and the work must move beyond traditional theological approaches.

Developments along both fronts have characterized the work in the field. Works have appeared that have begun to explore methodology. The 1995 book edited by Joel Martin and me, *Screening the Sacred,* consists of collected essays dealing only with popular films. And to avoid parochialism of either theological or disciplinary bent, the book is organized around three approaches to the study of film: theological, mythological, and ideological. In this typology is an incipient method for studying films that attempts to address shortcomings of any one method. The book argues that theological criticism treats religion traditionally and tends to find religion in films through theological categories such as grace, redemption, evil, sin, and forgiveness. The problem with theological criticism is its narrow focus, usually arising from Western symbols and religions. Mythological criticism universalizes the study of religion and film by treating religion as it is recognized through universal archetypes, symbols, and rituals. And finally, ideological criticism understands religion as it exists in relation to that which is not religion and includes categories ranging from the social order to gender relationships and race and class distinctions. By mapping out a threefold typology for the study of religion and film, the authors and editors of *Screening the Sacred* attempt to broaden the discussion to include a wide variety of understandings about what is religious in society.

Additional work on religion and film is emerging as noted scholars in religious studies are directing their attention to the topic at national conferences and in manuscripts in process. Thus, there seems to be a future for this pursuit in academia. In addition, if the anecdotal reports concerning pedagogy are any indication, using film in the classroom as an effective teaching tool seems to have a promising potential. If research and teaching in this protofield are to be successful, we can map out a few items scholars will have to accept as the field develops. Most of these challenges are already indicated in the scholarly works that exist at present. I will explore some of the issues here in hopes of stimulating dialogue about new approaches to the study of religion and film. In doing so, I will reflect on the future direction of religion and film studies but also suggest ways the film experience might mimic aspects of religious experience.

First, most of the current work on religion and film done by religious studies scholars and theologians grew out of and employs methodological procedures from literary and narrative studies. After all, as scholars, we have been trained to examine and produce texts, not films, and it is natural for us to proceed in this way. Although the approach has served the field well, it is necessary to explore methods unique to the film genre, and religious studies scholars need to learn more from the methods and insights of film studies. While we know how to "read" a film like literature, we might not know how to "see" a film critically.

Jann Cather Weaver has been sensitive to these questions on methodology and helps us to learn how to "see" films critically by differentiating between "seeing" and "watching" films. "Seeing" a film, for Weaver, goes beyond passive "watching" for entertainment. "Seeing is a disciplined task, not confined to the ocular function of sight. Rather, seeing is the critical discipline of delving beneath surface, affective, and customary (culturally coded) appearances. . . . To see a film is to engage a film in this intentional, participatory visual discipline."[29] Weaver gives religion and film scholars a vocabulary and working model for a methodology of seeing. In particular, Weaver, like Mason, challenges us to see the difference between films that are religious (function religiously) and films that merely employ religious symbols or draw upon the cultural context for religious images (i.e., the Christ figure or the Bible). Her method seems very effective in moving us "beyond watching, beyond the perpetual quest for the filmic Christ figure, and beyond using film as ILLUSTRATION of doctrine, moral lessons, or of a current religio-social issue."[30] The other real strength of Weaver's perspective is that it empowers the viewer and transfers power from the film producers/industry to the film viewers/consumers, both as individually engaged viewers and as a community of viewers.

Weaver's perspective implies that simply transferring the methods from literary studies is not sufficient because films represent a layering of narrative and images that is in many ways more complex than literature. This layering and intensification become clear when we look at the creative forces behind literature and film. When we deal with literature, we can usually focus on the author as the creative force behind the narrative; however, with film we must deal with layers of creative forces, including the screenplay writer, the director, and perhaps the author of a book if the screenplay was adapted from a novel. This complicates the critical task, as Alice Bach has reminded us in her work. As she implies in her comments on Bible films, the layering of film introduces contemporary culture into the process of interpretation of the subject matter. As a result, Bible films might reflect the contemporary situation more than the biblical one.[31] This is true of nonbiblical films as well, such as movies like *The Scarlet Letter*. *The Scarlet Letter* is based on a screenplay that takes liberties with the novel's story line. Such changes are not unusual when a novel is adapted for a screenplay, and revisions often reveal much about what the contemporary audiences will tolerate in their entertainment. In this case it tells us as much about twentieth-century preoccupations as about Hawthorne's nineteenth-century ones. Yet much of the critical analysis of the movie focuses simply on pointing out the changes made in transferring the classic novel to the screen rather than in trying to unravel the layering of intent and meaning behind the changes. This type of simple comparative analysis to the novel is not a sufficient standard of criticism because it does little to explore what the contemporary version tells us about our society or our sensibilities as a moviegoing public. We must explore new ways to deal with the dynamics of revision rather than simply judge the movie in relation to the book that bears the same title. We must fully consider this layering of creative intent.

But the creative force behind film is not the only element that is layered and intensified when moving from literature to film. All of the traditional elements of narrative undergo intensification. If in literary analysis we focus on character development, we must extend that examination with films to include not only the character in the screenplay but the actor's or actress's portrayal of that character. If with literature we look at setting, with a film the setting is intensified because of the images, special effects, and computer-generated visuals available to film-makers. And if plot analysis is our prime area of examination in litera-ture, we must note that plots in films unfold much more quickly (the action takes place in film time rather than in reading time), and filmic plots often unfold nonsequentially. With the elements of film, there is an intensification of effect and perhaps of influence, and we need to search for more productive ways to measure both effect and influence.

I have argued that images are extremely important in imparting meaning in our contemporary culture, perhaps even superseding texts for the task. If visual images are indeed replacing written texts as the conveyors of information and meaning, it might have important implica-tions for religious ideas.[32] And in film, visual images are further intensi-fied by soundtracks and other auditory effects. The result is an integrative experience unfolding before the moviegoer that is more intense, more riveting, more involving, and perhaps more participatory than the texts of previous generations. Add to this our own "realist" assumptions about what we see (i.e., seeing is believing),[33] and we can begin to sense the power attached to film images and their presentation. At least film seems to function powerfully in this way for my students, who are much more willing to watch a movie than to read a novel, and we need to be more sensitive to the effects of this integration of sensations.

This integrative experience of visual images and auditory presenta-tions are unfolding in more and more compact and graphic forms. For example, music videos represent a development of the film form that deserves serious attention. As conveyors of violence, sexual images, and plot lines, music videos are particularly effective in reaching a society that often does not demonstrate the patience for a two-hour plot to develop, let alone the several-hour experience of the novel. Perhaps the next technological development to deliver images will be virtual reality, which might be accompanied by tactile sensation as well. In any event, technology has made the proliferation of video images and auditory sen-sations possible and profitable and can provide the viewer a type of tran-scending possibility. One of the possibilities for the future of the study of religion and film must be to explore film's ability to provide this expe-rience of transcendence; it is through transcendence that we sense and explore the ways film might mimic religious experience.

Film gives us creative ways to approximate transcendence. Technology allows filmmakers to transport viewers to another world graphically, not simply through description.[34] Films can visually take us to outer space, to the jungles of the Congo, to a prehistoric rain forest inhabited by dinosaurs, or to a postapocalyptic setting. This transference takes us beyond ourselves and generally deals with topics that are beyond the ordinary, mundane experiences of our lives. As I wrote previously in *Screening the Sacred*, many popular films are characterized by "excess"; for example, violence and explicit sexuality. When films focus on excess, on that which is beyond the ordinary, they act religiously by allowing transcendence, freedom, and escape.[35] This transcendence through escape of the ordinariness of everyday life allows us to tap into what Janice Rushing and Richard Maltby identify as corporate beliefs through shared myths and ideals.[36] If films function in this way, then they function religiously or even mythically by shaping and reflecting shared values.[37]

This suggests that film provides an important way to study religion in contemporary America. In an age and society marked by individualism, films highlight societal and cultural truths. Richard Gollin comments on this by focusing on film's power to create in viewers the need to "sacrifice whatever their personal indulgences and rededicate themselves to higher public purposes."[38] So films like *Natural Born Killers* and *Pulp Fiction* tell us about ourselves, but so do films like *Apollo 13* and *Forrest Gump*. How are these films instructive about our society and, in Gollin's words, our "ideological covenants and obligations"?[39] Can they provide corporate truths and images? I am arguing they can and that other forms of our popular culture work on the societal level religiously by reflecting and affecting fundamental values and even behaviors.[40]

This corporate function of film as a clue to what society values suggests that we must be cognizant of the audience and of how meaning is relayed to that audience. We cannot simply assume the same type of audience we assume for a novel. Reading a novel is a solitary activity— watching a film, at least in the theater, has the potential for being a communal and thus ritualistic one.[41] We can ask questions concerning the communal consumption of film and what this means for the audience and the critic. We can also make assumptions and judgments about the effects of the VCR and the DVD player, rental movies, and other forms of cable and satellite TV that bring films into our living rooms. These technologies change a communal experience into a solitary one, in some ways paralleling the shift from storytelling to novel reading—a shift that requires a change in audience from communal to individual.

Therefore, our future study of popular film and religion should include sensitivity to what happens or might happen in the movie theater or at home and to what consequences this might hold for individuals and society. In other words, we must be concerned with the psychology of film and with what media experts call reception theory. Many scholars have suggested that popular culture can be a clue to understanding society's values and to recognizing what motivates individual and collective behavior.[42] The task for students of religion and film is to develop better ways to measure how films function religiously and how they might affect values and behaviors.

RELIGION, FILM, AND SECULARIZATION

The secularization thesis that forms the basis of this book is important to consider in light of film because film is the only cultural product studied here that is essentially a product of the postmodern world. Since secularization is generally associated with Western culture since the Enlightenment, film is the only cultural form considered here with its entire history occurring during the era when the secularization of Western culture has been at its height. This positions film uniquely to take over the functions religion is transferring to secular culture.

One of the major arguments underlying my work hinges on the idea that the secular and the religious worlds can coexist without religion becoming less significant. I am assuming that secularization does not destroy religion, and for the purposes of this study, I am defining secularization as a sociological process that blurs the boundaries between the sacred and the secular. Western religion is based on the idea of a transcendent God (a wholly and holy Other) and on a sacred realm that is completely separate from our mundane, secular, profane world. This division of reality into sacred and profane has also characterized much religious studies work. But in the postmodern era, the strict boundaries separating sacred and profane have become flexible, and from these flexible boundaries we see secularization taking place in two directions.[43] First, there is a tendency for tradition to secularize—for religious institutions to employ secular and popular cultural forms like television and the movies to make religious teachings relevant for a contemporary audience.[44] In this instance, we see contemporary religion making concessions to secular cultural forms. The second way secularization is proceeding is by the dispersion of the religious sensibility through a variety of contemporary secular cultural forms. As I argued in *Screening the Sacred*, when religious institutions no longer dominate culture, they forfeit some of their proprietorship over sacred sensibilities. With this loss of cultural hegemony, religious concerns surface elsewhere, so that secular culture can function religiously. In postmodern society, the religious impulse is disseminated through a variety of cultural forms like film, which are external to traditional religious institutions and expressions.[45]

As I have written previously in *Screening the Sacred,* the result of this secularization is a postmodern society defined by a secular paradox—a society that is uncomfortable with institutionalized and public religion but is often defined by religious categories through popular culture. As secularization of society continues, so does the dissipation of functions formerly reserved for religious institutions. We find popular culture functioning in some of the same ways as institutionalized religious ritual so that popular culture provides a context for understanding values, belief systems, and myths.[46]

NOTES

1. See Conrad Ostwalt, "Conclusion: Religion, Film, and Cultural Analysis," in Joel W. Martin and Conrad E. Ostwalt Jr., eds., *Screening the Sacred: Religion, Myth, and Ideology in Popular American Film* (Boulder: Westview, 1995), 153.

2. Parts of this chapter were previously published and are reprinted in edited version by permission of *Currents in Research: Biblical Studies,* Sheffield Academic Press, and Continuum. The full reference is Conrad Ostwalt, "Celluloid Religion: Reading Religion Scholars Watching Films: A Supplementary Response to Alice Bach's 'Cracking the Production Code: Watching Biblical Scholars Read Films,'" *Currents in Research: Biblical Studies* 8 (2000): 146–61, copyright © Sheffield Academic Press Limited, 2000. Portions of this chapter were also previously published in Ostwalt, "Conclusion: Religion, Film, and Cultural Analysis," in Martin and Ostwalt, *Screening the Sacred,* 152–59, and are reprinted or adapted here by permission of Perseus Books.

3. George Aichele and Richard Walsh, eds., *Screening Scripture: Intertextual Connections between Scripture and Film* (Harrisburg, Pa.: Trinity Press International, 2002).

4. Robert K. Johnston, *Reel Spirituality: Theology and Film in Dialogue* (Grand Rapids, Mich.: Baker, 2000).

5. Margaret Miles, *Seeing and Believing: Religion and Values in the Movies* (Boston: Beacon, 1996).

6. Martin and Ostwalt, *Screening the Sacred.*

7. Clive Marsh and Gaye Ortiz, eds., *Explorations in Theology and Film: Movies and Meaning* (Oxford: Blackwell, 1998).

8. John R. May, ed., *New Image of Religious Film* (Kansas City, Mo.: Sheed & Ward, 1997).

9. Michael Bliss, *The Word Made Flesh: Catholicism and Conflict in the Films of Martin Scorsese* (Lanham, Md.: Scarecrow, 1995).

10. See Johnston, *Reel Spirituality,* 31–39. See also 19–30 for a discussion on the power of film to change life.

11. Tom Hays, "Hollywood Gets Blame over Booth Torching," *Charlotte Observer,* 28 November 1996, 2A.

12. Joel Martin, "Redeeming America: *Rocky* as Ritual Racial Drama," in Martin and Ostwalt, *Screening the Sacred,* 126. See Michael Ryan and Douglas Kellner, *Camera Politica: The Politics and Ideology of Contemporary Hollywood Film* (Bloomington: Indiana University Press, 1988), 12–16.

13. See D. Grossman, "Trained to Kill," *Christianity Today,* 10 August 1998, 30–39.

14. Associated Press, "Get Used to It," *Reader's Digest,* November 1999, 155–56.

15. For a discussion, see Ostwalt, "Conclusion," *Screening the Sacred.*

16. Miles, *Seeing and Believing.*

17. Johnston, *Reel Spirituality,* 29–30.

18. See Ostwalt, "Conclusion," *Screening the Sacred,* 155–56.

19. Joel Martin, "Introduction: Seeing the Sacred on the Screen," in Martin and Ostwalt, *Screening the Sacred,* 4–5.

20. Martin, "Introduction," 4–5, 12.

21. Alice Bach, "Cracking the Production Code: Watching Biblical Scholars Read Films," *Currents in Research: Biblical Studies* 7 (1999): 21–22.

22. Conrad Ostwalt, "Armageddon at the Millennial Dawn," *Journal of Religion and Film* 4, no. 1; available from http://cid.unomaha.edu/~wwwjrf/. The bodhisattva reference first arose during a discussion following my presentation of a paper on *The Matrix* at the American Academy of Religion annual meeting in 1999.

23. Marilynne S. Mason, letter to the author, 12 February 1996.

24. M. S. Mason, "The Gospel According to Hollywood," *The Christian Science Monitor,* 23 July 1990, 10–11.

25. M. S. Mason, "Terry Gilliam Grabs the Spotlight," *The Christian Science Monitor,* 27 September 1991, 13.

26. Richard LaGravenese, quoted in M. S. Mason, "Terry Gilliam Grabs the Spotlight," 13.

27. Martin, "Redeeming America," 125–33.

28. See Martin and Ostwalt, *Screening the Sacred.*

29. Jann Cather Weaver, "Discerning the Religious Dimensions of Film: Toward a Visual Method Applied to *Dead Man Walking*" (paper presented at the annual conference of the American Academy of Religion, New Orleans, November 1996).

30. Ibid.

31. Bach, "Cracking the Production Code," 13, 16.

32. See Weaver, "Discerning the Religious Dimensions of Film," 2–3. See also Ostwalt, "Conclusion," *Screening the Sacred,* 153.

33. Richard M. Gollin, "Reading Films as They See Fit," *Christianity and Literature* 42 (spring 1993): 392–93.

34. Ibid., 401.

35. Ostwalt, "Conclusion," *Screening the Sacred,* 155.

36. Janice Rushing, "Evolution of 'The New Frontier' in *Alien* and *Aliens*: Patriarchal Co–optation of the Feminine Archetype," in Martin and Ostwalt, *Screening the Sacred,* 94–96; Janice Rushing, "Introduction to 'Evolution of the New Frontier' in *Alien* and *Aliens:* Patriarchal Co–optation of the Feminine Archetype," unpublished (September 1993), 2; and Richard Maltby, "Introduction," in *Dreams for Sale: Popular Culture in the 20th Century,* ed. Richard Maltby (London: Harrap, 1989), 11. See also John Storey, *An Introductory Guide to Cultural Theory and Popular*

Culture (Athens: The University of Georgia Press, 1993), 11ff.

37. See Matthew Fox, *Religion U.S.A.: Religion and Culture by Way of* TIME *Magazine* (Dubuque, Iowa: Listening Press, 1971), 7–10. Fox points out that secular culture has its own myths that reflect belief. See also Ostwalt, "Conclusion," *Screening the Sacred*, 155.

38. Richard M. Gollin, *A Viewer's Guide to Film* (New York: McGraw Hill, 1992), 180.

39. Ibid., 180.

40. See Ostwalt, "Conclusion," *Screening the Sacred*, 156.

41. Gollin, *A Viewer's Guide to Film*, 180.

42. This argument is common in studies dealing with popular literature. Kathryn Presley's work on popular literature in the Gilded Age draws upon a variety of works that establish a connection between popular literature and the social and moral values of an age. See William Darby, *Necessary American Fictions: Popular Literature of the 1950s* (Bowling Green, Ohio.: Bowling Green University Press, 1987), and Louis Schneider and Sanford M. Dornbush, *Popular Religion: Inspirational Books in America* (Chicago: University of Chicago Press, 1958). See also Catherine Albanese, *America: Religions and Religion*, 3d ed. (Belmont, Calif.: Wadsworth Publishing Co., 1999), 468–72.

43. See Ostwalt, "Conclusion," *Screening the Sacred*, 153–58.

44. Albanese, *America: Religions and Religion*, 17.

45. See Ostwalt, "Conclusion," *Screening the Sacred*, 158.

46. Ibid., 157–58.

7
MOVIES AND
THE APOCALYPSE

In the pages that follow, I will discuss how popular films have provided a secular context for understanding a traditional Western religious concept, the apocalypse, mirroring the two directions of secularization. Among theological images arising from Western, in particular Jewish and Christian, religions, none has received more popular attention recently than images associated with the end of the world. This preoccupation with the end of things is connected in a real way with the postmodern context that tends to deny anything absolute. With the destruction of absolutism, with the loss of certainty, it makes sense that theories and conspiracies about the end of the world would arise—if the absolute falls, so falls all else. But the end of the world does not simply result in the end of things, at least not theologically or in the movie versions. Almost invariably, the end brings about the ascendency of something to authority—some greatness to believe in. In a sense, the end-of-the-century preoccupation with the end of things was a response to postmodernism's relativism. This is seen very clearly in the recent theatrical preoccupation (particularly if you look at the pre-Y2K setting) with the end of the world—or at least with the end of life as we know it. By examining what movies have done with the Western concept of apocalypse, the cataclysmic end of the world, we can see how film secularizes a theological concept in the court of popular culture. And in doing so, the movies have recaptured and reinterpreted the Jewish and Christian concepts of the apocalypse where the context of a cosmic battle between good and evil destroys the earth, results in a sovereign God (good) defeating the forces of evil, and pictures a new kingdom, a transcendent, heavenly empire (a sacred realm) that replaces the destroyed world (the contemporary secular realm).

If we take the Jewish and Christian apocalyptic traditions and compare them to film's communication of those traditions, we can see some interesting dynamics taking place between postmodernity and tradition. For example, when the Christian apocalypse, John's *Revelation*, was written, it was produced by and for a group of Christians who were marginal and on the fringes of society. This marginalized group, persecuted by the Roman Empire at the end of the first century, produced and embraced a vision of the apocalypse that overturned the ruling powers. World destruction was pictured as God's sovereign vengeance on an evil empire that had oppressed the righteous. In other words, John's *Revelation* was an anti-secular manifesto, warning against the ways of the world, condemning the world and those whose allegiance was to the world because the world would be destroyed and only the righteous would inherit the kingdom of God.

Fast-forward twenty centuries: Where are the Christian apocalypticists now? By and large they are not in the mainstream of Christianity because the church has become so secularized, so worldly. In fact, mostly since Constantine's legitimization of Christianity in the fourth century, visions of the apocalypse have come from the fringe of the Christian tradition. The mainstream of the tradition, the secularized and worldly majority in the tradition, cannot sustain a critique of worldliness because a secularized church is so heavily invested in the world. In the modern church community, only those who reject secular culture can truly embrace an apocalyptic vision. The result is that the Christian version of the apocalypse in contemporary society has become muted. A secularized church might have some vague understanding of the end of time, but it does not act like it believes in an imminent apocalypse because it continues to raise money and build buildings.

So the situation is this: outside of those fringe groups in the Christian tradition, a real apocalyptic consciousness as an anti-secular theological position is largely missing from contemporary Christian theology. The exception is found in some segments of the evangelical community that invest heavily in a premillennial, dispensationalist view of world conquest, but at the same time this community is often more secularized than ever, so the anti-secular edge of the apocalyptic consciousness is muted. Does this mean that religiously, apocalyptic concerns have ceased to exist? Undoubtedly not, for fascination with the end of the world is strong as witnessed by the proliferation of end-of-the-world movies and books, some from religious organizations and some from secular popular culture. My guess is that anxiety over human contingency invests in apocalyptic scenarios. Secular apocalypses have supplemented religion in establishing an apocalyptic imagination in popular culture because a secularized church (because of its investment in the world) often avoids the topic.

Why does the apocalyptic imagination have the power to transcend theology and persist in the secular imagination? It persists because it is a fundamentally religious category, a way of making sense out of our world. The apocalyptic imagination is essentially a way of overcoming our angst over the realization of our finitude. Apocalypticism is a Western concept that is basically egocentric in origin. We see life around us and we observe it beginning and ending; we know birth and death, and as we imagine our own birth and death, we extrapolate and hypothesize world creation and world destruction as a way to make sense of time and a creation that outlives us. Hypothesizing egocentrically, we believe that if we are born and die, then surely the world had a beginning and will have an end. However, this reasoning results only if we reduce the totality of existence to the restrictive life of individuals; when we look at humanity or the world as a whole, origins and ends are not so obvious—humanity recycles itself, as does nature across the evolutionary cycle. Therefore, the apocalyptic imagination results when we construct a worldview based on our egocentric beliefs concerning life and time. As Frank Kermode has written, "The paradigms of apocalypse continue to lie under our ways of making sense of the world" by helping us to order our lives and time with a beginning and an end point that has some meaning.[1]

This egocentric angst about the end is accentuated in contemporary culture because mainstream secular religion has essentially dropped the apocalypse as a meaningful notion, so we seek other outlets for overcoming our anxiety about the end of things. We find these secular apocalypses in the burgeoning fascination with the end of the world in the film industry and in the Hollywood version of Armageddon—a secularized reappropriation of the traditional Christian apocalypse. Scores of secular movies as diverse as Jim Henson's children's epic, *The Dark Crystal*, to *Pale Rider*, *Apocalypse Now*, *Natural Born Killers,* and *Independence Day* explore various notions about the end of things. In addition, there are also movies about the end produced by evangelicals who try to counter secular philosophy with an evangelical version of the end of time. *The Omega Code* and the film version of *Left Behind* provide two examples of evangelical visions attempting to reclaim defining the apocalypse in popular culture. Virtually all of these films, secular or Christian, participate in the secularization of religion by secularizing the apocalypse in one of two ways. The evangelical films try to render traditional theology through the secular medium of film and thus demonstrate secularization in the first direction, the secularization of the sacred. The secular films arise from a completely secular vantage point but tap into a theological context that has been borrowed from traditional religion. As such, these secular apocalypses sacralize the secular by raising secular philosophies through the context of religious ideas. These approaches both participate in secularization but issue radically different visions of the end of the world based on fundamentally different worldviews. Because we find both secularists and conservative theologies competing in the secular arena of the theater to portray a vision of the end of the world, we see how thoroughly secularization has produced a blurring and bending of boundaries between the sacred and the secular.

THE SECULARIZATION OF THE SACRED: THE BIBLE AND THE EVANGELICAL APOCALYPSE ON THE SCREEN

Despite evangelical suspicion about secular culture, the evangelical tradition, at least in the twentieth century, has not been at all shy about employing secular culture to spread the Christian message. Christian radio, television, and music all employ secular tactics and media very effectively. Film as well constitutes fertile ground for the portrayal of religious topics, sometimes by religious people and sometimes by secular. When religious groups adopt secular forms, media, or tactics for presenting a message they perceive to be sacred, we see the secularization of the sacred in our secularization process. The blurring of distinctions continues, here promoted by the religious community.

An example of this willingness to adopt a secular medium to spread the sacred message comes through the very successful evangelical book on Jesus by Philip Yancey, *The Jesus I Never Knew*. Yancey, editor-at-large at *Christianity Today* magazine, wrote the book as an outgrowth of a Sunday school class he was teaching in Chicago in which he used portrayals of Jesus in film to study Jesus' life. The book chronicles the effect films about Jesus had on Yancey personally (in Yancey's words, "The films helped restore Jesus' humanity for me"[2]) and suggests that films can be powerful tools for communicating the evangelical message. The book, published by Zondervan, is accompanied by teaching materials and a video that uses clips from movies about Jesus. *The Jesus I Never Knew* was phenomenally successful in evangelical circles, winning the 1996 Gold Medallion Christian Book of the Year Award by the Evangelical Christian Publishers Association. The success of Yancey's pedagogy and book demonstrates again the blurring of sacred and secular realms in our culture, particularly evident in films.

Almost from the beginning of film, religious topics have found their way into the medium, and religious controversy has arisen in the context of film and the popular audience. In *Reel Spirituality,* Robert Johnston includes a chapter on the relationship between the church and the movies and provides an excellent brief history of religious themes and controversies through the history of the cinema. As he points out, many early films featured religious subjects and were made by religious people. As the cinema evolved, so did the presentation of religion and the Bible, but much of the subject matter was still biblical, such as Cecil B. DeMille's *The Ten Commandments.*[3] Alice Bach has written an insightful article on film and the Bible in which she differentiates between films about biblical subjects and films where analysts claim to find biblical influence. She rightly advises caution when dealing with film and reminds us not to go looking for biblical themes that may or may not be present.[4] Similarly, Jeffrey Mahan balances some of the theological and cultural concerns of presenting Jesus on film in his recent article, "Celluloid Savior: Jesus in the Movies,"[5] while Anton Karl Kozlovic has written an article entitled "Superman as Christ-Figure: The American Pop Culture Movie Messiah."[6] And a more recent volume edited by George Aichele and Richard Walsh, *Screening Scripture,* explores the enduring influence of biblical themes on secular movies.[7] I mention these examples from many to point out that from the beginning of film, the Bible has influenced and continues to influence the medium in terms of subject matter, theme, symbolism, and interpretive criticism. Sometimes the connection is made by religious moviemakers, sometimes by secular moviemakers, and sometimes by critics and analysts. So it should be no surprise that with the recent fascination with the end of the world there are movies depicting the apocalypse from a conservative Christian perspective as well as from a secular perspective. After all, what better topic than cosmic cataclysm could one hope for, given special effects in contemporary movies? The challenge to depict Satan, Armageddon, the rapture, and other eschatological images presents the right sort of task for special-effects crews and makeup artists.

During a paper presentation at a conference a few years back, I wondered aloud about the absence of major motion pictures depicting the apocalypse from a distinctly biblical perspective. In quick succession came films like *The Omega Code, Left Behind,* and *Megiddo:The Omega Code II,* all three films based on biblical rather than secular visions of the end times and all three coming from the perspective of evangelical Christianity. That these films appeared among other secular end-of-the-world movies makes for a fascinating comparison of worldviews. For while the medium, film, might be the same, the premise and message differ greatly.

One of the most intriguing issues arising from these evangelical films about the apocalypse is how much the forces behind the films want them to be a success—not only in the evangelical world but also in the popular culture.The films are not an attempt to reach believers so much as they are an attempt to tap into the secular culture on a popular mass-audience level. In a *Gentlemen's Quarterly* interview with Jim Nelson, Matt Crouch, the producer of *Megiddo,* describes his goal of reaching an evangelical movie audience, but he also admits his method was to use the "quality of Hollywood" to communicate the Christian message.[8] In addition, Tim LaHaye sued Namesake Entertainment and Cloud Ten Pictures in July 1999 because, at least in part, the film *Left Behind* did not realize the anticipated mass and blockbuster appeal.[9] And Peter Lalonde, one half of the Lalonde brothers who made the movie *Left Behind,* exclaimed in the same interview mentioned above, "Jack Nicholson! . . . How good an Antichrist would that guy be?"[10] Clearly, Crouch, LaHaye, and the Lalondes all want to render a film faithful to the biblical story of the apocalypse, but they want these films to be successful in the same sense that Hollywood blockbusters with Hollywood stars are successful with a popular audience.At the conclusion of the *Left Behind* video, Kirk Cameron, star of the film, urges viewers to spread the word so the film will have a greater popular effect.

However, these filmmakers are sensitive to the subtle blurring of lines involved when using secular media and forms for sacred purposes. In his article for *GQ,* "God Is on Line One," Jim Nelson recognizes the discontinuity. These evangelical films about the apocalypse require "fictive jumps . . . to fictionalize what you believe to be true."[11] The filmmakers and screenplay writers recognize this and accept responsibility for fictionalizing parts of the story that are not spelled out in the Bible in order to make the story credible.They are careful not to contradict the Bible in their writing, however.[12] So the result is a movie that stays mostly true to the biblical accounts of the apocalypse—however they may be interpreted—and that uses modern special effects and filming techniques to bring the more fantastic and visual parts of the story to life on the screen.The result is sometimes dazzling, sometimes horrific, and often effective, especially with the proper audience.

After a brief review of *The Omega Code, Left Behind,* and *Megiddo: The Omega Code II,* I will suggest some common characteristics of these few attempts at popular Christian apocalyptic movies before examining the more common and numerous examples of popular secular apocalyptic movies.

The Omega Code *and* Megiddo: The Omega Code II:
The Secularization of the Sacred Apocalypse

The Omega Code, a surprisingly successful evangelical vision of the apocalypse from 1999, is based on the notion that the Bible contains a secret code that will reveal the events of the end time. The idea that whoever controls the code can control the eternal souls of humans motivates the antichrist, embodied by the character Stone Alexander (played by Michael York), to steal the code and initiate the events that will lead to the end of time. An elaborate computer program allows Bible scholars and Stone to unravel the Bible code by reading the text in three dimensions. The plot of this action thriller proceeds as Stone tries to wrest control of the final code from the film's protagonist, Gillen Lane (played by Casper Van Diem), a self-absorbed human potential guru who in the end undergoes a religious conversion through his struggle to thwart the antichrist. The film ends ambiguously with the revelation of the final code that points to the new millennium as the beginning of the end. Whether the antichrist controls events and initiates his hellish kingdom or the kingdom of God is inaugurated awaits resolution in *Megiddo: The Omega Code II.*

The film's main characters, Stone and Gillen Lane, are introduced early in the film, and it is not clear at first who is supposed to represent the antichrist. Lane is a young, brilliant, handsome, and precocious Ph.D. in world religions and mythology from Cambridge. He has achieved success and fame as a human empowerment speaker and writer who appears as an evangelist for a secular humanist gospel. As the film progresses, it becomes clear that Lane is not the embodiment of evil but is simply the paradigm of human fallibility and sinfulness. While his motivational speeches and work appear to save others, he cannot save himself—he suffers from demonic visions and nightmares, his marriage is falling apart, and he is powerless to stop the film's more demonic character, the antichrist Stone Alexander. So the evangelical perspective of the film becomes clear—the battle in the movie is for the human soul, represented in concentrated form by the brash, confident Lane. And human pride in one's ability to save oneself becomes the chief avenue for falling into evil. Nevertheless, by the end of the film, Lane, tormented still by his demonic visions, prays a simple prayer, "God, Jesus, save me."

At once, his visions are lifted and his demons vanquished; while it is unclear if this prayer will deliver Lane and humanity from the evil of the antichrist, it is clear that Lane (and thus human beings) cannot save themselves but must depend on the saving grace of Jesus Christ. The movie obviously operates from an evangelical perspective, and the message is clearly enunciated through the transformation of Lane. That the action takes place in the context of the apocalyptic drama gives us a clue to the motivating force behind the film.

The film's other main character, Stone Alexander, the embodiment of evil, the antichrist, appears as a benevolent world leader who uses technology to solve problems of drought and food production while using his charisma to unite people under his goal of a one-world government. While his actions appear to benefit humankind, they produce a smoke-screen that hides his evil intent to capture the souls of human beings and enslave them in his ungodly kingdom. This vision of the antichrist is in accord with teachings of some who study biblical prophecy with a view toward the apocalyptic drama—a false peace breeds deception and blindness. Stone's demonic and supernatural nature unfolds as the plot does, particularly when he is resurrected after dying from a gunshot wound to the head, thereby fulfilling the prophecy associated with the beast, who "seemed to have a mortal wound . . . [to the head that] was healed."[13] From that point on, it is clear that the antichrist is embodied in Stone and that the cosmic battle is underway. Stone represents pure evil arrayed against God, while Lane represents human frailty. The battleground is earth—the spoils of victory, the souls of human beings.

The plot is difficult to follow without some grounding in the apocalyptic tradition that lies behind the film. Hal Lindsey, who wrote *The Late Great Planet Earth* in 1970, served as consultant to the film, and the apocalyptic drama unfolding bears the mark of the tradition he has represented during the latter part of the twentieth century. In the video version of *Megiddo,* the sequel to *The Omega Code,* Lindsey appears before the movie starts to reassert his position that the film chronicles the "precise pattern" of events that are foretold in biblical prophecy. He asserts his belief that the antichrist is now alive and that the second coming of Jesus is not long in the future. Paul Crouch (executive producer of the film and father of Matt Crouch, the producer of both *The Omega Code* movies) also appears in a short cameo to vouch for the veracity of the belief that we are situated at the end of time on earth when Bible prophecy points to the coming of the antichrist and the battle of Armageddon. *Megiddo* takes the viewer to that battle made famous in John's *Revelation* in the climax of the movie.

The 2002 *Megiddo: The Omega Code II* is a more sophisticated movie than *The Omega Code*. The plot is more suspenseful, less punctuated by the esoteric code that drives the action. And the moviemakers use special effects more liberally and with more dramatic results than in the earlier film: Stone Alexander spews from his mouth a plague of what appears to be locusts; a hellish scene of the battle of Armageddon (the hill of Megiddo) plays out under the red light of a sun turned to blood; a shaft of heavenly light descends from heaven; Stone is transformed into a beastly and horrific Satan who is cast into and chained in the lake of fire. With *Megiddo,* Matt Crouch employs cinematic special effects to portray the events presented in *Revelation.* The effect is dramatic, and this is the most interesting point about the movie. With *Megiddo* we see clearly the blurring of secular and sacred lines through the use of media, which the film decries, to help visualize a sacred story. The power of image, made possible by a secular, popular film medium, becomes part of creatively telling and recasting a sacred story. By presenting it in visual form, part horror film, part science fiction, part religious drama, the filmmakers take a bold step in exploring popular avenues for a sacred message.

After an initial narration by the antichrist, *Megiddo* begins in 1960 when Stone is a young boy and chronicles the development and maturation of the evil of antichrist. At a party, the young boy overhears a conversation between his father and a friend about the 1960 presidential election. Stone's father predicts Nixon cannot win the presidency because "he doesn't look good on television" and offers his assessment of the relatively new medium of television: "People will form their opinions" from television, he boldly asserts in a not-so-subtle foreshadowing of the role the media will play in the rise of the antichrist to world dominion. Later in the movie, Stone murders his father in order to control his father's media empire because it is key to distributing his message. In a bit of thematic irony, the film portrays mass media as the tool the antichrist will use to ascend to popularity while at the same time this story is told through the same mass media. In fact, as mentioned earlier, contemporary evangelicals have been adept at using various media formats for spreading the message, so it is not media per se that is evil. The point here is that secular media can be used for good or evil, and that it is suspect at best.

After Stone attempts to kill his baby brother, he is sent to military school in Rome where he receives the military training and leadership skills he later employs in his attempted rise to world dominion. The film chronicles Stone's rise to head of the European Union and ultimately to chancellor of the United World Union, seemingly bringing peace and ending world hunger through his attempts to create a unified world government, a united world with one currency and one language. Such a vision of world dominion has long been associated with the antichrist by some apocalypticists, so this plot is a predictable one based on this particular prophetic tradition. As in *The Omega Code,* Stone has a human obstacle to battle and overcome, his brother David (played by Michael Biehn), the same one he tried to murder as a baby. David (messianic overtones?) ascends from the vice presidency of the United States when Stone kills the president, and Stone then tries to force David to join the United World Union. The United States had been the chief holdout, joined tentatively by China and the "Latins" in their suspicion of Stone and his one-world government. Of course, David refuses, and the forces are quickly aligned—Stone and his United World Union against the United States with its allies, the "Latins" and China.

This good versus evil scenario quickly develops as David is discredited by Stone and by treasonous forces within the U.S. government, goes into hiding and, seeking strength through prayer, ultimately tries to assassinate Stone. He fails, and as in *The Omega Code,* the potential human savior falls short. Even David, with his goodness and honesty, with the force of the United States and its allies, cannot defeat the beast—this task must be left to the supernatural. The movie comes to its climax with the aforementioned battle of Armageddon, the appearance of the kingdom of God, the casting out of evil, and the establishment of God's kingdom. The last image of the movie is of a renewed earth: the scene abruptly changes from hellish battlefield to Eden-like paradise, punctuated by a cascading waterfall.

Left Behind

Left Behind, the 2000 movie based on the novel by the same name, was produced by the Canadian filmmaking duo Peter and Paul Lalonde. The film comes in a line of apocalypse theme movies written and produced by the brothers, including *Apocalypse, Revelation,* and *Tribulation.* The Lalondes and Cloud Ten Pictures' earlier movies were not largely known, although *Tribulation* boasted a sizeable budget and a cast with known names like Gary Busey, Margot Kidder, Howie Mandel, and Nick Mancuso. But *Left Behind* received the benefit of the blockbuster novel series by Tim LaHaye and Jerry Jenkins. Kirk Cameron, Brad Johnson, Chelsea Noble, and Clarence Gilyard give the movie recognizable stars, and the action-packed plot containing political intrigue gives the evangelical message a viable vehicle to attract a popular audience.

Many of the same elements found in *The Omega Code* movies are present here: the plot revolves around eschatological interpretations of biblical prophecy; underlying tension in Jerusalem between Jews and Muslims are key to the end of time; a charismatic and powerful antichrist rises to world popularity through the United Nations by combating world hunger and offering world peace; a global currency and global community are instituted; rebuilding the temple in Jerusalem is planned. Yet this film focuses on another element in the eschatological drama based on biblical prophecy. The premise of *Left Behind* turns on the rapture, the belief that true Christians will be caught up in heaven and mysteriously disappear in order to escape the prophesied tribulation period. This intriguing element adds drama to the film as people disappear from planes and cars and chaos and panic result. As dazzling as the special effects of Armageddon are in *Megiddo: The Omega Code II*, capturing the chaotic results of a rapture are much more believable, having a visceral and palpable impact. The movie ends with the revelation of the antichrist, the world poised on the brink of the seven-year period known as the tribulation, but with the assertion that "faith is enough."

The other major element that sets this film apart from *The Omega Code* movies is a more pronounced evangelical appeal. *Left Behind* portrays successful, attractive people making rational decisions to follow Jesus Christ, praying for forgiveness and guidance in light of the events of and following the rapture. By shifting focus from antichrist and Armageddon to rapture, the film is less like a horror film and more like an intriguing action flick, albeit with an evangelical message. The video, which was released before the movie came to theaters, ends with an appeal by star Kirk Cameron to spread the word about the film project so that others will see it but also so that Hollywood will take notice—notice that an audience exists who will pay to see movies with a spiritual message. The film becomes a purposeful evangelical tool to spread the message to as many people as possible through use of secular media. The hope that other such films will be produced by Hollywood lies at the core of the project. These evangelical Christian filmmakers understand the power of images and film to shape beliefs and attitudes and are beginning to capitalize on this aspect of the postmodern psyche.

This brief review of some evangelical films that have chosen the apocalyptic drama as their subject allows us to isolate a few characteristics of the secularization of the sacred drama.

While each film has its own individual characteristics, these films share the following emphases to one degree or another:

1. These films reflect a particular evangelical interpretation of the end of time that is tied to linking biblical prophecy to contemporary events. Not all evangelicals share this interpretation of the biblical apocalyptic literature, but there does exist a community that seeks within contemporary events signs that the end is approaching based on clues in the Bible. This stance involves an interpretive leap—beginning with the notion that the Bible is the key to understanding all of life, this evangelical apocalyptic stance believes that there are also hidden clues that will reveal the key to understanding the conclusion of history.

2. In these dramas, there is a focus on the apocalyptic antichrist rather than on a savior figure. This makes sense because in the evangelical apocalyptic drama, the savior is the risen and returning Christ, and none of the films depict the return of Christ.

3. The films accept the idea that this world is beyond saving and that events of the end are to be interpreted as those that will usher in God's kingdom.

4. The apocalyptic conflict is a cosmic one between good and evil for eternity and for human souls.

5. Human effort cannot save the planet or humankind—no human savior will be adequate. The final battle is a cosmic one waged on a supernatural level.

6. Certain signs are key and repeat themselves as enduring symbols in this prophetic tradition: the establishment of Israel as a nation; Middle East conflict, particularly between Jews and Muslims; creation of a global community by erasing national boundaries and creating a world currency; weather patterns and natural disasters; the deceptive and charismatic rise of antichrist.

7. Technology is key—a computer program unravels the secret code in *The Omega Code,* the media become the tools of the beast in *Megiddo,* and scientific technology to end world hunger is significant in all three movies.

8. Violence characterizes all three films but is much less a part of *Left Behind* than *The Omega Code* and *Megiddo*. Of course, violence in these films should not surprise us, even though they are meant to be spiritual films, because the subject matter is violent—world conquest, the antichrist, evil incarnate, and so on, must come wrapped in a certain amount of violence.

9. There can be no lasting world peace and no final solution to problems such as poverty and hunger. Peace and alleviation from suffering can only be achieved in God's kingdom.

10. These films use secular media and popular entertainment as vehicles for a particular sacred view of the apocalypse and constitute the secularization of the sacred. Filmmakers do this willingly in order to capture the imagination of a secular audience.

I enumerate these characteristics now in order to compare them to those found in apocalyptic films that begin from a secular viewpoint rather than from an evangelical one. The differences in worldview are interesting and enlightening.

THE SACRALIZATION OF THE SECULAR: SECULAR APOCALYPSES[14]

Although it is not surprising to see evangelicals making films about the apocalypse (except for the fact that evangelicals historically have been suspicious of the medium), one finds it at least intriguing to see the various movies made (particularly in the 1990s) about end-of-the-world themes. As Y2K anxieties mounted, moviemakers cashed in and a surprisingly wide range of movies emerged about the end of the world. These secular apocalypses were made not from the religious point of view at all, yet they participated in a sacralization of the secular because in many ways they functioned religiously by imparting an ideology (if not theology) of the end times that captured the imagination of the public. In doing so, they took on sacred function. Commentators such as Daniel Wojcik view apocalypticism as rampant in American society. In his insightful work on popular culture and the apocalypse, *The End of the World as We Know It: Faith, Fatalism, and Apocalypse in America,*[15] Wojcik sees apocalypticism everywhere in culture and examines apocalyptic philosophies that give serious response to our hopes and visions. Wojcik points to popular culture as an effective medium for communicating contemporary apocalyptic visions and the concerns accompanying them. When popular culture does this, it addresses a fundamental religious concern, so when secular cultural forms like movies tackle a worldview that traditionally has been ascribed to the religious imagination, we have secular culture taking up sacred functions, thus sacralizing the secular imagination. This sacralized, secular ideology, communicated through diverse films, sets forth a few recurring themes. After reviewing these themes through reference to a variety of secular apocalyptic films, we will look at three films in particular that embody the secular approach to the end of time. *Waterworld, 12 Monkeys,* and *Independence Day* provide us with examples of the extraordinary diversity of popular films based on eschatological themes. What will emerge is an apocalyptic consciousness in the popular secular sphere that contrasts drastically with the one established in evangelical apocalyptic movies.

The first point to keep in mind with these secular cinematic apocalypses is that although many borrow image and symbolism from the Jewish and Christian apocalyptic dramas, most are not apocalyptic per se in the sense that Jewish and Christian apocalypses "unveil" or "reveal" God's sovereignty. While they focus on the eschatological characteristics of the tradition and view the end of the world through the lens of religious apocalyptic renderings, these cinematic dramas ignore some salient features of apocalyptic texts.

Second, the cinematic apocalyptic dramas draw as much from contemporary science fiction as they do from apocalyptic texts, so the stories appear in radically altered forms. For example, whereas demonic beasts might predominate in the evangelical films, these apocalyptic culprits wear contemporary clothing in secular films. The cinematic apocalypses contemporize evil, the Prince of Darkness, and the antichrist. No longer the beast of *Revelation,* modern evil comes packaged in nuclear weapons, global warming, killer viruses, and aliens—ideas that can excite the imagination of contemporary secular audiences.

Third, in secular apocalyptic dramas, it is no longer the supernatural that initiates the apocalypse. Whereas in traditional Jewish and Christian eschatology the apocalypse comes from the transcendent realm,[16] in secular apocalypses, the end comes about more often than not from human stupidity and greed (for example, *Waterworld*). This is the ultimate secularization of the apocalypse, because world destruction has been removed from the realm of the sacred to the secular realm, from the hand of the supernatural to the will of humanity. The secular film version of the apocalypse removes the divine element from the apocalyptic drama yet retains religious symbolism, imagery, and language. Nor does it remove the notion of otherness as a necessary component of humanity's struggle with the end of the world. However, in these films, the divine Other is replaced by aliens, disease, meteors, and machines—an otherness that exists in "binary opposition" to humankind. So the secular apocalypse of film is postmodern in that it has undermined the binary opposition of God-human[17] by effectively removing God from the equation. Yet it retains a sense of opposition ("something-human") that is crucial for understanding threats to existence.

Fourth, in the traditional Christian apocalypse, the end of the world raises the righteous to the kingdom of heaven and judges the wicked, so Armageddon is something not only preordained to happen but welcomed by the righteous community. In the secular apocalypse, as I have noted in *Screening the Sacred,* there is no such fatalism and differentiation, and the emphasis is not on the end itself but on avoiding or surviving the end. In fact, surviving the end is one of the characteristics of the secular apocalypse, and we find that human ingenuity, scientific adaptations, and heroism allow humanity to survive and outlive the apocalypse or to avoid it entirely. This makes sense—since the secular apocalypse has humanity initiating the end, it casts human beings in the role of messiah, savior from destruction.[18] This characteristic stands in stark contrast to the evangelical films, which picture potential human heroes as powerless against supernatural forces, both good and evil. Thus, we see a secular apocalyptic imagination that removes Armageddon from God's hands and places it squarely in the hands of humanity—the fate of the world depends on no one but ourselves. This exclusion of God from the apocalypse defines the secularization of traditional apocalyptic imagination. This secularization of the end trivializes it, humanizes it, and makes it less threatening, if not inconsequential.

A fifth characteristic of the more recent apocalyptic films suggests a further refinement as well. Just a few years back, many apocalyptic films were based on the premise of nuclear holocaust, because at one time the idea of nuclear winter was foremost in our minds as the villain most likely to succeed in bringing about the end of the world as we know it.[19] Films such as the 1964 British black comedy *Dr. Strangelove: Or How I Learned to Stop Worrying and Love the Bomb, Def-Con 4,* or *The Day After* illustrate an earlier preoccupation with world destruction by nuclear means. And the idea still arises. For example, in *Independence Day,* nuclear destruction of the world becomes a fear but is minimal in light of the other threat of world destruction, alien invasion. In fact, nuclear destruction is considered in that film as a possible means of *saving* the world from apocalypse. Let us entertain the assumption that with the end of the Cold War, the nuclear threat no longer dominates our fears as it once did, so imaginative filmmakers and artists have gone in search of other world-ending scenarios, such as global warming in *Waterworld.* We will see this transition clearly when we examine *12 Monkeys,* an apocalyptic scenario based on a killer virus. The film was inspired by a 1962 French film that envisioned the end of the world through nuclear destruction. While nuclear annihilation was a real fear in 1962, it was less so at the end of the twentieth century, so *12 Monkeys* had to go in search of a more convincing culprit. What we learn from our secular apocalypses is that we tend to continually reinterpret the apocalypse in light of contemporary consciousness and fears.

Finally, when apocalypticism focuses on the end of things, it becomes a way of overcoming our angst over the realization of our finitude. But when apocalypticism focuses on violence, it becomes a way to control chaos and evil by identifying it, as in *12 Monkeys,* or by defeating it, as in *Independence Day.* The paradigms of violence, like the paradigms of world destruction, help us to make sense of our world by transferring judgment to human control. It is an egocentric attempt to achieve the sovereignty that God claimed in the Jewish and Christian apocalypses. The violence we see portrayed so frequently on our movie screens, the violence we are so fond of calling gratuitous, functions apocalyptically, and thus religiously as well. Or at least it can. What did violence bring us in John's *Revelation* and in the evangelical apocalyptic movies? The battle between good and evil and the ultimate destruction of evil. What does violence bring to the movie screen in secular apocalypses? If not the destruction of evil, then at least the identification of it. This is an important role for movies to play in a secular world where belief in the devil as the embodiment of evil carries little if any import.

Consider a few brief examples that flesh out the above characteristics of the secular cinematic apocalypse. The notion that while the threat of the end is inevitable, hope that the destruction of humanity is avoidable runs through virtually all of the recent secular films with eschatological emphases or allusions.[20] These films reject the idea of human extinction in favor of imagining humanity's salvation. We see this in films like *12 Monkeys,* in which there is hope that humanity will be rescued from a killer virus, or in *Waterworld,* which ends with an "ark" locating dry land, the promised land. In *Armageddon,* the sacrifice and heroism of one individual spares the world and humanity entirely. As a huge meteor bears down on the Earth, Harry Stamper (an oil-rig driller played by Bruce Willis) and a rag-tag group of misfits (similar to *Independence Day*) are recruited to fly a spaceship to land on the meteor, drill a hole, and drop a nuclear bomb into it to destroy it before it destroys the earth. Besides a subplot involving a romance between Stamper's daughter (played by Liv Tyler) and his protégé (played by Ben Affleck), that is as deep as the plot gets. A multinational mission is successful, but only after Stamper, in a final act of selflessness, sacrifices his life to save Earth. The movie's plot is weak, but it works well to demonstrate Hollywood's secular apocalyptic premise—the end is avoidable.

Deep Impact employs a plot that is a bit more complex. In this movie, Earth is threatened by a comet. Government officials, led by the U.S. president (played compassionately by Morgan Freeman), scramble to devise a plan to save the Earth. The basic plan is the same—fly a space-ship into the comet and blow it up. This time the mission is led by an ex-astronaut (played by Robert Duvall), but the complexity of dealing with a comet makes it clear to our heroes and the government that some fragments will hit the earth with catastrophic effects even if the mission is successful. Thus, the plot is more complicated, if only slightly so, and raises ethical questions about who will be saved and how. The heroic efforts of government ensure the survival of humanity even if it means great loss of life.

In *Contact*, we are treated to the movie adaptation of Carl Sagan's vision of humanity's first contact with alien intelligence in another world. We are also introduced to the idea that this event could bring mass extinction from the hands of an advanced and hostile civilization (similar again to *Independence Day*). Jodie Foster plays Dr. Eleanor Arroway, a brilliant young scientist who is obsessed with finding evidence of extraterrestrial life. The movie features a strong cast and does allow some debate of theology, even though most of the questions involve the existence of God rather than any serious consideration of eschatology. Nevertheless, the movie offers hope and comfort that humans are not alone to face the horror of extinction. Although not a guarantee, the notion that another intelligence exists out there comforts us. In this movie, government officials make it clear that they consider alien life a threat whether the aliens act aggressively or not, thus mirroring popular images of alien forces invading earth. Yet the alien "other" in *Contact* seems benign, fatherly, and almost divine to the secular scientific mind in which God is functionally absent.

Contact, as secular apocalypse, communicates serene comfort from the calming presence of extraterrestrial life and presents a stark contrast to religious apocalypse that is portrayed through disturbing scenes in the movie in which religious fanatics are depicted as apocalyptic terrorists. Whereas religious apocalypticists in *Contact* use violence (they destroy the costly machine built to allow contact with an extraterrestrial civilization), in Hollywood's apocalyptic drama the threat of human extinction breeds harmony, not violence. The threat of the end tends to bring people together in a unified stand against annihilation, evolving out of a deep faith in the powers of scientific ingenuity and human ability. This is also seen clearly in *Deep Impact* and *Armageddon,* in which individuals and government combine forces to save the day. The message is clear: together we can beat this thing. Note how different this is to the help-lessness of humanity in the face of a divinely ordained apocalypse one finds in evangelical apocalyptic dramas. So the secular apocalypse moves beyond some of the fatalism we often find in religious apocalypticism.

If the world is to be saved, it must have a savior in these cinematic dramas. While we see this messiah fixation in *12 Monkeys, Independence Day, Waterworld, Deep Impact, Armageddon,* and even *Contact,* we see it nowhere more powerfully than in *The Matrix.* In this film, a computer hacker who takes the name "Neo" (Keanu Reeves) stumbles onto secretive and life-threatening information. Neo learns that his world is all an illusion, an elaborate hoax played on his mind to obscure the real world where machines, computers, and artificial intelligence have enslaved humanity. This "unveiling" reflects the revelatory intent of much religious apocalypse. The plot taps into the underlying fear that society is too dependent on the computer (particularly in light at that time of Y2K anxieties) and that dependence will lead to humanity's downfall (i.e., enslavement).

In *The Matrix,* fear is developed through a scenario in which machines breed and sustain humans as power sources. At the same time, the machines construct an elaborate shadow world (a cyber world of illusion), and feed it to the imaginations of the catatonic human bodies. Neo is initiated into this awareness by an underground movement of humans who are seeking to overthrow the machines and establish a new city, the city of Zion, where hopes of restoration of the human race stay alive. A strong-willed Trinity (Carrie-Anne Moss) leads Neo to the leader of these revolutionaries, Morpheus (Laurence Fishburne), who looks for a "chosen one" to lead them to freedom. Morpheus is con-vinced that Neo is the one. Neo gradually emerges as the one who will lead the underground resistance, and the movie ends not with restora-tion but with hope of such.

Note the strong religious imagery present in names: Neo (new), Trinity (Christian overtones?), Morpheus (dream god from Greek mythology), city of Zion. This obvious use of religious language estab-lishes Neo as one of the strongest messiah figures in contemporary apoca-lyptic movies. Religious language and devotion predominate in Morpheus's selection of Neo as "the One." And Neo's initiation to mes-sianic ways becomes highly ritualized. Neo's training involves martial arts expertise and mind control, bringing an Eastern religious element into the picture as well. So Keanu Reeves becomes one in a line of macho messiahs (e.g., Bruce Willis and Kevin Costner) who use muscle and force to save humanity, but unlike other messiahs, this one must use mind control as well. And his literal "waking up" out of his catatonic state makes Neo as much a bodhisattva[21] as a Western-style messiah.

Neo's messianic cause brings to light yet another characteristic of the secular cinematic apocalypse. With the exclusion of the divine from the apocalyptic formula, the secular apocalypse seeks new relevance in redefining the end through science and human effort. Angelic armies and beasts no longer suffice to usher in the end. Even though the secular apocalypse uses science and human ingenuity to overcome the fatalism of religious apocalyptic myth, often these secular versions employ religious language and images. In *Armageddon,* the United States, Russia, France, and Japan join in a cooperative effort to save humanity using technology, but the president of the United States refers to the Bible in his effort to create a unified mission to save the world from collision with a massive meteor. When at the end of the film catastrophe has been averted, the movie portrays mass celebrations at religious shrines. So while the thanks for salvation should go to science and human sacrifice, the movie cannot quite divorce itself from the divine implications of global disaster. In a similar vein, the plot of *Deep Impact* also relies on science and secular government to save a remnant of the Earth, but these actions are couched in religiously symbolic language. For example, the spaceship carrying the nuclear weapon that eventually destroys the comet threatening Earth is christened "the Messiah," while the operation that selects and transports selected Americans to safe bunkers so they can repopulate the Earth is dubbed "Project Noah's Ark." The impact of these symbols suggests that the cinematic apocalypse is thoroughly secular in terms of substance—the actors, saviors, and heroes are governments and individuals while the threat comes not from some divine power but from natural forces. Nevertheless, the apocalyptic moment still carries religious imagery and symbolism. This might be the most telling comment on our secular society's appropriation of religion—while our culture is substantively secular, we legitimize it with reference to religion, and if our culture functions religiously as well, it is sacralized.

After undermining the God-human dichotomy and rejecting the supernatural as the agency for the apocalypse, the contemporary apocalyptic imagination has been in search of a new apocalyptic cause. As suggested earlier, the contemporary eschatological movie has redefined the agency of the end several times in the last twenty or so years. At one time, eschatological fears were attached to our fears of nuclear annihilation, yet by the late 1990s, nuclear weapons become the agency of salvation, as in *Deep Impact, Independence Day,* and *Armageddon.* Viruses (12

Monkeys and *Outbreak*), aliens (*Independence Day*), and global warming (*Waterworld*) have taken front stage as threats that concern contemporary Americans. And more recently, *The Matrix* has explored the possibility of artificial intelligence giving rise to the end of the civilization that produced it. The theme of humanity against machine is not a new one and recalls the Frankenstein theme of a human creation turning against the human creator.[22] *The Matrix* uses fears surrounding technology (e.g., Y2K fears were based on nervousness that our culture had created a monster— a computer-driven world that would wreck civilization) to continue the "Garden motif" in which creation turns against the Creator.

This element of *The Matrix* allows a further refinement of the secular cinematic apocalyptic myth made possible by the concept of virtual reality. To a greater extent than ever before in human culture, we can use technology to create a virtual reality. *The Matrix* raises an interesting question concerning the capabilities of this technology a couple of hundred years from now. The plot of the movie is based on the premise that computers have constructed an elaborate alternative reality that masks the postapocalyptic world. To the extent human beings exist in this world, they exist in ignorance of the real, actual state of their world or their lives. They have been duped by a virtual world that to them appears real. This contemporary revisiting of Plato's famous allegory of the cave and of neo-Platonic dualism of real and ideal adds an interesting twist to the idea of the apocalypse and raises the possibility that the apocalyptic moment has already passed—both in reality and out of human memory. The role of Morpheus (the Greek god of dreams) as the character who introduces the real versus the shadow world in this movie only complicates the matter. How can we be sure Morpheus's version of the Matrix is not the "dream" masquerading as his "reality" that is based on "illusion."

Most twentieth-century millennial groups are premillennial in their orientation and thus require a destruction scenario to fulfill their apocalyptic expectations. The secular cinematic apocalyptic drama capitalizes on this perception and stereotypes apocalyptic groups—this describes an additional characteristic of these cinematic apocalyptic dramas. Contemporary culture already tends to view apocalyptic groups as marginal, sometimes scary, sometimes dangerous, sometimes the agents of mass destruction. This image certainly does not describe all religious groups that are millennial in orientation, but it does describe the way secular movies have portrayed religious groups focusing on the apocalypse. As a result of this and other cultural characterizations, religion has largely forfeited its proprietorship of the apocalypse in our culture. In its place, science has stepped in with its fantastic theories about origins and endings in our universe.

The conflict between faith and science in dealing with cosmology is a main theme in *Contact*. In this movie, the protagonist, Dr. Arroway, exhibits unyielding faith in science while religious representatives appear as kooks (the apocalyptic terrorist), as right wing zealots (Rob Lowe's character, Richard Rank), or as compromised and unconvincing (Matthew McConaughey's character, Palmer Joss). In the end, this works against the scientist Arroway when she asks the world to believe her story, which cannot be proven or substantiated. In our secular eschatological dramas, science has wrested control of cosmic cataclysm away from religion, suggesting that the charges of secularists that religion is anachronistic (if not irrelevant) arise most convincingly over questions of eschatology. We have already witnessed more than a century of debate over creation and now see the movie medium sponsoring debate on the eschaton.

My main argument here is that a secularized apocalyptic imagination is fostered by or reflected in the contemporary film industry, and that this imagination of the end contributes in some way to a postmodern, secular vision of apocalypse that draws upon but revises the Jewish and Christian apocalyptic imagination. As such, films like the ones highlighted in the remainder of this chapter are re-visioning the apocalypse in ways that make sense to contemporary audiences and in ways that eclipse traditional religion's ability to do so. By eclipsing traditional religion's role in presenting apocalyptic themes, these secular apocalypses take on sacred roles and witness to a sacralization of secular culture. Sometimes this process draws on the traditional apocalypse's heavy eschatological emphasis—sometimes more generally on the apocalyptic cataclysm that envisions justice and judgment through violence and death. All of these themes can be found in many popular films—I will look more closely at three: *Waterworld*, *12 Monkeys*, and *Independence Day*. These movies all function religiously in that they present a secular apocalyptic story that helps the viewer come to grips with human finitude and world fragility.

Waterworld

The highly publicized and critically abused film *Waterworld* provides a good example of an apocalyptic film based on a contemporary dilemma. *Waterworld* takes the warnings of global warming and, like any good science fiction work, asks the question, "What if?" Then the film extrapolates a possible future scenario based on the idea of melted polar caps from a runaway greenhouse effect. The film is thus based on an earth largely covered by water, a new flood requiring, as in Noah's day, adaptation to life entirely on water. A world covered in water not only poses challenges to the remnant of humanity that survives the eco-catastrophe, but it also created major headaches for the production crew. Determined to avoid shooting with a blue screen, Dean Semler's crew encountered incredible difficulty shooting the film on water, particularly on the unstable trimaran that is the Mariner's (played by Kevin Costner) ark. The technical demands and artistic difficulties of shooting on water led to what was then the most expensive film in history, at about $175 million, and to a Universal Pictures production record of 166 days.[23] For all this cost and trouble, director Kevin Reynolds and producer-star Kevin Costner did make a technically advanced film, and a good one at that,[24] and the film anticipated residual income on ventures such as "Waterworld Live," a live sea-war spectacular and outdoor stunt show at Universal Studios Hollywood.[25]

The film itself follows a straightforward plot with predictable developments. The setting is a future inundated Earth, where survivors of the great eco-disaster exist on floating cities, atolls, or floating barges (minisocieties). Mariner is a loner, existing on his trimaran and adapting to life on the sea. The action of the movie begins when Mariner arrives at an atoll to trade for supplies. He possesses a few ounces of the most precious commodity in such a world, dirt, and seeks to trade his treasure for water and a scrubby tomato plant. The citizens of the atoll discover Mariner is a mutant with webbed feet and gills behind his ears. This mutation calls to mind the mutation themes of earlier postnuclear films. Mariner is caged and sentenced to death when the atoll is attacked by a band of smokers (pirates) who are led by Deacon (Dennis Hopper). In the confusion, Mariner is rescued by a beautiful woman, Helen, and a little girl, Enola, and the three escape together on Mariner's trimaran.

The point of the story is revealed when we learn that Deacon is pursuing Enola because of a tattoo on her back that is a map leading to the mythical dry land. Obviously, in *Waterworld*, if someone could find and master dry land, that person could enjoy unimaginable riches and pleasure. The plot develops as Deacon captures Enola; Mariner discovers a drawing Enola leaves behind that matches an old copy of *National Geographic* picturing trees with the caption, "Paradise Lost"; Mariner surmises that perhaps the mythical dry land actually could exist and that Enola might hold the key to paradise after all. This makes her rescue crucial.

Mariner locates and infiltrates Deacon's floating colony, a huge oil tanker. In great feats of daring, he saves Enola, destroys the tanker, and defeats Deacon and his evil minions. Once evil has been destroyed, Helen and Mariner employ the help of Gregor, an old inventor from Helen's atoll, and decipher the tattoo on Enola's back. In the end, they find dry

land, complete with fresh water and vegetation, and populate it with the
survivors of the atoll where Helen and Enola began. The righteous community, as opposed to Deacon's evil society, occupies dry land, paradise.
However, Mariner realizes he is not meant for dry land (remember his
mutations) and, having played his part as epic hero and savior, he leaves
the community behind and sails off alone.

The point of the story, the apocalyptic premise, is to find paradise,
dry land, a flooded world's version of the kingdom of God. *Waterworld*
thus defines a period of temporary trial and tribulation, a concept familiar to the Christian apocalypse, which will be followed by paradise. And
the vicinity of dry land is signaled in the same way as it was following
the biblical deluge, by the perching of a bird on the edge of the ark, in
this case, a balloon. Dry land is the metaphorical home for the inhabitants of Waterworld and literally home for Enola. When Enola arrives at
their paradise, she exclaims, "I'm home." Enola had once lived on the
island and was sent away when her parents were dying. Enola is a curious girl who has visions of and draws strange figures: what we know as
trees and horses but what were to the Waterworld inhabitants strange
unknown plants and animals. Her drawings came from her suppressed
memories from early childhood. So arrival at dry land is "going home"
for humans who were not meant to live on water, just as the postapocalyptic "new heaven and new earth" meant going home for first-
century Christians who were dispossessed in Roman society and for
true Christians in the evangelical apocalyptic movies.

Dry land was all but destroyed in the apocalyptic scenario of
Waterworld. Yet the promised land was never forgotten and attained
mythic proportions, and the righteous eventually inherit paradise in the
last scene of the movie. Mariner, who rescues Enola and leads the remnant to paradise, becomes the apocalyptic hero who appears on the
scene in order to deliver (save) the righteous, guide them to paradise,
and defeat the wicked, which Mariner does in his daring rescue of
Enola. I have written in *Screening the Sacred* about another apocalyptic
hero from an earlier film using apocalyptic imagery and categories,
Clint Eastwood's *Pale Rider*.[26] In that story, Eastwood (Preacher) rides
onto the scene as a young girl reads from the book of John's *Revelation*.
During the course of the story, Preacher befriends the residents of a
small community, defends their rights against the power of a large strip-
mining company, and defeats the wicked en route to securing the happiness of the righteous community. At the closing of the movie,
Preacher rides out of sight, just as Costner sails into the horizon in
Waterworld. The apocalyptic hero protects, delivers, and defeats wickedness,

but in the end, the hero is of a different order and cannot remain with the righteous remnant.

As a secular apocalypse, *Waterworld* reflects contemporary secular concerns rather than sacred ones in its depiction of the apocalyptic disaster. In this case, it is very clear the apocalypse occurred as eco-disaster, which came about as a direct consequence of human action. Director Kevin Reynolds commented, "I'm very concerned with ecological issues, because I think they are the overwhelming problems the world faces right now and will result in our own self-destruction . . . a whole world covered in water because of human stupidity and greed."[27] Note the emphasis on the apocalypse being self-induced—our secular apocalypse in this case will be self-destruction, not supernatural destruction, as in the evangelical apocalyptic movies.

The environmental theme is carried out with little subtlety in two major symbols of the movie. First, Deacon's tanker, the evil and ancient freighter in the story, turns out to be the Exxon Valdez, the infamous tanker that polluted the waters and was at the time of the movie a symbol of ecological disaster. And near the point when Mariner triumphs over Deacon, we learn that the patron saint of Deacon and his evil empire is none other than Captain Joe Hazelwood, the doomed captain of the Valdez.[28] So in this movie of eco-apocalypse, the predominant symbol of evil turns out to be a symbol of ecological and environmental disaster. The second apocalyptic and environmental symbol here is Enola, whose name brings to mind the Enola Gay, the B-29 that dropped that atomic bomb on Hiroshima. In this movie, Enola delivers not the apocalypse but escape from it; not nuclear annihilation but the key to paradise. These two symbols draw upon contemporary ecological, environmental, and apocalyptic imagery to construct a secular apocalypse set on the watery world of our future.

12 Monkeys

From *Waterworld*, which is straightforward in terms of plot, we move to an examination of *12 Monkeys*, Terry Gilliam's convoluted story that jumps from future to past to past-future and back again. Gilliam, who also directed *The Fisher King* and the cult favorite *Brazil*, is known for his "inventively convoluted design."[29] The inspiration for this movie came from Chris Marker's 1962 *La Jetée*, a short work of stills that chronicles time travel after the apocalyptic nuclear destruction of Paris and, one would assume, the world. Gilliam Americanizes Marker's classic[30] and in the process produces a challenging secular apocalyptic image for the twenty-first century.

The film is set in Philadelphia in 2035. Ninety-nine percent of the world's population has been destroyed by a killer virus that was released in 1996. The survivors of the virus have now retreated underground, to a subterranean hell beneath the city. Scientists in this underground world send criminals to the surface periodically to monitor conditions. They decide to send one such subject, James Cole (played by Bruce Willis), on a time-traveling mission to 1996 to locate the source of the virus, thus allowing them to plot a strategy to defeat the bug and once again populate the Earth's surface—in other words, to go home. The scientists believe a group called the Army of the Twelve Monkeys was responsible for the outbreak. Cole is selected partly because of his keen powers of observation and memory (he is haunted by a childhood memory of a man shot down in an airport). Cole's first foray into the past lands him by mistake in Baltimore in 1990, where his mad apocalyptic ranting leads to his confinement in a mental hospital as a schizophrenic. There he meets Dr. Kathryn Railly (Madeleine Stowe), his psychiatrist, and Jeffrey Goines (Brad Pitt), a mental patient he befriends. Cole's attempts to contact the future fail, but he is finally returned to 2035, where his scientist interrogators make a second attempt and land him in 1917 in the middle of World War I. There, Cole is shot in the leg before landing in Baltimore in 1996. The time-travel sequences confuse past, present, and future so much that not only the viewer but Cole himself begins to doubt the reality of the quest. When Cole locates Dr. Railly in 1996, she is giving a lecture about a doomsday scenario based on a great plague. Her lecture is complete with references from John's *Revelation,* apocalyptic prophecies, and artwork symbolizing the end. Cole and Railly begin an adventure that leads them to the Army of the Twelve Monkeys, which is headed by none other than Goines. Dr. Railly begins to believe Cole's story when she discovers the bullet in his leg is from World War I. In the meantime, it turns out that the Army of the Twelve Monkeys had nothing to do with the virus but was an animal activist group aimed at freeing the research animals in the lab of Dr. Leland Goines (Jeffrey's father). An assistant to Dr. Goines, Dr. Peters, an "apocalypse nut" in the words of Dr. Railly, plans to scatter the virus.

Believing they had communicated sufficient information to the future and averted the release of the virus, Cole and Dr. Railly travel to the airport to pursue an amorous life together. Once at the airport, they encounter Dr. Peters and realize he is the one releasing the virus, and Cole tries to stop him. In the process, Cole himself is shot down by a security guard as a younger James Cole watches (hence the vivid memory of the adult Cole who saw or imagined his own death as a child).

The movie ends aboard a plane with a scientist from the future seated next to the plotting Dr. Peters.[31] One assumes the scientist acquires the needed information, returns to the future, defeats the virus, and allows humankind to go home, to once again populate the Earth or to establish a new world.

One of the most remarkable characteristics of this secular apocalypse is the time-travel element. With this tool, the viewer is allowed to see that human initiative both created the apocalypse and perhaps averted it; therefore, the confusion of time (which could also be considered a characteristic of postmodernity based on relativity theory) is the central element driving the plot. Jeffrey Beecroft, production designer for the movie, comments, "You have pieces of the past and the future and the present in all scenes," so that the plot ends with Cole's past memory of his future death.[32]

Beecroft's comments bring to mind an interesting possibility in terms of interpreting this film. In Marker's classic *La Jetée,* time travel seems to be imaginative mind extension,[33] so the possibility exists that the same is true in *12 Monkeys.* Since the story is told from Cole's point of view, it is not at all clear whether the story depicts reality or the distorted view of a real schizophrenic. In other words, the viewer has no way of knowing whether the story is based in 1990 in the mind of a mental patient or in 2035 with time travel and futuristic scientists. This apocalyptic scenario could present the eschaton or simply the delusions of a psychologically disturbed man rather than the real eschaton.[34]

The movie could be about an apocalypse that is human-caused with the help of a virus and human-averted with the help of futuristic ingenuity. This option fits our paradigm of secular apocalyptic movies, because it places world destruction at the feet of humanity and reinterprets the apocalypse in light of contemporary fears, mutated viruses, and biological terrorism. However, the other option, the imagined eschaton, raises some interesting possibilities for our secular apocalypse as well. If James Cole's illness leads to a vision of the end,[35] then the movie is less about a scenario of the end than it is about the visionary experience.

Now, let us imagine another famous visionary, John of Patmos, and the psychological dynamics that went into play in producing his revelation, his vision. If we look at *12 Monkeys* in the same way, we can understand apocalyptic scenarios as visionary attempts to imagine our own finitude (i.e., Cole's vision of his death) in a world that continues without us. In John's case, this scenario drew upon a storehouse of Jewish and Christian images to produce a vision of world destruction and God's kingdom. In Cole's case, he could have drawn upon a store of images from his twentieth-century paranoia and anxieties concerning deadly germs to produce a hellish end to civilization and the possibility of establishing a new Earth. The end being unimaginable, Cole then fabricated an alternative ending that saves humankind.

This alternative interpretation of *12 Monkeys* supports the idea that apocalyptic concepts are born out of Western and human egocentrism as a way of dealing with human finitude. Since time inscribes humanity to a limited existence, in a secular apocalyptic imagination, it makes sense that transcending time (time travel) could free humanity. John's apocalypse freed humanity by transcending space, by ascending to and viewing the kingdom of heaven. But the secular apocalypse, which has no transcendent realm in its arsenal of images, transcends time, the great limiter of human experience. And it is this transcendence of time that defines the end and the thwarting of the end for this secular apocalypse. With no transcendent kingdom of heaven, the secular apocalypse is limited to envisioning a new, regenerated Earth, a secular kingdom. In doing so, it sacralizes the secular.

Independence Day

With *Independence Day*, we have a movie that includes a different perspective of the apocalypse than our other two films. Whereas *Waterworld* and *12 Monkeys* are both postapocalyptic in respect to the events that bring about the end (they take place between destruction and reinhabitation of the earth—they are about going home), *Independence Day* portrays events that threaten to bring about the end. By the time humans figure out what is going on, the world's major cities have been destroyed and a thirty-six-hour countdown to complete world destruction is underway. So *Independence Day* is less about going home than it is about saving home; less about finding a new earth than it is about saving the old.

The premise is an old one lifted directly from H. G. Wells' *War of the Worlds* in which the fate of humanity and civilization is directly threatened by hostile aliens with superior technology bent on destroying human life and conquering Earth. The film opens on July 2 with views of an American flag planted on the moon and appropriate American symbols such as Washington monuments and the Statue of Liberty. Then we see a huge alien ship approach the planet. The mother ship then dispatches smaller ships (still fifteen miles in diameter) that travel to and hover over major cities like Washington, Los Angeles, and New York. The gargantuan ships dwarf the cities and provide eerie apocalyptic scenes as they arrive at their appointed destinations around the globe. As they approach, they come from the sky in mountains of fire and smoke, like some fiery chariots from another world. And when they arrive, they darken the skies and threaten total annihilation from another world. With government officials scrambling to respond appropriately and with the cities in panic, the aliens attack on July 2 and destroy the targeted cities—millions die around the world. The images are dramatic, sensational, and highly symbolic—major buildings and monuments are obliterated, the Statue of Liberty lies face down with a destroyed Manhattan in the background, and in a scene that is the ultimate apocalyptic image for American civil religion, the White House is destroyed.

July 3 opens with the cities in ruin and government officials at a loss for what to do. We learn that the U.S. government knew about these aliens from a crashed ship from years ago and that there is a top-secret area (Area 51—a creative reference to the theorized Roswell secret military installation) where scientists have been studying the aliens with little success for years. The secretary of state and former CIA director knew about the facility but failed to tell the president; the implication is that because of governmental secrecy, more people will die. So even though the apocalypse in this movie comes from above, human action and inaction and governmental deception are at least partially responsible for the disaster. With this twist in the film, it is probably appropriate that the movie was shot largely at Hughes Aircraft in Culver City, California, where top-secret weapons were designed and built during the Cold War.[36]

Meanwhile, an unlikely coalition of heroes begins to emerge who ultimately team up to save the world. The U.S. Air Force is gearing up to respond with one of the movie's heroes, Captain Steven Hiller (Will Smith), emerging as a top-gun fighter pilot who wants to join the NASA shuttle team. Russell Casse (Randy Quaid), one of the great comic characters of the movie, is a drunken crop duster who suffers from post-combat trauma from his service in Vietnam. Casse was also abducted by aliens in the past and wants payback. David Levinson, an electronics specialist played by Jeff Goldblum, emerges as an eccentric genius inspired by his equally offbeat father (Judd Hirsch). And, of course, President Whitmore (Bill Pullman) provides inspirational leadership who pulls together a force of fighter pilots and who even straps himself into a jet fighter to do battle with the aliens (the president had been a fighter pilot during the Gulf War). As the movie develops, our team of saviors is a politically correct coalition of African American, Jewish, and WASP heroes who are undergirded by the strength and inspiration of women and the elderly and who join talents to defeat evil. Levinson conceptualized the plan to defeat the aliens and flies with Captain Hiller to plant a computer virus on board the mother ship. Captain Hiller flies an alien

craft to the mother ship and returns home safely and heroically with
Levinson. Casse sacrifices his life to destroy the aliens. And Whitmore
provides the energy and leadership to inspire his warriors in a wonderful speech just before climbing into a fighter jet: in his speech he declares
the Fourth of July no longer an American holiday but worldwide
Independence Day, when humankind will join forces to gain "freedom
from annihilation," that is, freedom from apocalyptic destruction.

Our heroes are successful, the alien threat is defeated, and somehow
humankind was able to put aside political differences to join together in
a united effort against a common foe and save the world. This rather trite
point of the movie demonstrates the seriousness of the secular apocalyptic idea—apocalypse is a real threat that will require extraordinary
means to defeat, but the apocalypse can be avoided, even if it is initiated
by some greater force. It can be averted through human ingenuity, technology, and unity. Again, this avoidance of the end is one of the characteristics of the secularization of the apocalypse—no longer do we
picture the apocalypse as beyond our control, initiated by supernatural
forces as in evangelical apocalyptic movies. Also, in this and in other
secular apocalyptic movies, we see world unity as a key to avoiding the
end, while in evangelical movies, world unity is a sign of the antichrist.

Nevertheless, *Independence Day* introduces a new element into our
secular apocalypse. In this movie and others like it, the impending doom
is not the direct result of human failure, as it was in *Waterworld* and *12
Monkeys*, but comes from a force greater than and beyond our control.
As Caron Schwartz Ellis has argued, aliens constitute another type of
otherness,[37] so that aliens can become our secular "other," descending
from the heavens, the transcendent realm. And this is problematic for a
postmodern secular worldview that basically no longer accepts the idea
of a transcendent realm. So how does *Independence Day* deal with this
dilemma? It familiarizes the alien and makes it vulnerable. In one of the
great comic lines of this movie (and by the way, this is a very humorous
film—no dark disaster film here), U.S. pilots are plotting strategy for
counterattack when Captain Hiller is reprimanded by his superior officer for talking during the meeting. When called down by his officer,
Hiller quips, "I'm just a little anxious to get up there and whup E.T.'s
ass." This comic line makes the aliens, the other, vulnerable and familiar,
because we immediately recall the loveable and vulnerable Spielberg
creation, E.T. This is how the secular apocalypse deals with otherness: it
makes the alien familiar and less threatening as a way of controlling what
is beyond our control. This is one of the characteristics of our secular
apocalypses. They bring world destruction and those forces that threaten

to destroy the world under human control. There is no helplessness in the face of the Almighty here, and in our secular cinematic apocalyptic dramas, humankind, not God, emerges as sovereign.

SUMMARY

My contention here is that the process of secularization has affected some of our traditional religious categories, one of them being the idea of the apocalypse. With a sacred worldview, one that dichotomizes the transcendent realm and the world, cosmic cataclysm initiated from another realm to destroy the world makes sense and is almost inevitable. However, in a secular world, where our worldview no longer dichotomizes the transcendent and this world, where we view reality through a secular lens rather than through a sacred one, we have difficulty conceptualizing world destruction from the hands of a sovereign ruler. Part of the process of secularization involves raising humanity to the sovereign level so that humans control their own destiny, and this has even spilled over into our ideas of the apocalypse. Because mainstream religion by definition has become so secularized it rarely deals with the scenario of the apocalypse, one might think it would simply go away. But the apocalyptic imagination is alive and well, because the human imagination (at least the Western imagination) must incorporate the end point in order to make sense out of time and death. So with religion's minimizing the eschaton because of the secularization of mainstream traditional religion, popular culture has co-opted what was the religious business of apocalyptic thinking. In that it provides an apocalyptic consciousness, it functions religiously and witnesses to the sacralization of a secular viewpoint. Popular movies have taken up the charge and created an alternative secular apocalyptic imagination in which the end is less threatening and can even be avoided.

The secularization of the apocalyptic consciousness in movies, like elsewhere in our popular culture, takes place in two directions: 1) evangelical apocalyptic films start with a sacred worldview and portray the apocalypse using secular media and contexts, thus secularizing the sacred; 2) secular apocalyptic films proceed from a secular worldview and substitute a secular vision of the end for the traditional religious apocalypse. That this new vision functions religiously to deal meaningfully with the problem of the end of existence results in a sacralization of the secular. In either case, we see the secularizing blurring of boundaries between the sacred and secular unfold in our end-of-time imaginations.

NOTES

1. Frank Kermode, *The Sense of an Ending: Studies in the Theory of Fiction* (London: Oxford University Press, 1967), 3–5, 17, 28. See also Ostwalt, "Hollywood and Armageddon: Apocalyptic Themes in Recent Cinematic Presentation," in Joel W. Martin and Conrad E. Ostwalt, Jr., *Screening the Sacred: Religion, Myth, and Ideology in Popular American Film* (Boulder: Westview Press, 1995), 61–62.

2. Philip Yancey, *The Jesus I Never Knew* (Grand Rapids, Mich.: Zondervan, 1995), 22.

3. See Robert K. Johnston, *Reel Spirituality: Theology and Film in Dialogue* (Grand Rapids: Baker, 2000), 31–37.

4. See Catherine Bach, "Cracking the Production Code."

5. Jeffrey H. Mahan, "Celluloid Savior: Jesus in the Movies," *Journal of Religion and Film,* 6, no. 1 (April 2002); available from http://cid.unomaha.edu/~wwwjrf/ celluloid.htm. See also Jeffrey H. Mahan, *Christianity and the Arts* 8, no. 2 (spring 2001) for another version of the article.

6. Anton Karl Kozlovic, "Superman as Christ-Figure: The American Pop Culture Movie Messiah," *Journal of Religion and Film* 6, no. 1 (April 2002); available from http://cid.unomaha.edu/~wwwjrf/superman.htm.

7. Aichele and Walsh, *Screening Scripture.*

8. Matt Crouch, interview by Jim Nelson, "God Is on Line One," *Gentlemen's Quarterly*, March 2001, 314.

9. Michael Smith, "Author LaHaye Sues *Left Behind* Film Producers," *Christianity Today,* 23 April 2001, 20.

10. Peter Lalonde, interview by Jim Nelson, "God Is on Line One," 353.

11. Jim Nelson, "God Is on Line One," 353.

12. Ibid.

13. The quotation is from Revelation 13:3, Revised Standard Version. The bracket is mine to add the context of the head wound.

14. Portions of this chapter were previously published in *The Journal of Religion and Film* and are reprinted here in edited and expanded form by permission of the editor of the journal. The full bibliographic records follow: Conrad Ostwalt, "Armageddon at the Millennial Dawn" 4, no. 1; "Religion and Popular Movies" 2, no. 3; and "Visions of the End: Secular Apocalypse in Recent Hollywood Film" 2, no. 1, all in *The Journal of Religion and Film;* available from http://cid.unomaha. edu/~wwwjrf/.

15. See Daniel Wojcik, *The End of the World as We Know It: Faith, Fatalism, and Apocalypse in America* (New York: New York University Press, 1997).

16. See Norman Cohn, *The Pursuit of the Millennium* (Oxford: Oxford University Press, 1980), 15–22; and John J. Collins, *The Apocalyptic Imagination: An Introduction to the Jewish Matrix of Christianity* (New York: Crossroad, 1987), 9.

17. See John Storey, *An Introductory Guide to Cultural Theory and Popular Culture* (Athens: The University of Georgia Press, 1993), 73–86, for a discussion of binary oppositions, particularly in Claude Lévi-Strauss's work on myth.

18. See Ostwalt, "Hollywood and Armageddon," *Screening the Sacred*.

19. Ibid.

20. Ibid.

21. The ideas on *The Matrix* were initially presented at the 1999 annual conference of the American Academy of Religion. The bodhisattva reference came from the discussion that followed the presentation of that paper.

22. The Frankenstein connection was suggested to me by Dr. Kelly L. Searsmith.

23. See Donald E. Williams, "An Oceanic Odyssey," *American Cinematographer* 76, no. 8 (August 1995): 40; Ron Magid, "The End of the World as We Know It," *American Cinematographer* 77, no. 7 (July 1996): 43–50; and Ron Magid, "Taking the Plunge on *Waterworld*," *American Cinematographer* 76, no. 12 (December 1995): 73–76.

24. See Stuart Kawans, "Films," *The Nation*, 28 August 1995, 216.

25. See Robert Cashill, "Waterworld Live," *The Business of Entertainment Technology and Design (TCI)*, April 1996, 38.

26. For a more complete discussion of *Pale Rider*, see Ostwalt, "Hollywood and Armageddon."

27. Kevin Reynolds, quoted in Williams, "An Oceanic Odyssey," 40–41.

28. See Williams, "An Oceanic Odyssey," 41, and Jose Arroyo, "*Waterworld*," *Sight and Sound*, September 1995.

29. John Calhoun, "*12 Monkeys*," *TCI*, March 1996, 35.

30. See Thomas Delapa, "Déjà vu . . . again," *Boulder Weekly*, 11 January 1996, 24.

31. For a detailed plot analysis of the movie, see Philip Strick, "*12 Monkeys*," *Sight and Sound*, April 1996, 56ff.

32. Jeffrey Beecroft, quoted in Calhoun, "*12 Monkeys*," 36.

33. See Strick, "*12 Monkeys*," 56.

34. David Morgan, "Extremities," *Sight and Sound*, January 1996, 18–20.

35. Keith Simanton, "Terry Gilliam, *La Jetée*, and the *Omega Man*," 1996 review, World Wide Web.

36. David Williams, "Worlds at War," *American Cinematographer* 77, no. 7 (July 1996): 32.

37. Caron Schwartz Ellis, "With Eyes Uplifted: Space Aliens as Sky Gods," in *Screening the Sacred*, 83–93. For aliens as an example of cinematic otherness, see Ostwalt, "Conclusion," *Screening the Sacred*, 155.

CONCLUSION:
Theological Appropriation
of Secularization:
A Cooperative Model

"Since religion is dead, religion is everywhere. . . . Religion was once an affair of the church; it is now in the streets in each man's heart. Once there were priests; now every man's a priest."

—Richard Wright, *The Outsider*[1]

For over three years now, I have enjoyed the opportunity each day to drive my daughter to and from preschool to begin and end the workday. Sometimes these short twenty-minute commutes pass with hardly a word spoken, sometimes in chatty silliness. I have fielded the types of penetrating questions that make the most hardened parent cringe, and I have helped make up nonsense rhymes and songs. These rides have become sacred time, because they are ritualized; because they take me beyond myself, my daily concerns, and my work worries; because they introduce me to another's world; and because and not least, the interaction that occurs has sharpened my awareness and consciousness more than hours of prayer or meditation. Never am I more focused than during these too few moments of the day—focused on driving safely, for one, but also focused on the surrounding environment that becomes for my daughter a source of endless curiosity and questioning.

After three years, I notice things I failed to notice before. For example, I read bumper stickers at stoplights because I never know when I might have to answer a question about one. I have learned there are developed theologies on the bumpers of automobiles ranging from apocalyptic predictions to glorification of the goddess. And I have noticed a curious "evolution" of symbols on the backs of cars that highlights the ever-shifting boundaries that merge sacred and secular. Consider the following:

Most of us have seen the familiar Christian symbol of the fish. In its most rudimentary form, it appears as two curves, meeting at one end to form a head and crossing near the opposite end to create a tail. The use of the symbol dates to early Christianity and is deeply ingrained in Christian iconography. It appears in churches, on Christmas trees, on billboards, in advertisements, and on cars. The Greek word for fish, *ichthus,* is an acronym for a Christian confession: Jesus Christ, Son of God, Savior. Early Christians could identify themselves secretly during times of persecution by initiating or completing the fish symbol in the presence of someone they suspected of sharing their faith. So the contemporary, public display of the fish symbol represents a quiet and respectful proclamation of faith, not an aggressive evangelistic tool or social commentary—simply an unobtrusive way of claiming faith. It is not surprising that a fair number of these fish symbols (at least where I live) are displayed on automobiles—some of them are plain and some have *Jesus* or the Greek letters for *ichthus* printed inside of them.

A while back, another symbol began to appear on the backs of cars that at first glance resembled the simple ichthus. However, upon closer examination, one could see that the ichthus had sprouted legs and that in the new symbol, now an amphibian, the name Jesus had been replaced by the name Darwin. The editorial comment is clear: this Darwinian amphibian is a direct response to the Christian declaration of faith through display of the fish. The secular response proposes to replace the fish with a more highly evolved creature, science, through its evolutionary representative, Darwin. The display of the Darwinian amphibian suggests that Christianity is antiquated and inferior to science and to rationalism, that a sacred worldview is to be discarded for a secular one. What at first appeared to be an attempt at clever commentary presented some interesting and disturbing questions as I began to think about the evolution of ichthus. Why would a secular-minded person want to co-opt a religious movement's symbol and openly mock the underlying commitment attached to the symbol? There was no provocation in displaying the fish—why the deliberate insult in response?

The exchange does not end with the appearance of the evolved amphibian. The next evolution in popular cultural exchange appeared just a few weeks ago, when I first spotted on the back of the car in front of me a new version of the symbol. This time, the Darwinian amphibian was being swallowed by a bigger fish that had TRUTH inscribed inside it. With this Christian response, this time provocative, the symbol co-opts not only the secular symbol (Darwinian amphibian) but also the secular philosophy behind it (survival of the fittest) to debunk the secular "truth." The irony is obvious. The secular amphibian used the Christian fish to attack Christian thought while the Christian response used secular philosophy to attack the secular amphibian.

The exchange is instructive and brings to light an attempt from both perspectives to mount a worldview/culture war that pits Christian fundamentalism against science, the sacred against the secular. The stakes are high—Truth. This public exchange also demonstrates the level of public, secular saturation of religion and religious dialogue. The evolution of the ichthus represents an ideological debate on the nature of creation and on the validity of the sacred worldview. The crux of the debate is not so much creationism versus evolutionary theory as it is about the basic worldview behind these theories: sacred versus secular.

Nevertheless, I was careful above with my choice of words. I suggested this exchange represents an attempt to mount a culture war, not the actual pitting of worldviews against one another. I believe the deeper truth found within this apparent conflict is not irreconcilable positions but rather an assimilation of one worldview into another—a melding of one into the other—a blurring of boundaries between secular and sacred, not retrenchment into clearly defined worlds. Each evolutionary step of the ichthus incorporates elements of the opposing worldview to develop its own stance: the secular amphibian incorporates the Christian fish just as the Christian carnivore assimilates the secular. The secular amphibian embodies the ichthus. Conversely, and even more telling, perhaps, if the popular adage holds, "We are what we eat," then the Christian carnivore takes into itself (sacramentally?) the secular amphibian and becomes the secular worldview. The secular is sacralized by incorporating ichthus; the sacred is secularized by eating the amphibian. We see this exchange everywhere—the process of these dissolving boundaries between sacred and secular is secularization.

LOOKING ELSEWHERE FOR SECULARIZATION

Popular culture is a rich repository for evidence of this secularization process. As I have noted throughout this book, the process takes place in two directions. What we normally consider sacred culture or institutions constantly adopt secular means to an end. They take on secular ways when convenient or advantageous. This secularization of the sacred is inherent in Western religion and marks the history of Christianity from virtually the beginning. But secular culture also participates in secularization by taking on religious functioning on many levels. When culture functions to create ideologies that grant meaning to individuals or cultures, we have secular ideologies functioning religiously, and we witness the sacralization of the secular. The two directions mark a dialogue in society, a two-way reaching out that blurs the distinctions and boundaries we sometimes like to imagine existing between the secular and the sacred. Such a dialogue of blurring is the secularization process.

I organized this book around three aspects of cultural production: space, text, and image. I chose these three because it seems to me that we see most clearly—in the spaces we construct for specific purposes, the texts we revere, and the images we view—the attempts to define certain objects as sacred, certain functions as secular, and so forth. In other words, in our culture we tend to divide space, text, and image into sacred and secular camps. I chose these three as well because they define roughly a historical development of Western ways of conveying meaning. Before texts, we had spaces, and more recently, we tend toward images, which in some ways brings us full circle to a pre-textual situation where spaces and their arrangements become supreme in conveying meaning. I hope that by looking at these three areas, my thesis that sacred and secular are in constant dialogue in society has been strengthened.

However, it should be noted that space, text, and image do not exhaust the areas of culture where one finds the secularization process. Many other areas of popular culture might be examined—popular magazines help define issues of gender in our culture;[2] television might help shape adolescent appropriations of violent attitudes;[3] art has long been allied to religious expression as well as to secular; music and, more recently, music videos seem to act in particularly powerful ways to capture the attention of adolescents and potentially shape their ideologies.[4] These and other products of culture neatly fit or are related to one of my three organizing categories: space, text, or image. However, music in some sense does not fit these categories and in some sense fits them all. While music is neither space, text, nor image, in some ways it embodies spatial, textual, and visual characteristics—the spatial arrangement of sound through rhythm and speed is reflected in music texts with notation and is often punctuated by images accompanying performance. In any event, music in our culture operates in many of the ways our other categories do and can be used to illustrate the secularization thesis. And when music becomes music video, then it definitely contains aspects of at least text and image. Music alone and music with video demonstrate not only the secularization process but also how we can construct a postmodern theology of popular culture that is large enough and open enough to allow both sacred and secular religious functioning.

We need look no further than the genre of music known as "Christian pop" or "Christian rock" to see the secularization of the sacred in full swing. Some of what passes as contemporary Christian music is hardly recognizable from "Top 40" music that plays constantly on commercial stations. The only difference arises with the lyrics, which are distinctly Christian. Some of this music has a hard edge to it and resembles rock and roll in every respect except for lyrics. From light rock to rap to punk to hard rock—these forms have been adopted by the contemporary Christian music scene. The popularization of Christian rock/pop music witnesses to a purposeful adaptation of a secular medium for the propagation of the Christian message. The strategy is to tap into youth culture and Christianize it.

The genesis of this movement in the evangelical community seems to have been motivated by the desire to give evangelical youth what they wanted (pop music) but at the same time to make sure it was ideologically in line with evangelical truths. So early contemporary Christian music appealed to a subculture of evangelical youth and could be purchased in Christian bookstores. However, by the mid-1990s, the music began to reach beyond Christian bookstores and musicians began to play in secular venues. The direction of the music changed—no longer an internal cultural form, the music was directed to secular audiences, using secular forms with Christian lyrics to become an evangelical tool. By 1995, the growing Christian music empire was moving beyond evangelical audiences and was gaining ground in the secular mainstream. The growing popularity of the movement was due, probably in large part, to popular crossover artists like Amy Grant, who performed secular songs as well as songs with Christian lyrics. With this growing popularity in the secular realm, Christian music moved from the shelves of Christian bookstores to the aisles of Wal-Mart.[5] Whether or not this music is reaching an expanded secular audience or simply reaching the evangelical market in secular venues is difficult to determine. However, it is clear that such marketing of the message marks a definite adoption of the secular medium for theological purposes.

This secularization of Christian music creates some confusion with many fans and critics of Christian music. For example, one of the most popular and successful stars of the contemporary Christian music scene,

Amy Grant, has often confused and even dismayed followers of the genre. Winner of several Grammy and Dove awards, her huge popularity among evangelicals was translated to the popular music scene by the mid-1980s, as Grant was able to move almost seamlessly between the worlds of secular pop and Christian music. That the Christian music diva could record such songs as "Baby, Baby" created suspicion among some evangelical fans. More recently, the release of her album *Behind the Eyes* has created a renewed round of confusion and doubt over the intent of her music from some evangelical circles. Even though the songs on the album deal with themes such as temptation, struggle, love, and fidelity (Christian themes if there ever were some), the lyrics are hard to identify as Christian. As a result, some religious radio stations chose not to play the album because it contained "no evangelical bent, no mention of God."[6] So while the most recognizable artist in the Christian music scene continues her crossover success, some are uncomfortable with what they consider the secularization of sacred music, or at least the secularization of a sacred music artist.

This discomfort is directed at other Christian artists as well and demonstrates that the secularization of this cultural form is perhaps proceeding more completely than those marked by space, text, or image. Perhaps it is more difficult to draw the lines with music. Some religious fans of contemporary Christian music seem to believe that some artists adopt the forms of secular culture too well in their attempts to be relevant. For example, the Christian ska group (ska has been characterized as upbeat punk rock with horns[7]) Five Iron Frenzy has seemingly crossed the line with some fans. The group is fond of playing secular venues and tends to shy away from "preaching" at their concerts. And they seem to have offended some Christian fans when they donned Star Trek outfits for one of their concerts. Some critics seem to question the band's commitment to its Christian cause because there exists little to distinguish the group from secular ska bands. Nevertheless, the group's lead singer defends their style by suggesting that some audience members are "saved" by attending their concerts rather than through preaching.[8] While disagreement remains among evangelicals concerning the appropriate limits of adopting secular culture as a vehicle for the sacred message, there seems to be unanimity that the purpose for using secular media in the first place is for propagation of the gospel. So the purposeful secularization of the sacred is meant to reach the secular audience with the sacred message.

We even see this same secularization tendency in more traditional "gospel" music formats. Record production companies are purposely pushing gospel music and artists into the secular arena to garner more mainstream audiences and venues. According to Jazzy Jordan of Verity Records, "Gospel artists are starting to resemble a lot of secular artists . . . bringing the hip-hop beats and feel of the street to gospel."[9] Pulling off such a secularizing market strategy is no easy task, as recognized by Demetrus Alexander Stewart of Atlantic Christian in the following comment for *Billboard* magazine concerning imaging of the secularized gospel music: "The mainstream side didn't want it to look too churchy and, for gospel, it couldn't look too worldly, so we were trying to strike a balance."[10] This perceived balance gives us a clue to the extent that blurring of boundaries has taken place. No longer do sacred musicians reject secular culture, nor do the fans and promoters of sacred music. Rather, extensive blurring of malleable boundaries between the sacred and secular components of our culture is not only accepted but manipulated from the sacred side and, as we shall see, also from the secular side.

Just as contemporary Christian musicians use a secular medium to communicate a sacred message, we also see secular artists whose seemingly secular music communicates religiously meaningful lyrics. That represents the sacralization of the secular in which originally secular cultural forms take on sacred or religious functions through the subject matter or presentation of the art. Examples abound: Tori Amos singing "God" or "Muhammad My Friend"; Joan Osborne's lyrics asking, "What if God Was One of Us?"; Garth Brooks singing about "unanswered prayers." These secular folk, pop, and country songs represent a small fraction of many contemporary secular songs that employ religious language, themes, or images to create a kind of secular theology through music. Religion is everywhere in popular music and videos, and it is not coming from religious bodies or from any recognizable religious community. Perhaps the most interesting pop star whose work touches upon and implicates religious themes is Madonna, whose work includes songs and videos such as "Like a Prayer" and music where she chants "Om Shanti."[11]

What can we make of this contemporary sacralization of secular music? It witnesses the extent to which our society has become religion-saturated throughout its popular culture in and through venues that are distinct from and separate from religious institutions and official religious bodies. Does this mean that religion, far from losing power through secularization, might actually be more potent in our culture than ever, albeit without the official backing of institutions? The possibility exists that religion dissipated throughout the culture, arising authentically in the hands and creations of representatives who are removed from the restrictions of orthodoxy, can become a religion that empowers and functions to grant meaning to a more diverse population than can official religious bodies alone.[12]

If this in fact is happening, is there something about music that inspires a more powerful religious response than other cultural forms? We can at least recognize, as does the work of Andy Bennett, that popular music operates collectively in political and social ways.[13] Music can be a powerful means to express theology or ideologies of any sort and is thus an important vehicle for the secularization of popular culture and religion. Consider the important work of James C. Scott in *Domination and the Arts of Resistance: Hidden Transcripts*[14] and of theomusicologist Jon Michael Spencer in *Blues and Evil*.[15]

Scott argues that the relationship between dominant and subordinate groups in society is often marked by public and hidden transcripts. Because of their subordinate status, marginalized groups are not free to publicly communicate some messages. Therefore, these groups create hidden transcripts, messages that can be understood within the group but that are hidden from the dominant group. In this way, the subordinate group can communicate rebellious or factious messages.[16] Such hidden transcripts can function to bolster morale or create group cohesion, and they constitute important ideologies of groups. It is often within the hidden transcripts of a group that one finds truth. In this way, African American religious traditions could operate in the South to make religion meaningful even in the context of slavery and Jim Crow. Therefore, gospel music and other forms of African American hidden transcripts gave voice within the African American community to a meaningful version of Christianity that promised social reversal while critiquing white Christianity and society.

Spencer's work on blues music recalls this social dynamic as he examines some of the stereotypes surrounding blues music. He contends that blues music contains an essentially religious character even though it is often characterized as the devil's music. This misinterpretation of the genre results when critics from outside the tradition misread the hidden transcripts contained within the music. Spencer goes on to construct mythologies of the blues based on African traditions and Christianity; theologies of the blues, which allow blues music to function religiously in the African American community while critiquing the traditional church; and theodicies of the blues that function religiously in addressing oppression of African Americans. In these theodicies, Spencer suggests that code in blues lyrics equates white oppressors with evil and that such music establishes a rebellious theodicy. Thus, embedded within blues music as an African American cultural product are a mythology, theology, and theodicy (theological categories) that authenticate African traditions while critiquing white religion and society.[17] In this case, it is blues music, generally considered secular, that represents an authentic theological stance within the black community—not the black church and certainly not the white. Where the institution fails, the secular culture functions religiously and the secular is sacralized and becomes more powerful than sacred institutions in functioning religiously.

Jon Michael Spencer spoke at a conference in 1996 where he eloquently elaborated on this point.[18] In making the case for theo-musicology, Spencer suggested that secular music contains layers of theological meaning. He noted that popular music has contributed to American spirituality and has affected behavior and that it is perhaps better suited for these purposes than sacred music. Whereas sacred music is defined by, bounded by, and limited by doctrine and dogma, secular music has no such limitations. Thus, according to Spencer, it is in secular music that we learn what we really believe, and it is through our response to secular music that we can fashion an ethic that is meaningful and relevant. Secular music, therefore, provides a more reliable measure of authentic belief, relevant ethics, and real commitment than sacred music, which can be defined by standards of belief that are no longer owned by those in the tradition.

Scott's thesis and Spencer's enlightened work on blues demonstrate the power music can claim in the religious sphere and in constructing values and ethics that we live by and respond to. That music claims this power to create all kinds of ideologies and value systems has been well documented in the literature, and we find sociologists, theologians, and even pediatricians writing about the powerful effect music can have on society and individuals. The effectiveness of music to create and strengthen ideologies and behaviors seems to be multiplied when music is coupled with image to produce the very popular cultural form, the music video.[19] Music videos are short, visually rich, intense, loaded with images of violence and sexuality, and devoured by young people in such a way that they affect values and attitudes toward gender, sexuality, and violence.[20] With this in mind, we need to be cognizant of the power music and music videos exert in shaping the attitudes of young people, for example, because these forms function in a most meaningful way— by acting religiously, they shape ideological covenants.

Much of the work on music and music videos centers on the extent to which they help shape youth attitudes, particularly toward sexuality and violence. The concern comes from the shared assessment that the values being transmitted through popular music and videos are harmful.

As early as the 1930s we see popular music playing a significant role in portraying women, using a complex combination of images ranging from innocent sweetheart to sexual vixen.[21] Many scholars now agree that contemporary popular music plays a significant role, perhaps even a leadership role, in constructing and deconstructing gender images in the culture.[22] The problem arises because it seems the predominant images conveyed in popular music lean toward objectifying women as sexual objects and often portray women as victims of sexual violence. Much of the literature suggests that music videos promote stereotypes about sexuality and dramatize sexual relationships through a model of antagonistic relationships between men and women that cast women in submissive roles.[23] The disturbing implication is that popular music and music videos perpetuate certain myths of sexuality and gender relationships that youth incorporate uncritically from the culture.

Sut Jhally has created an important and provocative video that supports the above research suggestions that music videos create and support cultural stories of sexuality. Jhally challenges us to think critically about the impact of those stories on the consumers of music videos (mainly young people). Jhally's videos, *Dreamworlds* and the updated *Dreamworlds II*, argue with narration that accompanies video and music clips that music videos create cultural stories about sexuality based on male "adolescent fantasy." These stories are potentially harmful to women because of objectification within a dream world of sexual fantasy.[24] Jhally's videos argue persuasively that the dream world of music video portrays women from a male perspective that is absorbed into youth culture. The women in these videos play a "decorative role," exposing their bodies through undressing, bathing, and stripping. These women are schoolgirls, teachers, and prostitutes, and the dominant behavior they exhibit is nymphomania. The implication is that all women, schoolgirls as well as prostitutes, exhibit strong, aggressive sexual desire. In the music video dream world, these women make themselves available to men through easy, casual sexual encounters, devoid of any meaningful relationship.

The most disturbing aspect of this male dream world, according to Jhally, takes this "decorative role" to its logical conclusion. If videos support a cultural story that puts women's bodies on display for males, then women's bodies become nothing more than objects; women in the videos "lose subjectivity" and, thus, their humanity. In the dream world, men do not have to respect women or sexual boundaries because women have no subjective status. This, according to Jhally, leads to attitudes that legitimize and normalize sexual violation of women. Jhally underscores this warning by ending the video with a clip of a gang rape from the movie *The Accused,* while interspersing clips from music videos and by posting statistics that suggest that adolescent attitudes demonstrate a disturbing acceptance of sexual violence. If Jhally is right and music videos create a powerful cultural story that promotes an ethos of easy sex with women as objects, then we see this cultural form playing a significant religious role by functioning to create and grant validity to moral and ethical standards that stand in contradiction to many other religious teachings on sexual morality and the value of persons and bodies. These secular stories function as mythic truth and thus sacralize the secular.

Music and the music video provide powerful avenues for teaching youth through their culture. Thus, Jhally's film is disturbing and illustrates the negative power of religious functioning. However, music and music videos do not have to solely promote negative values any more than full-length films only promote violence and sexuality. Music can also function religiously in positive ways, making meaningful transcendence of the mundane possible and enlightening. Music can function as an avenue to enlightened and heightened living, not simply degraded living. There are no doubt many positive examples of popular music and popular music videos, but a uniquely American form of popular music, jazz, captures the essence of the sacralizing possibility of secular music.

If Ferdinand "Jelly Roll" Morton did not give birth to jazz music according to his own claims, then he at least was midwife to the movement. It is probably more accurate to consider him one of the earliest important composers of jazz music in the early twentieth century.[25] It was in jazz that Jelly Roll located the power of truth and a type of transcendent immortality. As a jazz composer, Jelly Roll sometimes found himself defining jazz differently than those jazz musicians who found the power of jazz in improvisation, the original creation of music in unscripted fashion. But Jelly Roll did not reject improvisation—he simply jealously guarded his composition and limited improvisational freedom to a select few musicians.[26] Thus, we find in Jelly Roll a type of elitism of talent, but for those talented individuals, himself and a handful of musicians, finding power in the creative process was a reality. For a few enlightened and blessed individuals, jazz could become a means to achieve a heightened relation to creativity and could lead to a type of transcendent approach to truth.

This brings to mind the philosophy of transcendentalism of Emerson and Thoreau. For the transcendentalists, Emerson especially, only those who achieved a heightened awareness, communicated through metaphors of "seeing" could claim "imagination, . . . a very high sort of seeing," and could become poets of "true naming."[27] Emerson's poetic awareness, Thoreau's walking meditation, Jelly Roll's meditative improvisation all suggest that transcendence is available to those who can imagine the poetry or the melody, and that truth is available through the creative relationship of artist and the divine. Through music, secular music as well as sacred, we hear the possibility of transcendence through creativity— music is poetry, music is myth, music is vibration that resonates not only physically but at the deepest level of our consciousness—as such, music functions religiously as an avenue to truth. Music allows us to participate in the creative moment, the transcendent moment, and can become an important transmitter of cultural truths and power, of Scott's "hidden transcripts," of Spencer's "mythologies," of Jhally's "cultural stories," of gospel music's secular gospel, of Jelly Roll's creative transcendence. As such, we see music and its accompanying images and trappings functioning in the ongoing secularizing process, both secularizing sacred music and sacralizing secular tunes, blurring and bending the boundaries between sacred and secular.

THE POSTMODERN SECULARIZATION OF RELIGION: MEDITATIVE IMPROVISATION

We know that religious diversity in America is increasing;[28] people are redefining God, as Wade Clark Roof reminds us, in more personal and individualistic ways;[29] Robert Wuthnow points out that contemporary Americans feel comfortable searching for religious meaning in extra-ecclesiastical activities and institutions;[30] we see our popular culture influencing religion in very public ways. Does all this suggest, as some have argued, that religion in our culture, or at least traditional religious institutions, is falling by the wayside, that it will lose power over culture or over individual lives, that secularization will result in the obliteration of religion as a major part of American culture? Far from it. Leigh Eric Schmidt has eloquently described the process of secularization in *Consumer Rites: The Buying and Selling of American Holidays*. Schmidt recalls Reinhold Niebuhr's sacred-secular "paradox" to suggest that we witness in our culture "a dance of the sacred and the secular, sometimes graceful, sometimes awkward."[31] Secularization is not warfare where one side will acquiesce; rather, it is Schmidt's dance, with partners in relation, touching and separate, flowing and faltering, self-conscious and confident, seducing and holding at arm's length. Secularization, as dance, flows into dissolving and bending boundaries as sacred and secular exist in relation to one another.

So we want to see secularization not through a paradigm of antagonism but through a model of relational tension in which one cannot exist without the other and each mutually props up the other. Secularization describes a situation of codependence. The antagonistic model of secularization is a postmodern attempt to explain a modern challenge to a Christian worldview. In its postmodernness, secularization theory has tended to deconstruct truth claims and ideologies and is dependent on such deconstruction to explain reality. Deconstruction itself suggests antagonism between authority structures in society, so religion as authority structure has come under attack as part of the larger postmodern challenge to authority. Thus, postmodernism has attempted to describe the modern scientific deconstruction of Christianity as secularization but has failed to demonstrate that such deconstruction is actually happening.

Nevertheless, the antagonistic, deconstructing model, which reached its peak in postmodern critique but maintains its roots in modernism's rationalism, is beginning to soften. We can reconstruct the evolution of sacred-secular codependence by looking at the concept of "binary opposition"[32] as fundamental in reality construction. If we can say that premodern binary opposition was defined by a God-human dichotomy, the modern opposition became sacred-secular, and the postmodern negates the sacred from the dichotomy entirely with the ascendancy of the secular. So with postmodernism's deconstruction of the sacred, binary opposition is defined solely in secular terms, as in human-human, human-nature, human-machine, or the like. However, as John McClure has argued, we may now find ourselves in a "post-secular culture," a post-postmodernism if you will, where philosophical, theological, and popular voices alike "refuse to silence" either sacred or secular voices but draw from each in nondualistic ways.[33] McClure points out that representatives of the oppositional model such as Edward Said recognize a return to religion in postmodern culture but decry it as regressive. McClure then reviews other secular philosophers such as Michel Foucault, Jürgen Habermas, and Jacques Derrida, who maintain more openness to religious worldviews. What we see in McClure's work is the possibility of religious meaning in a secular world that can be free from dogmatism and be embedded in popular cultural forms.[34] Thus, our postmodern binary oppositions become more cooperative binary relations.

What we have then is a more cooperative view of the sacred-secular continuum that replaces the oppositional model, that moves beyond acceptance of a sacred-secular dichotomy revealed by modern rationalism, and that unveils the long partnership that has characterized the relation between sacred and secular since before the rise of modern worldviews. This model of partnership holds that sacred and secular are not dichotomous in Western culture but dialogic in constant relation. The secularization/sacralization process as described in this book predates modernity, the Enlightenment, and the rise of modern science. The partnership is as old as notions of transcendence, because it is the birth of the idea of the transcendent, something beyond self, that gives rise to the search for meaning beyond self, an objective rather than subjective truth. This objectification battles the existential horror of imagining nothing beyond the self, existential aloneness. Once truth is objectified, the sacred and the secular become the partnered repositories of truth tucked away in transcendental as well as in this-worldly reality. Both realms become external and objective places for truth, which is external to the self and to subjective reality, to reside.

What postmodernism tries to do is to resubjectivize truth by undermining truth claim systems—Christianity, capitalism, Marxism, Americanism, as examples. In this sense, postmodern deconstruction can be seen as a corrective to objectification. This is where classical secularization theory has risen to supremacy in the effort to undermine the idea of the sacred as a way of deconstructing the idea of ultimate truth. However, secularization theory does not undermine the idea of ultimate truth but merely replaces the sacred with the secular as the repository of such truth. Classical secularization theory, based on oppositional models, simply replaces one kind of objective truth with another, and this postmodern approach to resubjectivize truth fails. What we have instead are sacred/secular, other/this, beyond/here, transcendent/immanent tandem polarities of externalized truth claims that represent in different ways the human need to objectify truth. We see this even in the postmodern task of undermining truth claims, because if postmodernism refuses to adopt an ethic or morality and depends on subjective appropriation of principles, we face the prospects of unchallenged evil, injustice, slavery, and other atrocities that arise throughout human history.[35] And postmodernism ultimately fails in that it either replaces one set of truth claims for another or, as Robert Royal in his quotation of G. K. Chesterton points out, the process of undermining a truth claim only solidifies that claim, pushing it to unprecedented dogmatism.[36] Thus, postmodernism either objectifies itself or that which it hopes to undermine, undercutting the notion of subjectivity, undermining the attempt to undermine, imploding, or shall we say, deconstructing itself.

So rather than seeing sacred and secular as oppositional whereby one must capitulate to the other, it is more helpful to see sacred and secular worldviews on a continuum along which we attempt to define "the good, the true, and the beautiful"[37] in commonly held value structures including religion, popular culture, literature, music, and community. Be it categorized as secular or conceived as sacred, the compartmentalization of culture matters less than legitimation of value for a group, either formally or informally, conceived within a common cultural context. So postmodernism brings not the end of religion, not even the end of religious institutions. But it can lead to a secularization of religion wherein the sacred and secular exist in dialogical, reciprocal, and cooperative relationships.

We can see this in the United States where there exists less separation of sacred and secular values than there is separation of the sources of authority for those values. While sacred worldviews may differ from secularly conceived reality structures in terms of their authoritative ground, two supposedly opposed worldviews may in fact espouse similar value systems because they exist in cooperative, not oppositional, relationship, especially in the popular culture. Likewise, values from sacred and secular realms are shared in America in social context because the sources of authority for values nurture one another and support one another, defined as they are in relation to one another. So we can have civil religious dialogue that falls in line with religious institutions because of common cultural grounding even though American civil and governmental institutions and religious institutions maintain a formal wall of separation between them. This wall does not separate sacred and secular values, only institutional sponsorship.

The nonestablishment clause of the First Amendment to the U.S. Constitution maintains secular, political neutrality (and thus secular independence) toward sacred matters, while the freedom of worship clause seeks religious independence from secular powers. And in this separation we hold sacrosanct, the real cooperative relationship emerges—both religion and government are independently defined but inextricably bound: one's freedom is defined through relation to the other. If no one religion is established, then all or none are valid harbingers of truth while secular philosophy guides the process. If U.S. citizens are free to choose or not choose, then secular powers validate all or none. The relationship between religion and the secular in the United States is not separate if by separate one means oppositional. Quite the contrary, they are separate in their reciprocity, which defines a broadly diverse religious landscape that is closely connected to and dependent on secular life.

The pluralist experiment in the United States guarantees that no one truth position can claim authoritative ascendancy: thus, the legitimacy of all is established and upheld by secular authority, and the pluralistic religious situation legitimizes the philosophical ideological base that allows it. In other words, the American religious-political experiment demands, and at the same time depends on, a vital religious pluralism. A vital religious pluralism in turn depends on recognition of varieties of religious truth claims and at least implicitly encourages and supports infidelity toward denominationalism and dogmatism. This infidelity is what we see in contemporary America—appropriate and expected infidelity toward dogmatic formulation, not toward religion itself. This infidelity toward institutionalized doctrine and ritual has been misconstrued as secularization that leads to the demise of religion. While secularization in America rightly might lead to the demise of institutional dogmatism, it does not spell the end of religion; in fact, it gives us a more vital and multifarious religious landscape than would exist without the secular mandate. Infidelity to institutionalized religion does not equate with illegitimacy—one can be devoted to truth while not devoted to any particular truth claim. So the reciprocal, cooperative relationship that exists between secular worldviews and sacred realities can breed a cooperative quest for "the good, the true, and the beautiful"[38] when this transcendental journey beyond self can be directed toward the world as easily as toward the heavens.

If such a quest toward meaning is to lead to healing rather than to disruption, to reconciliation rather than to demonizing, it must be predicated upon the recognition that religious truth is larger than any dogmatism, larger than any institution, and can be glimpsed by embracing the sacred-secular dance, by remaining open to truth where and when it arises, by "departing the text"[39] with mindful awareness of truths rather than Truth. Such a quest must be meditative in intent and open to surprise at any moment. Such an approach requires improvisation rather than enslavement to notation and mindful awareness rather than mindless faith. Meditative improvisation allows us to glimpse truth in the midst of this sacred-secular partnership.

FINAL WORDS

Secularization paradigms are usually based on the sacred-secular dichotomization, which in turn arose out of Western dualism and is heightened by modernism as historicism and empiricism rose to primacy through science. In many manifestations of this dualism, religion takes a reactionary stance toward the secular while the secular remains suspicious toward religion. Perhaps postmodernism, which in its most trenchant forms reinforces the secular–sacred antagonism, will lead us beyond the postmodern disenchantment with the sacred to a place where sacred and secular are not oppositional but rather integrated and infused with one another. This perspective must recognize and maintain healthy and legitimate theological tension between the·two, for any merger carries risk. The danger of sacralizing the secular is that it can occur without moral or ethical grounding and can become relativistic to the extent of meaninglessness.[40] The risk of the secularization of the sacred is functional. If the sacred adopts secular functions while refusing to revise its theological orientation, then it runs the risk of delegitimizing that particular theological perspective (the example is the church that becomes so identified with secular culture that it loses its prophetic voice in society).[41]

Risks aside, if the contemporary church can accept a cooperative model for secularization and embrace the world, its travails and its beauties, perhaps then the world can embrace religion, its truths and its ecstasies. Herein lies grace: when reconciliation between the world and religion, between the secular and the sacred, occurs, then so, in the words of Andrew Johnson, "the lion and the lamb shall lie down together."[42]

NOTES

1. Richard Wright, *The Outsider* (New York: Harper & Row, 1953), 359. I first ran across this quote in Lama Surya Das, *Awakening to the Sacred: Creating a Spiritual Life from Scratch* (New York: Broadway Books, 1999), 323.

2. See Linda Kalof, "Stereotyped Evaluative Judgments and Female Attractiveness," *Gender Issues* 17, no. 2 (spring 1999): 68–82.

3. See Michael Rich, Elizabeth R. Woods, Elizabeth Goodman, S. Jean Emans, and Robert H. DuRant, "Aggressors or Victims: Gender and Race in Music Video Violence," *Pediatrics* 101, no. 4 (April 1998): 669–74.

4. See Rich et al., "Aggressors or Victims," 670.

5. See Steve Rabey, "Pop Goes the Gospel: Contemporary Christian Music Secures an Unprecedented Secular Market Push," *Christianity Today*, 15 May 1995, 55.

6. William D. Romanowski, "Where's the Gospel? Amy Grant's Latest Album Has Thrown the Contemporary Christian Music Industry into a First-Rate Identity Crisis," *Christianity Today*, 8 December 1997, 44–45.

7. Ken Steinken, "Where No Ministry Has Gone Before: To Be More Effective Ministers, Five Iron Frenzy Resists the Packaging of Christian Rock Bands," *Christianity Today*, 24 May 1999, 74–75.

8. Ibid.

9. Jazzy Jordan, interview by L. C., in "Going Mainstream," *Billboard*, 5 August 2000, 46–48.

10. Demetrus Alexander-Stewart, interview by L. C., in "Going Mainstream," *Billboard*, 5 August 2000, 46–48.

11. See Das, *Awakening to the Sacred*, 308–9, for the spiritual significance of Madonna's chanting.

12. Amanda Porterfield raises this question in the introduction to *The Transformation of American Religion: The Story of a Late Twentieth-Century Awakening* (Oxford: Oxford University Press, 2001).

13. Andy Bennett, *Cultures of Popular Music* (Buckingham: Open University Press, 2001), 1.

14. James C. Scott, *Domination and the Arts of Resistance: Hidden Transcripts* (New Haven: Yale University Press, 1990).

15. Jon Michael Spencer, *Blues and Evil* (Knoxville: University of Tennessee Press, 1993).

16. Scott, *Domination and the Arts of Resistance*.

17. This paragraph represents my understanding of Spencer's book, *Blues and Evil*.

18. Jon Michael Spencer (paper presented at the American Academy of Religion, New Orleans, November 1996).

19. See Rich et al., "Aggressors or Victims."

20. See ibid; and Linda Kalof, "The Effects of Gender and Music Video Imagery on Sexual Attitudes," *The Journal of Social Psychology* 139, no. 3 (1999): 378–85.

21. See T. E. Scheurer, "Goddesses and Golddiggers: Images of Women in Popular Music of the 1930s," *Journal of Popular Culture* 24, no. 1 (summer 1990): 23–38.

22. See Susan McClary, "Women and Music on the Verge of the New Millennium," *Signs: Journal of Women in Culture and Society* 25, no. 4 (summer 2000): 1283–86. McClary suggests that music might "foreshadow" developments and issues that occur in other cultural forms (1285). See also Gayle Wald, "Just a Girl? Rock Music, Feminism, and the Cultural Construction of Female Youth," *Signs: Journal of Women in Culture and Society* 23, no. 3 (spring 1998): 585–610; Kalof, "The Effects of Gender and Music Video Imagery"; and Rich et al., "Aggressors or Victims."

23. See Rich et al., "Aggressors or Victims"; and Kalof, "The Effects of Gender and Music Video Imagery."

24. For this and other references to the Jhally video, see *Dreamworlds II: Desire, Sex, and Power in Music Video*, written, edited, and narrated by Sut Jhally (Media Education Foundation, 1995).

25. Alan Lomax, *Mr. Jelly Roll Morton: The Fortunes of Jelly Roll Morton, New Orleans Creole and "Inventor of Jazz"* (New York: Grosset & Dunlap, 1950), 68.

26. Ibid.

27. Ralph Waldo Emerson, "The Poet," *Essays* (1841; Cambridge: Riverside Press, 1903), 3:26.

28. See Susan Mitchell, *American Attitudes: Who Thinks What about the Issues That Shape Our Lives*, 2d ed. (Ithaca, N.Y.: New Strategist Publications, 1998); and 3d ed. (2000).

29. Wade Clark Roof, quoted in Karin Evans, "Journeys of the Spirit," *Health*, April 2001, 123.

30. Robert Wuthnow, quoted in Evans, "Journeys of the Spirit," 123, 178.

31. Leigh Eric Schmidt, *Consumer Rites: The Buying and Selling of American*

Holidays (Princeton: Princeton University Press, 1995), 14. For the Niebuhr reference, see Reinhold Niebuhr, *Pious and Secular America* (New York: Scribner's, 1958).

32. See John Storey, *An Introductory Guide to Cultural Theory and Popular Culture,* 2d ed. (Athens: University of Georgia Press, 1998), 78–81, for a discussion of binary oppositions, particularly in the work of Claude Lévi-Strauss.

33. John A. McClure, "Post-Secular Culture: The Return of Religion in Contemporary Theory and Literature," *CrossCurrents* 47 (fall 1997): 340.

34. See McClure, "Post-Secular Culture," 334–41.

35. See Robert Royal, "Christian Humanism in a Postmodern Age," *The New Religious Humanists: A Reader,* ed. Gregory Wolfe (New York: Free Press, 1997), 94–95.

36. See Royal, "Christian Humanism in a Postmodern Age," 103. Royal quotes G. K. Chesterton from *Heretics* (New York: John Lane Co., 1909, 1905), 304–5.

37. Royal, "Christian Humanism," 92.

38. Ibid.

39. Thank you to my daughter and her book *Goodnight Opus* by Berkeley Breathed (Boston: Little, Brown, 1993) for giving me this wonderful phrase.

40. This is the danger suggested by Royal, "Christian Humanism." See also Sam Keen, *To a Dancing God* (New York: Harper & Row, 1970), on the danger of losing a theistic perspective.

41. See Keen, *To a Dancing God.*

42. From *The Papers of Andrew Johnson,* ed. L. P. Graf and R. W. Haskins (Knoxville: 1970), 2:176–77, as quoted in Winthrop S. Hudson, *Religion in America,* 4th ed. (New York: Macmillan, 1987), 149. See Dixon Wector, *The Saga of American Society* (New York, 1937), 100; and Donald G. Mathews, *Religion in the Old South* (Chicago: University of Chicago Press, 1977).

WORKS CITED

Adams, E .M. *Religion and Cultural Freedom*. Philadelphia: Temple University Press, 1993.

Aichele, George, and Richard Walsh, eds. *Screening Scripture: Intertextual Connections between Scripture and Film*. Harrisburg, Pa.: Trinity Press International, 2002.

Albanese, Catherine. *America: Religions and Religion*. 3d ed. Belmont, Calif.: Wadsworth Publishing Co., 1999.

Arnold, Edwin T. "An Interview with Lee Smith," *Appalachian Journal* 11 (spring 1984): 240–54.

Arroyo, Jose. "*Waterworld*." *Sight and Sound* 5, no. 9 (September 1995).

Associated Press. "Get Used to It." *Reader's Digest*, November 1999, 155–56.

Bach, Alice. "Cracking the Production Code: Watching Biblical Scholars Read Films." *Currents in Research: Biblical Studies* 7 (1999): 11–34.

Bandera, Cesareo. *The Sacred Game: The Role of the Sacred in the Genesis of Modern Literary Fiction*. University Park: Pennsylvania State University Press, 1994.

Baudrillard, Jean. *Simulations*. New York: Semiotext(e), 1983.

Beattie, Melody. *Codependent No More*. San Francisco: Harper & Hazelton, 1987.

Bell, Daniel. "The Return of the Sacred? The Argument on the Future of Religion." *British Journal of Sociology* 28 (December 1977): 419–49.

Bennett, Andy. *Cultures of Popular Music*. Buckingham, U.K.: Open University Press, 2001.

Bennett, Tanya Long. "The Protean Ivy in Lee Smith's *Fair and Tender Ladies*." *Southern Literary Journal* 30, no. 2 (spring 1998): 76–95.

Benson, Dennis. *Electric Evangelism*. Nashville: Abingdon Press, 1973.

Berger, Peter L. "Religion in Post-Protestant America." *Commentary* 85, no. 5 (May 1986): 41–46.

————. "Secularism in Retreat." *The National Interest* (winter 1996/97): 3–12.

————. *The Sacred Canopy: Elements of a Sociological Theory of Religion*. Garden City, N.Y.: Doubleday, 1967.

Blanchard, Kenneth H., Patricia Zigarmi, and Drea Zigarmi. *Leadership and the One-Minute Manager: Increasing Effectiveness through Situational Leadership*. New York: William Morrow, 1985.

Bliss, Michael. *The Word Made Flesh: Catholicism and Conflict in the Films of Martin Scorsese*. Lanham, Md.: Scarecrow Press, 1995.

Bloom, Harold, ed. *Amy Tan*. Philadelphia: Chelsea House, 2000.

Blossom, Jay. "'An Ideal Summer Resort for Christian Families': Wholesome Entertainment in Early-20th-Century Winona Lake." Paper presented at the annual meeting of the American Academy of Religion, Boston, November 1999.

Board, Stephen. "Moving the World with Magazines: A Survey of Evangelical Periodicals." In Quentin J. Schultze, ed., *American Evangelicals and the Mass Media: Perspectives on the Relationship between American Evangelicals and the Mass Media*. Grand Rapids, Mich.: Zondervan, 1990.

Boyer, Paul. *When Time Shall Be No More: Prophecy Belief in Modern American Culture*. Cambridge: Cambridge University Press, 1992.

Breathed, Berkeley. *Goodnight Opus*. Boston: Little Brown, 1993.

Bremer, Thomas S. "From Pilgrims' Sacred Topography to Tourists' Sacred Landscape: A Brief Tour of Western Religious Travel." Paper presented at the annual meeting of the American Academy of Religion, Boston, November 1999.

Brooks, Cleanth. *Community, Religion and Literature*. Columbia: University of Missouri Press, 1995.

Brown, W. Dale. *Of Fiction and Faith: Twelve American Writers Talk about Their Vision and Work*. Grand Rapids, Mich.: Eerdmans, 1997.

Bruce, Steven, ed. *Religion and Modernization: Sociologists and Historians Debate the Secularization Thesis*. Oxford: Clarendon Press, 1992.

Burton, Thomas. *Serpent-Handling Believers*. Knoxville: University of Tennessee Press, 1993.

Butler, Jon. *Awash in a Sea of Faith*. Cambridge: Harvard University Press, 1990.

Byrd, Linda J. "The Reclamation of the Feminine Divine: 'Walking in My Body Like a Queen' in Lee Smith's *Fair and Tender Ladies*." In *He Said, She Says: A RSVP to the Male Text*. Edited by Mica Howe and Sarah Appleton Aguiar. London: Fairleigh Dickinson University Press, 2001.

Cahill, Thomas. *The Gifts of the Jews: How a Tribe of Desert Nomads Changed the Way Everyone Thinks and Feels*. New York: Doubleday, 1998.

Calhoun, John. "12 Monkeys." *The Business of Entertainment Technology and Design* (March 1996): 34–37.

Campbell, Joseph. *Reflections on the Art of Living: A Joseph Campbell Companion*. Edited by Diane K. Olson. New York: HarperCollins, 1991.

Carey, Phyllis, ed. *Wagering on Transcendence: The Search for Meaning in Literature*. Kansas City: Sheed & Ward, 1997.

Carter, Stephen L. *The Culture of Disbelief: How American Law and Politics Trivialize Religious Devotion*. New York: Basic Books, 1993.

Cashill, Robert. "Waterworld Live." *The Business of Entertainment Technology and Design* (April 1996): 38–41.

Chadwick, Owen. *The Secularization of the European Mind in the Nineteenth Century.* Cambridge: Cambridge University Press, 1975.

Chappell, Fred. "Family Time." *The Southern Review* 28 (October 1992): 937–43.

Chaves, Mark. "Secularization as Declining Religious Authority." *Social Forces* 72, no. 3, 749–74.

Chen, Victoria. "Chinese American Women, Language, and Moving Subjectivity." In Harold Bloom, ed., *Amy Tan.* Philadelphia, Chelsea House, 2000.

Chesterton, G. K. *Heretics.* New York: John Lane, 1905, 1909.

Cohn, Norman. *The Pursuit of the Millennium.* Oxford: Oxford University Press, 1980.

Collins, John J. *The Apocalyptic Imagination: An Introduction to the Jewish Matrix of Christianity.* New York: Crossroad, 1987.

Cox, Harvey. *The Secular City: Secularization and Urbanization in Theological Perspective.* New York: Macmillan, 1966.

Crouch, Matt. Interview by Jim Nelson. "God Is on Line One." *Gentlemen's Quarterly,* March 2001, 310–15, 352–53.

Darby, William. *Necessary American Fictions: Popular Literature of the 1950s.* Bowling Green, Ohio: Bowling Green University Press, 1987.

Delapa, Thomas. "Deja vu . . . again," *Boulder Weekly,* 11 January 1996, 24.

Demerath, N. J. III. "Varieties of Sacred Experience." *Journal for the Scientific Study of Religion* 39, no. 1 (March 2000): 1–11.

Dorgan, Howard. *The Airwaves of Zion: Radio and Religion in Appalachia.* Knoxville: University of Tennessee Press, 1993.

———. *Giving Glory to God in Appalachia: Worship Practices of Six Baptist Subdenominations.* Knoxville: University of Tennessee Press, 1987.

———. *The Old Regular Baptists of Central Appalachia.* Knoxville: University of Tennessee Press, 1989.

Doty, William G. *Contemporary New Testament Interpretation.* Englewood Cliffs, N.J.: Prentice Hall, 1972.

Dowling, Claudia Glenn. "A Light in the Desert." *Life,* June 1996, 66–72.

Drane, James. *The Possibility of God: A Reconsideration of Religion in a Technological Society.* Towota, N.J.: Littlefield, Adams, & Co., 1976.

Dvorak, Angeline Godwin. "Cooking as Mission and Ministry in Southern Culture: The Nurturers of Clyde Edgerton's *Walking Across Egypt,* Fannie Flagg's *Fried Green Tomatoes at the Whistle Stop Café,* and Anne Tyler's *Dinner at the Homesick Restaurant.*" *Southern Quarterly* 30, nos. 2–3 (winter-spring 1992): 90–98.

Edgerton, Clyde. *Killer Diller.* Chapel Hill, N.C.: Algonquin Press, 1991.

———. *Raney.* New York: Ballantine, 1985.

———. *Walking Across Egypt.* Chapel Hill, N.C.: Algonquin Press, 1987.

Eliade, Mircea. *The Sacred and the Profane: The Nature of Religion.* Translated by Willard R. Trask. New York: Harcourt Brace Jovanovich, 1959.

Eliot, T. S. "Religion and Literature." In *Selected Essays.* New York: Harcourt Brace Jovanovich, 1932. Repr. in G. B. Tennyson and Edward E. Ericson Jr., eds., *Religion and Modern Literature: Essays in Theory and Criticism,* 21–30. Grand Rapids, Mich.: Eerdmans, 1975.

Ellis, Caron Schwartz. "With Eyes Uplifted: Space Aliens as Sky Gods." In Joel W. Martin and Conrad E. Ostwalt Jr., eds., *Screening the Sacred: Religion, Myth, and Ideology in Popular American Film.* Boulder: Westview, 1995.

Emerson, Ralph Waldo. "The Poet." In *Essays*, 14. 1841. Cambridge: Riverside Press, 1903.

Evans, Karin. "Journeys of the Spirit." *Health*, April 2001, 118–23, 178–79.

Finke, Roger. "An Unsecular America." In Steve Bruce, ed., *Religion and Modernization: Sociologists and Historians Debate the Secularization Thesis*. Oxford: Clarendon Press, 1992.

Finke, Roger, and Rodney Stark, *The Churching of America, 1776–1990: Winners and Losers in our Religious Economy*. New Brunswick, N.J.: Rutgers University Press, 1992.

Foster, Hal, ed. *The Anti-Aesthetic: Essays on Postmodern Culture*. Port Townsend, Wash.: Bay Press, 1983.

Fowler, Robert Booth. *Unconventional Partners: Religion and Liberal Culture in the United States*. Grand Rapids, Mich.: Eerdmans, 1989.

Fox, Matthew. *Religion U.S.A.: Religion and Culture by Way of* TIME *Magazine*. Dubuque, Iowa: Listening Press, 1971.

Freud, Sigmund. *The Future of an Illusion*. Edited and translated James Strachey. New York: Norton, 1961.

Gabriel, Trip. "MTV-Inspired Images, but the Message for Children Is a Moral One." *New York Times*, 16 April 1995, 14.

Galloway, Paul. "Media Are Poor Substitute for the Family." *Chicago Tribune*. Repr. in *Charlotte Observer*, 3 June 1996, 9A.

Gallup, George, and Jim Castelli, *The People's Religion: American Faith in the '90s*. New York: MacMillan, 1989.

Garfield, Ken. "Nontraditional Church Appealing to Many." *Charlotte Observer*, 24 May 1993.

Gaustad, Edwin S., Darline Miller, and G. Allsion Stokes. "Religion in America." *American Quarterly* 31, no. 3 (1979): 250.

Geertz, Clifford. *The Interpretation of Cultures*. New York: Basic Books, 1973.

Gilkey, Langdon. *Naming the Whirlwind: The Renewal of God Language*. Indianapolis: Bobbs-Merrill, 1969.

———. *Society and the Sacred: Toward a Theology of Culture in Decline*. New York: Crossroad, 1981.

Gilmore, Michael T. *American Romanticism and the Marketplace*. Chicago: University of Chicago Press, 1985.

Gollin, Richard M. "Reading Films as They See Fit." *Christianity and Literature* 42 (spring 1993): 391–401.

Graf, Leroy P., and Ralph W. Haskins, eds. *The Papers of Andrew Johnson*. Knoxville: University of Tennessee Press, 1970.

Greeley, Andrew. "The Persistence of Religion." *CrossCurrents: The Journal of the Association for Religion and Intellectual Life* 45, no. 1 (spring 1995): 24–41.

Gregory, Joel. *Too Great a Temptation: The Seductive Power of America's Super Church*. Fort Worth: Summit Group, 1994.

Griffin, Michael. "Religion, Literature and the Arts (RLA) in Australia: An Introduction to This Special Issue of *Literature and Theology*." *Literature and Theology: An International Journal of Theory, Criticism and Culture* 10, no. 3 (September 1996): 202–3.

Grossman, Cathy Lynn. "Charting the Unchurched in America." *USA Today*, 7 March 2002, 1–5. Available from www.usatoday.com.

Grossman, D. "Trained to Kill." *Christianity Today*, 10 August 1998, 30–39.

Guelzo, Allen C. "Selling God in America: How Christians Have Befriended Mammon." *Christianity Today*, 24 April 1995, 27–30.

Guinn, Matthew. *After Southern Modernism: Fiction of the Contemporary South.* Jackson: University Press of Mississippi, 2000.

Gunn, Giles. *The Interpretation of Otherness: Literature, Religion, and the American Imagination.* New York: Oxford University Press, 1979.

Hadden, Jeffrey K. "Desacralizing Secularization Theory." In Jeffrey K. Hadden and Anson Shupe, eds., *Secularization and Fundamentalism Reconsidered: Religion and the Politicial Order.* Vol. 3. New York: Paragon House, 1989.

Hammond, Phillip E., ed. *The Sacred in the Secular Age: Toward Revision in the Scientific Study of Religion.* Berkeley: University of California Press, 1985.

Hatch, Nathan O. *The Democratization of American Christianity.* New Haven: Yale University Press, 1989.

Hays, Tom. "Hollywood Gets Blame over Booth Torching." *Charlotte Observer*, 28 November 1995, 2A.

Herion-Sarafidis, Elisabeth. "Interview with Lee Smith." *Southern Quarterly* 32 (winter 1994): 7–18.

Hesla, David. "Religion and Literature: The Second Stage." *Journal of the American Academy of Religion* 46, no. 2 (summer 1978): 181–92.

Hill, Dorothy Combs. *Lee Smith.* New York: Twayne Publishers, 1992.

Hoover, Stewart M. *Mass Media Religion: The Social Sources of the Electronic Church.* Newbury Park, Calif.: SAGE Publications, 1988.

———. "The Meaning of Religious Television: The '700 Club' in the Lives of Its Viewers." In Quentin J. Schultze, ed., *American Evangelicalism and the Mass Media.* Grand Rapids, Mich.: Zondervan, 1990.

Horsfield, Peter G. *Religious Television: The American Experience.* New York: Longmans, 1987.

Howe, Mica, and Sarah Appleton Aguiar, eds. *He Said, She Says: An RSVP to the Male Text.* London: Fairleigh Dickinson University Press, 2001.

Hudson, Winthrop S. *Religion in America.* 4th ed. New York: MacMillan, 1987.

Hulsether, Mark. "Interpreting the 'Popular' in Popular Religion." *American Studies* 36, no. 2 (fall 1995): 129–33.

Hunt, V. "A Conversation with Randall Kenan." *African American Review* 29, no. 3 (fall 1995): 413–16.

Hunter, George G. III. *Church for the Unchurched.* Nashville: Abingdon, 1996.

Hunter, James D., and Stephen C. Ainlay, eds. *Making Sense of Modern Times: Peter L. Berger and the Vision of Interpretive Sociology.* New York: Routledge & Kegan Paul, 1986.

Huntley, E. D. *Amy Tan: A Critical Companion.* Westport, Conn.: Greenwood Press, 1998.

Husband, Timothy, and Jane Hayword. *The Secular Spirit: Life and Art at the End of the Middle Ages.* New York: E. P. Dutton, 1975.

ICF. www.icf.ch/

ICF Church News 4 (1996): 4.

Iannaccone, Laurence. "The Consequences of Religious Market Structure: Adam Smith and the Economics of Religion." *Rationality and Society* 3 (April 1991): 156–77.

Iannaccone, Laurence, and Rodney Stark. "A Supply Side Reinterpretation of the 'Secularization' of Europe." *Journal for the Scientific Study of Religion* 33, no. 3 (1994): 230–52.

Jameson, Frederic. "Postmodernism and Consumer Society." In Hal Foster, ed., *The Anti-Aesthetic: Essays in Postmodern Culture,* 111–25. Pottownsend, Wash.: Bay Press, 1983.

———. "Postmodernism, or the Cultural Logic of Late Capitalism." *New Left Review* 146 (1984).

Jarrett, Bill. "The Lively Experiment: American Evangelicalism and Twentieth-Century Technology." Paper presented at the North Carolina Religious Studies Association, Boone, North Carolina, October 1993.

Jasper, David. "Art and the Biblical Canon." Keynote address at Religion, Literature and the Arts Conference, North Sydney, Australia, 1994. Quoted in Michael Griffin, "Religion, Literature and the Arts in Australia: An Introduction to This Special Issue of *Literature and Theology.*" *Literature and Theology: An International Journal of Theory, Criticism and Culture* 10, no. 3 (September 1996): 202–3.

———. "Formal Response Given to the Arts, Literature, and Religion Section." Paper delivered at the Southeastern Conference for the Study of Religion, Columbia, South Carolina, March 1996.

———. *The Study of Literature and Religion: An Introduction.* Minneapolis: Fortress, 1989.

Jhally, Sut. *Dreamworlds II: Desire, Sex, and Power in Music Video.* Media Education Foundation, 1995.

Johnston, Robert K. *Reel Spirituality: Theology and Film in Dialogue.* Grand Rapids, Mich.: Baker, 2000.

Jones, Anne Goodwyn. "The World of Lee Smith." *Southern Quarterly* 22 (fall 1983): 115–39.

Kalof, Linda. "The Effects of Gender and Music Video Imagery on Sexual Attitudes." *The Journal of Social Psychology* 139, no. 3 (1999): 378–85.

———. "Stereotyped Evaluative Judgments and Female Attractiveness." *Gender Issues* 17, no. 2 (spring 1999): 68–82.

Kaufman, Peter Iver. "Religion on the Run." *Journal of Interdisciplinary History* 25, no. 1 (summer 1994): 85–94.

Kawans, Stuart. "Films." *The Nation* 261, no. 6 (28 August 1995): 215–16.

Kazin, Alfred. *God and the American Writer.* New York: Knopf, 1997.

Keen, Sam. *To a Dancing God: Notes of a Spiritual Traveler.* New York: Harper & Row, 1970.

Keirsey, David, and Marilyn Bates. *Please Understand Me: Character and Temperament Types.* Del Mar, Calif.: Prometheus Nemesis, 1978.

Kenan, Randall. *A Visitation of Spirits.* New York: Anchor, 1990.

Kermode, Frank. *The Sense of an Ending: Studies in the Theory of Fiction.* London: Oxford University Press, 1967.

Ketchin, Susan. *The Christ-Haunted Landscape: Faith and Doubt in Southern Fiction.* Jackson: University Press of Mississippi, 1994.

Kidd, James L. "Megachurch Methods." *Christian Century* 114, no. 16 (14 May 1997): 482–85.

Kimbrough, David. *Taking Up Serpents: Snake Handlers of Eastern Kentucky.* Chapel Hill: University of North Carolina Press, 1995.

Kort, Wesley. *Narrative Elements and Religious Meaning.* Philadelphia: Fortress, 1975.

———. "'Religion and Literature' in Postmodernist Contexts." *Journal of the American Academy of Religion* 58, no. 4, 575–88.

Kotler, Philip. *Marketing Management: Analysis, Planning, Implementation, and Control.* 6th ed. Englewood Cliffs, N.J.: Prentice Hall, 1988.

Kozlović, Anton Karl. "Superman as Christ-Figure: The American Pop Culture Movie Messiah." *Journal of Religion and Film* 6, no. 1 (April 2002). Available from http://cid.unomaha.edu/~wwwjrf/superman.htm.

Kromer, Allen. "Clyde Edgerton's Comic Vision." Master's thesis, Baylor University, 1992.

L. C. "Going Mainstream." *Billboard,* 5 August 2000, 46–48.

LaHaye, Tim, and Jerry Jenkins. *Left Behind: A Novel of the Earth's Last Days.* Wheaton, Ill.: Tyndale, 1995.

Lalonde, Peter. Interview by Jim Nelson. "God Is on Line One." In *Gentlemen's Quarterly,* March 2001, 310–15, 352–53.

Lechner, Frank J. "The Case Against Secularization: A Rebuttal." *Social Forces* 69 (1991): 1103–9.

Lewis, R. W. B. "Hold on Hard to the Huckleberry Bushes." *Sewanee Review* 67, no. 3 (summer 1959).

Lindsey, Hal, with C. C. Carlson. *The Late Great Planet Earth.* Grand Rapids, Mich.: Zondervan, 1970.

Loewenstein, Claudia. "Unshackling the Patriarchy: An Interview with Lee Smith." *Southwest Review* 78 (fall 1993): 486–505.

Lomax, Alan. *Mr. Jelly Roll Morton: The Fortunes of Jelly Roll Morton, New Orleans Creole and "Inventor of Jazz."* New York: Grosset & Dunlap, 1950.

Luecke, David S. "Is Willow Creek the Way of the Future?" *Christian Century* 114, no. 16 (14 May 1997): 479–83.

Lukacs, John. "It's the End of the Modern Age." *The Chronicle of Higher Education,* 26 April 2002, B9.

Lyotard, Jean-Francois. *The Postmodern Condition: A Report on Knowledge.* Manchester: Manchester University Press, 1984.

Magid, Ron. "The End of the World as We Know It." *American Cinematographer* 77, no. 7 (July 1996): 43–50.

———. "Taking the Plunge on *Waterworld.*" *American Cinematographer* 76, no. 12 (December 1995): 73–76.

Mahan, Jeffrey H. "Celluloid Savior: Jesus in the Movies." *Journal of Religion and Film* 6, no. 1 (April 2002). Available from http://cid.unomaha.edu/~wwwjrf/celluloid.htm.

Makarushka, Irena. "Framing the Text: A Reflection on Meanings and Methods." Paper, Bowdoin College, Brunswick, Maine, October 1993.

Maltby, Richard, ed. *Dreams for Sale: Popular Culture in the 20th Century*. London: Harrap, 1989.

Marsden, George M. *Fundamenatalism and American Culture: The Shaping of Twentieth-Century Evangelicalism 1870–1925*. Oxford: Oxford University Press, 1980.

Marsden, George M., and Bradley J. Longfield, eds. *The Secularization of the Academy*. New York: Oxford University Press, 1992.

Marsh, Clive, and Gaye Ortiz, eds. *Explorations in Theology and Film: Movies and Meaning*. Oxford: Blackwell, 1998.

Martin, David. *A General Theory of Secularization*. New York: Harper & Row, 1978.

———. *The Religious and the Secular*. New York: Schocken Books, 1969.

Martin, Joel W., and Conrad E. Ostwalt Jr., eds. *Screening the Sacred: Religion, Myth, and Ideology in Popular American Film*. Boulder: Westview, 1995.

Marty, Martin E. *The Modern Schism: Three Paths to the Secular*. New York: Harper & Row, 1969.

Mason, Marilynne S. Letter to the author, 12 February 1996.

———. "The Gospel According to Hollywood." *Christian Science Monitor*, 23 July 1990, 10–11.

———. "Terry Gilliam Grabs the Spotlight." *Christian Science Monitor*, 27 September 1991, 13.

Mathews, Donald G. *Religion in the Old South*. Chicago: University of Chicago Press, 1977.

Mathisen, James. "From Civil Religion to Folk Religion: The Case for American Sport." In *Human Kinetics*. Edited by S. J. Hoffman. Champagne: University of Illinois Press, 1992.

May, John R., ed. *New Image of Religious Film*. Kansas City, Mo.: Sheed & Ward, 1997.

McCauley, Deborah Vansau. *Appalachian Mountain Religion: A History*. Urbana: University of Illinois Press, 1995.

McClary, Susan. "Women and Music on the Verge of the New Millennium." *Signs: Journal of Women in Culture and Society* 25, no. 4 (summer 2000): 1283–86.

McCloughlin, Merrill. "From Revival Tent to Mainstream." *U.S. News & World Report*, 19 December 1988, 52–57.

McClure, John A. "Post–Secular Culture: The Return of Religion in Contemporary Theory and Literature." *CrossCurrents* 47 (fall 1997): 332–47.

McFee, Michael. "'Reading a Small History in a Universal Light': Doris Betts, Clyde Edgerton, and the Triumph of True Regionalism." *Pembroke Magazine* 23 (1991): 59–67.

McGlohon, Loonis. Lyrics to "Love Valley," 1960s.

McManners, John, ed. *The Oxford History of Christianity*. Oxford: Oxford University Press, 1993.

Mecklenburg Community Church. *In Touch*. November 1993.

Meland, Bernard Eugene. *The Realities of Faith: The Revolution in Cultural Forms*. New York: Oxford University Press, 1962.

———. *The Secularization of Modern Cultures*. New York: Oxford University Press, 1966.

Melville, Herman. *Moby Dick*. New York: New American Library, 1961.

Metcalf, Harold E. *The Magic of Telephone Evangelism*. Atlanta: Southern Union Conference of Seventh-Day Adventists, 1967.

Metropolitan Museum of Art. *The Secular Spirit: Life and Art at the End of the Middle Ages*. New York: E. P. Dutton, 1975.

Milbank, John. *Theology and Social History: Beyond Secular Reason*. Oxford: Basil Blackwell, 1990.

Miles, Margaret. *Seeing and Believing: Religion and Values in the Movies*. Boston: Beacon Press, 1996.

Mitchell, Susan. *American Attitudes: Who Thinks What about the Issues That Shape Our Lives*. 2d ed. Ithaca, N.Y.: New Strategist Publications, 1998.

Montell, William Lynwood. *The Saga of Coe Ridge: A Study in Oral History*. Knoxville: University of Tennessee Press, 1970.

Moon, Duncan. *Morning Edition*. National Public Radio, 20 April 2001. Transcript 14–17.

Moore, R. Laurence. *Selling God: American Religion in the Marketplace of Culture*. New York: Oxford University Press, 1994.

Morgan, David. "Extremities." *Sight and Sound* 6, no. 1 (January 1996): 18–20.

Morgan, Timothy C. "Cyber Shock: New Ways of Thinking Must Be Developed for the Church to Keep Pace in the Coming Information Age." *Christianity Today*, 3 April 1995, 78–86.

Moseley, James G. *A Cultural History of Religion in America*. Westport, Conn.: Greenwood Press, 1981.

Nash, David. *Secularism, Art and Freedom*. Leicester: Leicester University Press, 1992.

Nasser, Haya El. "Giant Churches Irk Some Neighbors." *USA Today* online, 23 September 2002. Available from www.usatoday.com.

Nathanson, Paul. *Over the Rainbow: The Wizard of Oz as a Secular Myth of America*. Albany: State University of New York Press, 1991.

Nelson, Jim. "God Is on Line One." *Gentlemen's Quarterly*, March 2001, 310–15, 352–53.

Newell, William Lloyd. *The Secular Magi: Marx, Freud, and Nietzsche on Religion*. New York: Pilgrim Press, 1986.

Niebuhr, Gustav. "The High Energy Never Stops." *New York Times*, 16 April 1995, 14.

———. "Where Religion Gets a Big Dose of Shopping-Mall Culture." *New York Times*, 16 April 1995, 1, 14.

Niebuhr, Reinhold. *Pious and Secular America*. New York: Scribner's, 1958.

Noll, Mark. *A History of Christianity in the United States and Canada*. Grand Rapids, Mich.: Eerdmans, 1992.

O'Brien, Tim. *The Things They Carried*. New York: Broadway Books, 1990.

O'Connor, Flannery. *Mystery and Manners: Occasional Prose*. Edited by Sally Fitzgerald and Robert Fitzgerald. New York: Farrar, Straus, & Giroux, 1957.

O'Keefe, Mark. "The Megachurch: Oregon." *Sunday Oregonian: Forum*, 22 September 1996, E1, E7.

Ostling, Richard N. "Many Are Called: Dialing for Jesus." *Time*, 27 February 1989, 79.

Ostwalt, Conrad E. Jr. *After Eden: The Secularization of American Space in the Fiction of Willa Cather and Theodore Dreiser*. Lewisburg, Pa.: Bucknell University Press, 1990.

————. "Armageddon at the Millennial Dawn" (4, no. 1); "Religion and Popular Movies" (2, no. 3); and "Visions of the End: Secular Apocalypse in Recent Hollywood Film" (2, no. 1). Available from *The Journal of Religion and Film,* http://cid.unomaha.edu/~wwwjrf/.

————. "Celluloid Religion: Reading Religion Scholars Watching Films: A Supplementary Response to Alice Bach's 'Cracking the Production Code: Watching Biblical Scholars Read Films.'" *Currents in Research: Biblical Studies* 8 (2000): 146–61.

————. "*Dances with Wolves*: An American *Heart of Darkness.*" *Literature/Film Quarterly* 24, no. 2 (1996): 209–16.

————. *Love Valley: An American Utopia.* Bowling Green, Ohio: Bowling Green State University Press, 1998.

————. "Love Valley: A Utopian Experiment in North Carolina." *North Carolina Humanities* 1, no. 1 (fall 1992): 101–8.

————. "Witches and Jesus: Lee Smith's Appalachian Religion." *Southern Literary Journal* 31, no. 1 (fall 1998): 98–118.

Parker, Everett C., Elinor Inman, and Ross Snyder. *Religious Radio: What to Do and How.* New York: Harper, 1948.

Parrish, Nancy. "'Ghostland': Tourism in Lee Smith's *Oral History.*" *Southern Quarterly* 32 (winter 1994): 37–47.

————. *Lee Smith, Annie Dillard, and the Hollins Group: A Genesis of Writers.* Baton Rouge: Louisiana State University Press, 1998.

————. "Lee Smith: Interviewed by Nancy Parrish." *Appalachian Journal* 19 (summer 1992): 394–401.

Payne, Elke Worley. "In Search of the Female Voice: Religious Experience in the Fiction of Lee Smith." Master's thesis, Western Carolina University, 1997.

Peacock, James L., and Ruel W. Tyson Jr. *Pilgrims of Paradox: Calvinism and Experience among the Primitive Baptists of the Blue Ridge.* Washington, D.C.: Smithsonian Institution Press, 1989.

"Pope Accepts Theory of Evolution." *Raleigh News and Observer,* 25 October 1996, 1A, 16A.

Porterfield, Amanda. *The Transformation of American Religion: The Story of a Late Twentieth-Century Awakening.* Oxford: Oxford University Press, 2001.

Postman, Neil. *Amusing Ourselves to Death.* New York: Viking Penguin, 1985.

Potter, G. R. *Zwingli.* Cambridge: Cambridge University Press, 1976.

Powers, John. "Shangri-la Comes to Hollywood, or Hollywood Comes to Shangri-la: Tibet and Popular Culture in the 1990s." Paper presented at the annual meeting of the American Academy of Religion, Boston, November 1999.

Pratt, Vernon. *Religion and Secularization.* London: Macmillan, 1970.

Pritchard, G. A. *Willow Creek Seeker Services: Evaluating a New Way of Doing Church.* Grand Rapids, Mich.: Baker, 1996.

Rabey, Steve. "Pop Goes the Gospel: Contemporary Christian Music Secures an Unprecedented Secular Market Push." *Christianity Today,* 15 May 1995, 55.

Reed, Eric. "Willow Creek Church Readies for Megagrowth." *Christianity Today,* 24 April 2000, 21.

Reilly, Rosalind B. "*Oral History:* The Enchanted Circle of Narrative and Dream." *Southern Literary Journal* 23 (fall 1990): 79–92.

Rich, Michael, Elizabeth R. Woods, Elizabeth Goodman, S. Jean Emans, and Robert H. DuRant. "Aggressors or Victims: Gender and Race in Music Video Violence." *Pediatrics* 101, no. 4 (April 1998): 669–74.

Robbins, Kenn. "Clyde Edgerton's *Killer Diller.*" *Southern Quarterly* 30, no. 1 (fall 1991): 66–69.

———. "A Conversation with Clyde Edgerton." *Southern Quarterly* 30, no. 1 (fall 1991): 58–65.

Roof, Wade Clark, and William McKinney. *American Mainline Religion: Its Changing Shape and Future.* New Brunswick, N.J.: Rutgers University Press, 1987.

Romanowski, William D. "Where's the Gospel? Amy Grant's Latest Album Has Thrown the Contemporary Christian Music Industry into a First-Rate Identity Crisis." *Christianity Today*, 8 December 1997, 44–45.

Ross-Bryant, Lynn. *Imagination and the Life of the Spirit: An Introduction to the Study of Religion and Literature.* Chico, Calif.: Scholars Press, 1981.

Rowe, Noel. "The Choice of Nothing." *Literature and Theology: An International Journal of Theory, Criticism and Culture* 10, no. 3 (September 1996): 224–29.

Royal, Robert. "Christian Humanism in a Postmodern Age." In *The New Religious Humanists: A Reader.* Edited by Gregory Wolfe. New York: Free Press, 1997.

Rushing, Janice. "Introduction to 'Evolution of "the New Frontier"' in *Alien* and *Aliens:* Patriarchal Cooptation of the Feminine Archetype." Essay, September 1993.

Ryan, Michael, and Douglas Kellner. *Camera Politica: The Politics and Ideology of Contemporary Hollywood Film.* Bloomington: Indiana University Press, 1988.

Saylor, Gregory, and Robert Detweiler. *Literature and Theology at Century's End.* Atlanta: Scholars Press, 1995.

Schaller, Lyle E. *The Seven-Day-a-Week Church.* Nashville: Abingdon, 1992.

Scheurer, T. E. "Goddesses and Golddiggers: Images of Women in Popular Music of the 1930s." *Journal of Popular Culture* 24, no. 1 (summer 1990): 23–38.

Schmidt, Leigh Eric. *Consumer Rites: The Buying and Selling of American Holidays.* Princeton: Princeton University Press, 1995.

Schneider, Louis, and Sanford M. Dornbush. *Popular Religion: Inspirational Books in America.* University of Chicago Press, 1958.

Schuller, Robert. *Your Church Has Real Possibilities!* Glendale, Calif.: Regal, 1974.

Schultze, Quentin J., ed. *American Evangelicals and the Mass Media: Perspectives on the Relationship between American Evangelicals and the Mass Media.* Grand Rapids, Mich.: Zondervan, 1990.

———. *Winning Your Kids Back from the Media.* Westmount, Ill.: InterVarsity Press, 1994.

Scott, James C. *Domination and the Arts of Resistance: Hidden Transcripts.* New Haven: Yale University Press, 1990.

Simanton, Keith. "Terry Gilliam, *La Jetée,* and the *Omega Man.*" Review, World Wide Web, 1996.

Slaven, Julie. "Lights! Cameras! Religion!" *Charlotte Observer*, 1 June 1996, G1, G4.

Smart, Ninian. *Beyond Ideology: Religion and the Future of Western Civilization.* San Francisco: Harper & Row, 1981.

Smith, Lee. *Black Mountain Breakdown.* New York: Ballantine, 1980, 1982.

———. *The Christmas Letters: A Novella.* Chapel Hill, N.C.: Algonquin Books, 1996.

———. *The Devil's Dream.* New York: Ballantine, 1992, 1993.

———. *Fair and Tender Ladies.* New York: Ballantine, 1988, 1989.

———. *Oral History.* New York: Ballantine, 1983, 1984.

———. *Saving Grace.* New York: Putnam, 1995.

———. "Tongues of Fire." In Lee Smith, *Me and My Baby View the Eclipse.* New York: Ballantine, 1990, 1991.

Smith, Michael. "Author LaHaye Sues *Left Behind* Film Producers." *Christianity Today,* 23 April 2001, 20.

Smith, Rebecca Godwin. "Gender Dynamics in the Fiction of Lee Smith: Examining Language and Narrative Strategies." Ph.D. diss., University of North Carolina at Chapel Hill, 1993.

———. "Writing, Singing, and Hearing a New Voice: Lee Smith's *The Devil's Dream.*" *Southern Quarterly* 32 (winter 1994): 48–62.

Smith, Virginia A. "Between the Lines: Contemporary Southern Women Writers Gail Godwin, Bobbie Ann Mason, Lisa Alther, and Lee Smith." Ph.D. diss., Pennsylvania State University, 1989.

———. "Luminous Halos and Lawn Chairs: Lee Smith's *Me and My Baby View the Eclipse.*" *Southern Review* 27 (April 1991): 479–85.

Sommerville, C. John. *The Secularization of Early Modern England: From Religious Culture to Religious Faith.* New York: Oxford University Press, 1992.

Spadafora, David. "Secularization in British Thought, 1730–1789: Some Landmarks." In W. Warren Wagar, ed., *The Secular Mind: Transformations of Faith in Modern Europe.* New York: Holmes & Meier, 1982.

Spencer, Jon Michael. "Formal Response to the North American Religious Section, 'Popular Music and American Religion in the 20th Century.'" Paper presented at the annual meeting of the American Academy of Religion, New Orleans, November 1996.

———. *Blues and Evil.* Knoxville: University of Tennessee Press, 1993.

"The Spirit Within." In *The Salon Interview: Amy Tan.* Available from http://www.salon.com/12nov1995/feature/tan.html.

Stark, Rodney, and William Sims Bainbridge. *The Future of Religion: Secularization, Revival and Cult Formation.* Berkeley: University of California Press, 1985.

Steinken, Ken. "Where No Ministry Has Gone Before: To Be More Effective Ministers, Five Iron Frenzy Resists the Packaging of Christian Rock Bands." *Christianity Today,* 24 May 1999, 74–75.

Stewart, Randall. *American Literature and Christian Doctrine.* Baton Rouge: Louisiana State University Press, 1958.

Stock, Phyllis H. "Proudhon and Morale Independante: A Variation of French Secular Morality." In W. Warren Wagar, ed., *The Secular Mind: Transformations of Faith in Modern Europe.* New York: Holmes & Meier, 1982.

Storey, John. *An Introductory Guide to Cultural Theory and Popular Culture.* Athens: University of Georgia Press, 1993.

Strick, Philip. "12 Monkeys." *Sight and Sound* 6, no. 4 (April 1996): 56.

Strobel, Lee. *Inside the Mind of Unchurched Harry and Mary: How to Reach Friends and Family Who Avoid God and the Church.* Grand Rapids, Mich.: Zondervan, 1993.

Surya Das, Lama. *Awakening to the Sacred: Creating a Spiritual Life from Scratch.* New York: Broadway Books, 1999.

Sylvan, Robin. "Burning Man and Rave Culture: A Pre-Millennial, Postmodern, Future Primitive Popular Religious Revival." Paper presented at the annual meeting of the American Academy of Religion, Boston, November 1999.

Tan, Amy. *The Hundred Secret Senses.* New York: Putnam, 1995.

———. *The Kitchen God's Wife.* New York: Putnam, 1991.

Tate, Linda, ed. *Conversations with Lee Smith.* Jackson: University of Mississippi Press, 2001.

Teem, William M. IV. "Let Us Now Praise the Other: Women in Smith's Short Fiction." *Studies in the Literary Imagination* 27 (fall 1994): 63–73.

Tennyson, G. B., and Edward E. Ericson Jr., eds. *Religion and Modern Literature: Essays in Theory and Criticism.* Grand Rapids, Mich.: Eerdmans, 1975.

Thumma, Scott. "Exploring the Megachurch Phenomena: Their Characteristics and Cultural Context." Available from Hartford Institute for Religion Research, hirr.hartsem.edu.

———. *The Kingdom, the Power, and the Glory: Megachurches in Modern American Society.* Ph.D. diss., Emory University, 1996.

Titon, Jeff Todd. *Powerhouse for God: Speech, Chant, and Song in an Appalachian Baptist Church.* Austin: University of Texas Press, 1988.

de Tocqueville, Alexis. *Democracy in America.* Chicago: University of Chicago Press, 2000.

Toynbee, Arnold. *An Historian's Approach to Religion.* New York: Oxford University Press, 1956.

Trueheart, Charles. "The Megachurch." *Sunday Oregonian: Forum,* 22 September 1996, E1.

Tschannen, Olivier. "The Secularization Paradigm: A Systematization." *Journal for the Scientific Study of Religion* 30, no. 4 (1991): 395–415.

Tweed, Thomas, and Stephen Prothero, *Asian Religion in America: A Documentary History.* New York: Oxford, 1999.

Underwood, Gloria Jan. "Blessings and Burdens: Memory in the Novels of Lee Smith." Ph.D. diss., University of South Carolina, 1991.

Vahanian, Gabriel. *The Death of God: The Culture of Our Post-Christian Era.* New York: George Braziller, 1961.

Vaughan, John N. *The Large Church: A Twentieth-Century Expression of the First-Century Church.* Grand Rapids, Mich.: Baker, 1985.

Wagar, W. Warren, ed. *The Secular Mind: Transformations of Faith in Modern Europe.* New York: Holmes & Meier, 1982.

Wald, Gayle. "Just a Girl? Rock Music, Feminism, and the Cultural Construction of Female Youth." *Signs: Journal of Women in Culture and Society* 23, no. 3 (spring 1998): 585–610.

Wald, Kenneth D. *Religion and Politics in the United States*. New York: St. Martin's, 1986.

Wall, James. "Viewing the Megachurch: Between a Gush and a Smirk." *Christian Century* 112, no. 10 (22 March 1995): 315–16.

Wallis, Roy, and Steve Bruce. "Secularization: The Orthodox Model." In Steve Bruce, ed., *Religion and Modernization: Sociologists and Historians Debate the Secularization Thesis*. Oxford: Clarendon Press, 1992.

Walsh, William. "Interview." In *Conversations with Lee Smith*. Edited by Linda Tate. Jackson: University of Mississippi Press, 2001.

Warner, Steven H. "Work in Progress toward a New Paradigm for the Sociological Study of Religion in the United States." *American Journal of Sociology* 98, no. 5 (1993): 1044–93.

Weaver, Jann Cather. "Discerning the Religious Dimensions of Film: Toward a Visual Method Applied to *Dead Man Walking*." Paper presented at the annual conference of the American Academy of Religion, New Orleans, November 1996.

Wector, Dixon. *The Saga of American Society: A Record of Social Aspiration, 1607–1937*. New York: Scribner's, 1937.

Wells, David. *Turning to God*. Grand Rapids, Mich.: Baker, 1989.

Wells, H. G. *The War of the Worlds*. London: William Heinemann, 1898.

Wesley, Debbie. "A New Way of Looking at an Old Story: Lee Smith's Portrait of Female Creativity." *Southern Literary Journal* 30, no. 1 (fall 1997): 88–101.

White, James Emery. "Churches, Listen to the Unchurched." *Charlotte Observer*, 27 March 1995, 7A.

————. *Opening the Front Door: Worship and Church Growth*. Nashville: Convention Press, 1992.

Wieland, Lisa Cade. "Old Times Not Forgotten: Family and Storytelling in Twentieth-Century Southern Literature." Ph.D. diss., Marquette University, Milwaukee, Wisconsin, 1998.

Williams, David. "Worlds at War." *American Cinematographer* 77, no. 7 (July 1996): 32–42.

Williams, Donald E. "An Oceanic Odyssey." *American Cinematographer* 76, no. 8 (August 1995): 40–51.

Williams, Peter. *Popular Religion in America: Symbolic Change and the Modernization Process in Historical Perspective*. Englewood Cliffs, N.J.: Prentice Hall, 1980, 1989.

Wilson, Bryan. "Aspects of Secularization in the West." *Japanese Journal of Religious Studies* 3, no. 4 (December 1976): 259–76.

————. "New Images of Christian Community." In *The Oxford History of Christianity*. Edited by John McManners. Oxford: Oxford University Press, 1993.

————. "Secularization: The Inherited Model." In Phillip E. Hammond, ed., *The Sacred in a Secular Age: Toward Revision in the Scientific Study of Religion*. Berkeley: University of California Press, 1985.

Wojcik, Daniel. *The End of the World as We Know It: Faith, Fatalism, and Apocalypse in America*. New York: New York University Press, 1997.

Wolfe, Gregory, ed. *The New Religious Humanists: A Reader*. New York: Free Press, 1997.

Wright, Richard. *The Outsider*. New York: Harper & Row, 1953.

Yamane, David. "Secularization on Trial: In Defense of a Neosecularization Paradigm." *Journal for the Scientific Study of Religion* 36, no. 1 (1997): 109–22.

Yancey, Philip. *The Jesus I Never Knew*. Grand Rapids, Mich.: Zondervan, 1995.

Ziolkowski, Eric. "History of Religions and the Study of Religion and Literature: Grounds for Alliance." *Literature and Theology: An International Journal of Religion, Theory and Culture* 12, no. 3 (September 1998): 305–25.

INDEX

acculturation, 59, 71, 117, 119
Affleck, Ben, 172
African American community, 132, 196
Agee, James, 101
Aichele, George, 161
alcohol, attitudes toward, 111
Allman Brothers Band, 85
America, secularization in, 51–52, 203–4. *See also* secularization, in Europe versus in America
American Revolution, 19
Amos, Tori, 195
Anabaptists, 49
anti-secularism, 46
apocalyptic dramas, 157–86
 antichrist figures in, 163–66, 168
 Christ figures in, 145, 147
 evangelical, 160–69
  characteristics of, 168–69
 secular, 169–86
  characteristics of, 170–72
  exclusion of God in, 170, 171
  messiah fixation in, 174
 world unity in, 185

See also specific movie titles
apocalyptic imagination, 159, 171, 175, 177, 186
apocalypticism, 159, 172
Apollo 13, 152
Appalachian religious traditions, 135n.14. *See also* Smith, Lee, fiction of
Armageddon, 172, 173–74, 175
Arnold, David, 99
Augustine *(The City of God),* 47–48
authority. *See* religious authority; secular authority

baby boomers, 66–67
Bach, Alice, 145, 150, 161
Bainbridge, William Sims *(The Future of Religion),* 3, 11, 12, 19, 29
Bakker, Jim and Tammy, 51, 53
Barker, Andy, 81–86
Baudrillard, Jean, 26, 27
Beecroft, Jeffrey, 182
Bell, Daniel, 3
Bennett, Andy, 196
Berg, Don, 85